WORLD TENSION

WORLD TENSION

The Psychopathology of International Relations

edited by

GEORGE W. KISKER

Prentice-Hall, Inc.   New York

HM291
.K5

FOREWORD

J. R. Rees, M.D.

Late Medical Director of the Travistock Clinic,
London; Honorary Consulting Psychiatrist to the
British Army; Director, World Federation of Mental Health.

I HAVE been greatly honored by being asked to write a Foreword to this symposium. There can be no doubt of the importance of the subject or of the value of gathering together the ideas of a considerable number of representative psychiatrists, psychologists, and social scientists from different countries on this topic of world tension.

I suspect that some of the reviewers of this book will complain—as they usually do about symposia—that there is overlapping and variation of style and probably direct contradiction discernible in some of the contributions. To me this does not seem at all discouraging. In fact, I should feel that there was something artificial or unsatisfactory if these criticisms could not be made. This is an international symposium. Those who have written have done so out of their own experience, each independently of the other. The task which faces the reader is to extract for himself the points of view which tally or conflict and to assess them afresh from his own angle, to try and comprehend the differences of opinion and to discover what points of importance have been left out. In any international discussion it is surely just as important to know the disagreements as the agreements, and it is likewise very important to be able to pinpoint those areas in which only further careful thought and research can yield results. My hope is that many of the contributors will, when they have seen the whole book, set about the rewriting of their contributions, for it seems possible that in this way we might make some real advance in the study of this vast problem.

If that were to happen, then the inspiration and labors of Dr. Kisker will not have been in vain.

Any international discussion of a scientific topic comes quickly up against certain difficulties. Language and semantics constitute the two outstanding problems in international communication. These are really greater problems than the difficulties which arise from the different disciplinary training of those who contribute.

In dealing with a vast problem such as we have now before us, it is important for us to avoid generalization wherever possible. What we aim at or wish to do is to clarify the underlying causes of tensions which lead to war, and to do this well enough to be able to suggest a remedy. It would seem at times as though nearly all the remedies that had been suggested for the disorder of the world had been too glib and superficial. In medicine we know that the hit-or-miss method of treatment is dangerous, and that it is rarely possible to prescribe treatment without a painstaking and accurate diagnosis. This book aims at contributing the diagnosis.

Contributions to the book are primarily from the point of view of psychopathology and from that of sociology, while a number of them might best be called sociopsychiatric in their approach. It is perhaps relevant to quote a short paragraph which was appended to a recent report put out by the Group for the Advancement of Psychiatry in the United States on the position of psychiatrists in the field of International Relations. This says:

In order to clarify some past confusion regarding the verbal semantics and functions of the interdiscipline approach the following definition is offered by the Committee on International Relations:—

The term interdiscipline approach (also called multidiscipline, interprofessional, or multiprofessional), refers to teamwork by experts in diverse fields of specialization on a mutually agreed project. This approach has been developed in response to the difficulties encountered in defining and analyzing problems which are complex and many-sided in their causes and effects. In most cases the understanding of such problems and the planning of concerted action toward their solution transcend the confines of a particular profession or discipline. A synthesis is called for, therefore, which the interprofessional approach aims to accomplish, through integration of the knowledge and skills developed in diverse fields of scientific endeavor having relevance to the problem on hand.

Dr. Margaret Mead first introduced me to the concept of the "orchestration" of the various professional points of view, and it is to be hoped that this book will be not merely a source of new ideas and a stimulus to think further into the problem, but the beginning of some sort of synthesis of the contributions made by many different people from many countries throughout the world.

As social scientists, psychologists, and psychiatrists, we can make no pretense to know the answer to the problem of tension in the world. But if we cannot make some contribution to the work of our colleagues in the diplomatic and the economic fields, then no one can. There are very few problems that do not yield to an approach which is made with due humility and with persistence, imagination, and determination.

Some of the contributions to this symposium provide what may be called case studies in the field of national disorder and tension, and we who are in medicine know the value of such studies for elucidation of the problem. All of us who read this book will, I am confident, find ourselves more determined to stimulate the researches into leadership and into the problems of aggression and the psychopathology of interpersonal relationships; and from these we shall move on to more adequate studies of the dynamics of groups. I hope that everyone who reads the book will ask himself: "What sort of contribution to the furthering of such studies, however small it may be, can I personally attempt?

PREFACE

THE purpose of this book is to explore the psychological implications of the tension and anxiety gripping our world. A number of distinguished specialists in human behavior, each representing a different country, have attempted to explain the present-day social and psychological crisis in terms that can be readily understood by everyone who takes an intelligent interest in what is happening, and what is likely to happen, to the world in which we live.

The psychological approach to international relations can be reduced to four major clinical problems of diagnosis, etiology, therapy, and prognosis. Each of these terms asks a question. The question posed by diagnosis is: What is wrong with the world today? Etiology asks the question: What has caused the present state of world tension? The question of therapy is: What can be done about it? And finally, the question raised by prognosis is: What is the outlook for the future?

This clinical approach—the viewing of the world as a patient—represents a departure from the more usual approach of the economist, the political scientist, the militarist, and the diplomat. While no serious student of the problem of international relations would insist that there is a single simple answer to any of the questions we have raised, it is becoming increasingly apparent that we need to know a great deal more about the human side of war and peace.

Psychologists, psychiatrists, and social scientists in fifty-three countries of the world were consulted in the preparation of this book. It is significant that not all of these scientists felt the same freedom to contribute to these pages. It is no accident that there is no chapter from Russia. Every effort was made to secure Soviet representation through official, semi-official, and non-official channels. More than a hundred letters sent to Russia, including one to Premier Stalin, have remained unanswered and unacknowledged. Similarly, scientists in Finland, Poland, Czechoslovakia, Hungary, Rumania, and Yugoslavia found it desirable to be excused from taking part in this project. The situation with reference to China demands special comment. Arrangements for a chapter from China were made many months ago. Free contact was maintained with Chinese psychologists and psychiatrists until the Communists drove out the Nationalist Government. From that day, there has been no word from any one of the several Chinese scientists who had been collaborating on this book. The failure to include other countries has been due to technical and editorial reasons.

A statement in the first paragraph of this preface bears repetition. Each of the contributors represents his own national interest. Each has, of course, been allowed complete freedom of expression. By the same token, each must take full responsibility for his own ideas. Some are Communist in their leanings, others Fascist, others Democratic. The purpose of the book is not to reconcile such differences, contradictions or inconsistencies, but to shed as much light on the subject of tensions as possible, from every angle. The reader should not expect the editor, the publishers, nor any contributor to be in agreement with everything expressed in these pages.

Many hands, heads, and hearts contributed to the development of this book. I must first of all express my deepest gratitude to the contributing authors for their enthusiastic reception of the idea and for their willing cooperation in meeting the requirements which were placed upon them. I must also thank the many other individuals who assisted, directly or indirectly, with the innumerable problems inherent in the collection, translation and preparation of manuscripts. Special thanks are due to Mr. Herbert T. Marcus of Cincinnati, Ohio, for his translation of the chapter on Germany, and to Professor I. P. Thibeau of Dichrich, Luxembourg, for his translation from that country. Finally, I give my warmest and sincerest thanks to my wife, Florence Ray Kisker, for her endless enthusiasm and for her wise and patient editorial assistance, and to my secretary, Celeste Renner, whose skill and determination materially lightened my task.

GEORGE W. KISKER

CONTENTS

AUSTRALIA

John Bostock, D.P.M.

Research Professor of Medical Psychology at the
University of Queensland; President of the Aus-
tralian-American Association (Queensland); Former President of the Australian Association of Psychiatrists.

THE story of man is largely the story of psychological tension. Man has of necessity always had tensions in
likes and dislikes of food and living conditions. Primitive man,
exposed to the dangers of fang and claw, lightning, flood and
famine, falling tree and avalanche, was initiated into a life of
fear. He could only survive by adjusting his tensions to reality
and living literally a life on tenterhooks.

At the outset it must be realized that man has a normal and
intricate psychological make-up for dealing with his environment. Even when asleep he may be aware of noise and time.
Through the day he is paying attention to his daily tasks. There
is such a degree of tension that holidays are needed to make
mind and body relax.

Down the years man changed his social life but not the bases
of his psychology. In order to decrease his tensions due to fear of
being attacked and to remove persistent anxieties of obtaining
food, he began to live in tribes. During the course of years these
expanded to become nations.

It is obvious that a hundred individuals with spears are more
than a match for a beast of prey. They can also organize food
supplies better than one individual. They can therefore live in
such security that the tensions of fear are lessened. The progress,
however, has been dearly bought, since we have acquired new
fears and new aggressions.

Mankind in the main is selfish, acquisitive, inquisitive, critical and power-loving. Such qualities inevitably produce tensions in the tribe. Envy, hatred and greed make their appearance. In addition, powerful individuals introduce a tyranny from which is born a new terror. It is not our purpose, however, to discuss the fascinating problem of intratribal tension, of which every individual living in town or city is acutely aware and about which he is intensely interested, but to consider the growth of tension between tribes.

When individuals combined to offset danger from beasts of prey, they created the infinitely greater danger of assault by other groups of men. The moment tribes are formed, intertribe problems occur. Tribal tensions are not placid. A few individuals or even one man can foment mass fear, mass distrust, mass greed or mass hatred. The psychological forces are never still; they simmer and are liable to sudden eruptions. The tension rises, to boil over in panic or aggression.

Tribal warfare became an accepted practice over the whole world. It ceased only when the tribes coalesced to form nations. Today the evil effects of mass tension on an international plane are enormously increased, owing to the rapidity of transportation, refinements in communication, and perfection in arms. The scope has passed from small sectors of tension in every continent until it has become a gigantic tension embracing the earth in its entirety.

So enormous is this scope that in the next global war its baneful effects will be felt by almost every inhabitant of every country. It is folly to await the catastrophe in a spirit of dumb resignation. The machinery of science must be organized to discover the way out from tragedy. It has already harnessed colossal forces for destruction. The psychiatrist believes that a remedy lies in the study of the mind.

He claims that since warfare is due to psychological tension on a large scale, it is logical to suppose that it can be eliminated, neutralized or diverted. In order to do this, the field of tensions must be surveyed in a broad manner. Each country has special problems from which important deductions can be made. Australia's contribution is chiefly dependent on its isolation. Disturbing international influences have been minimized. For more than a hundred years there has never been any major warfare on the continent. This factor is important since interracial feelings have been mellowed. When they are intense the vision is apt to be clouded by sentiment and prejudice. *The message from Australia is that tension is not part and parcel of race, but results from group aggression.*

The degree of psychological tension between peoples can be aptly illustrated by conditions in Australia before the coming of the white man put an end to intertribal warfare. Within easy walking distance of the place where this chapter was written, warfare between three tribes of Aboriginals was a regular if not indeed an annual feature. Each was jealous of any infringement of rights to its hunting ground, its women, or it ways of life. Any infringement raised the tempo of tension to a pitch at which hostility was inevitable.

It is a mistake to deny the existence of a large measure of intelligence in primitive people. They realized the evil results of intertribal tension and took measures for its limitation. Although unaware of the modern concept of universal brotherhood, the Australian Aboriginal glimpsed the essential methods for harnessing the emotions. Sentiments were fostered to such a degree that they became the guiding factor of tribal behavior. Boys and girls were initiated into a totem belief. They were taught to regard themselves as belonging to the fish, opossum, kangaroo, emu or some other family. Henceforward they must obey the totem law and befriend others who belonged to the same totem group.

The strength of these emotional bonds was so strong that it was possible for an individual Aboriginal to traverse the continent in safety, provided he was fortunate enough to encounter only those of his own totem grouping.

The direct use of a symbolic machinery to allay intertribal tension is shown in *ngia ngiampe,* as practiced by the Narrinyeri tribe of South Australia. A portion of a human umbilical cord, specially treated, is wrapped in a roll of emu feathers and bound with fiber from the Mallee tree. The finished product is called a *kalduke*. It signifies integrity and the linking of mother and child; it is emblematic of love and fellowship. If two tribes are at war, peace may be restored if another tribe can persuade them to accept the gift of a *kalduke*, thereby making them firm friends who can on no account fight each other.

Ngia ngiampe and the Totem system are examples of the control of group tension by the creation of an overriding sentiment, the greater grouping taking precedence over the smaller. The overriding sentiment can be used with almost the exactness of an algebraical formula to harness psychology to the great problem of community living.

It cannot be denied that Aboriginal psychology sheds light on modern international conditions. There is revealed the necessity for an overriding sentiment between peoples and the use of an object as a symbol of brotherhood, kindliness and humanity. It shows the utility of a degree of isolation so that nationals can live their own lives with the minimum amount of outside interference, and a forceful injunction against the use of arms on a national basis.

A great deal of misunderstanding has arisen because the average man, and many writers as well, regard international affairs as peculiar, complicated and isolated phenomena. The essential and underlying principles are identical with those which faced primitive people.

There must be a spiritual union in brotherhood, the use of a symbolic emblem, the right to live unmolested in one's own territory, and an embargo on the use of armed warfare.

There is, in fact, a close resemblance between *ngia ngiampe* in the role of tension-remover and the methods adopted by the white settlers of Australia. The first settlement of Australia by the British occurred in 1788, when Governor Phillip sailed to Port Jackson and founded the colony of New South Wales. In the succeeding years, colonies were established at other places. As the colonies grew in population and importance, clashes of interests occurred. In spite of the overriding sentiment for Britain and the use of the symbolic object in the British flag, feelings ran so high at times that the colonies, although not actually at war with each other, were in a condition of considerable interstate tension. The problem was satisfactorily solved in 1901 by creating a Federation of States on the pattern of the United States of America. It created a brotherhood of Australians, with a common symbol in the Australian flag.

Machinery was evolved for the guarantee of State rights and adequate State isolation. War was banned by the direct control of the armed forces through an all-Australian authority held in common. There is not now, nor is there ever likely to be, any serious interstate tension. Interstate war is unthinkable and impossible.

The miracle is no mystery to be conjured from a magician's hat. The process is simple, requiring ordinary intelligence and a will to action within the compass of every man. In psychological terms, it is the creation of an overriding sentiment and the sublimation of aggressive forces into other channels.

The cunning brains which produced *ngia ngiampe* and Federation have discovered a process of infinite worth, a pattern which will eventually solve the major problems of international tension. However, before embarking further on such prophecy, it is essential to analyze more completely the causes of racial prejudice. The illustrations so far considered have concerned tensions within groups of the same peoples—Aboriginals who practiced *ngia ngiampe* and British settlers who initiated Federation. It must be clear that differences of race do not create insuperable difficulties.

The population of Australia is predominantly Anglo-Saxon. The latest figures show a total population of 7,579,358, of whom 99.5% are British and .5% other nationals. There are 47,620 Aboriginals. The latter are largely scattered through the barren uninhabited portions. Some thousands are in reservations. There is no racial tension between the white and the black Australian. No major issues of conflict and rivalry are involved in their life and husbandry. There is no conflict to create hatred or jealousy. The average white Australian regrets that the Aboriginal is becoming less numerous.

Let us now consider international tension between European

settlers from countries other than Great Britain and the native white Australian.

From the legal viewpoint, the Australian nationalization laws are broad and humane. Australian nationality can be acquired with little difficulty after five years' residence, except in the case of certain ex-servicemen who served under the British command during World War II. Here the term is shortened. The law courts are open to all. There are no barriers to travel throughout the continent. Individual freedom is of a high order.

As might be expected, there is very little international tension. An Australian Jew has become Governor General, another has been Commander-in-Chief of the armed forces. Germans, Frenchmen, Greeks, and Russians have been and are still accepted as leaders in many spheres of Australian life. They are judged as men and as Australians.

The freedom from international tension has been demonstrated in a curious manner in World War II. Our prisoners of war at the hands of the Japanese suffered intolerable cruelties and hardships, yet they returned to their homeland with a marked absence of racial hate. They recalled the decent Japanese and made allowances for the others on the score of training and education.

In general, it may be said that the average Australian shows little trace of international tension. His homogeneity, isolation and the democratic form of government have contributed to a state of affairs in which continued or vivid racial hostility is incomprehensible. Man is judged as man. Color and race are of little importance and not primary factors. The Australian has a broad tolerance, in spite of insistence on a White Australian Policy and the overpublicized accounts of "color" incidents.

This broad picture of Australian internationalism is not, however, complete. Here and there ill-defined but fairly conclusive evidence of racial discrimination, amounting to tension, exists in certain racial groups. Some Italians working in the canefields, Germans in farming areas, Greeks in catering, Jews in industry attract a measurable degree of racial hostility.

Analysis indicates that the antagonism is not primarily racial. It exists because certain units live in groups which refuse to be assimilated. They encourage marriage within the group. Often the women do not learn the language of the land of their adoption. The groups work longer hours than the Australians and take little or no part in local affairs and sport. They save money and outbuy their Australian neighbors, who regard their activity as an aggression which foreshadows the coming of more group members to dispossess more and yet more Australians.

The Australians in the vicinity resent the exploitation of labor conditions, work for low wages, or abuse of the soil. The attitude is strengthened by the arrogance of those who regard an Australian venture as a means of achieving prosperity in order to provide for return in opulence to their homeland.

From time to time the placid interracial front has been disturbed by ideological differences based on religions with racial backgrounds. It is idle to refuse to admit their existence. Happily, they are accepted in the spirit of compromise, and with tolerance born of long usage. Except in rare instances, there has been no direct interference with the business or personal life of the individual. One might call the tension an ideological aggression of a mild order. It is not confined to any one religion. The tensions are mild and do not lead to armed or social violence.

During the last few years the spread of the Communist ideology has introduced an entirely new factor. Hitherto the struggle concerned God as a spiritual being. The Communists, by regarding God as the State, have evolved a system wherein aggression is an article of faith. At the dictates of a central executive any aggressive act upon man or property, if ideologically desirable, is justified. Armed and social violence are regarded as essential steps in evolution. The end is greater than the means. Man has no rights. The State has no limitations.

The Communist religion has fanatical devotees who have crusaded with ruthless enthusiasm. They have produced strikes in key industries. The waterfront has been paralyzed at their will. The coal industry is often hamstrung. Their political influence has such far-reaching consequences that the seeds of interracial tension are being faithfully sown by the disciples of the Russian cult.

As might be expected, long freedom from international problems has assisted Communism. The tension, though present, is diffuse and unorganized. In spite of this, there is no doubt that we are viewing the birth of a serious factor in international tension. A means must be found to counter the aggression which creates such far-reaching results.

Communism has gained adherents through its dreamlike vision of a wonderful Utopia. The democracies have a sounder basis in realistic visions of high standards based on free enterprise and broad legislation. They must bring their platform closer to the public ear and create a new enthusiasm through the prospect of benefits which can be created by closer union and cooperation.

The Australian experiment in citizenship reveals that racial differences do not of themselves lead to tension. In all cases where such tension exists, there is the additional factor of aggression. The moment that interference with the personal way of life occurs, the victim is in a state of psychological tension. It is important to understand that this reaction is quite normal, and is, indeed, universal in the human race.

There are many who tell us that every man should be able to overcome feelings of hostility through the use of moral precepts. While it is true that many reach heights of selflessness, these heights are quite inaccessible to the average man.

The reason for this is shown by a recent research on one hundred pre-school children in Brisbane, Queensland. A trained observer spent a year in watching children in the age groups of two to five at a kindergarten. It was discovered that the majority of children are occasionally aggressive, and that if unchecked they readily become habitual aggressors. The chief situations which lead to aggression in children are when coveted articles are in short supply or when the playing area is so restricted that there is too little elbow room.

While it may seem a long way from a nation to a nursery, the realities of food sufficiency and living space are fundamentally the same.

Not merely does the act of aggression produce tension in the individual child who has been victimized, but group tension also can occur. The latter resembles an epidemic; the children are "on edge" for a considerable period of time. It is significant that the main circumstance which produced the reaction was the introduction of new children into the group. The chief offender was a substandard child who did not conform to the social usages of the others. To them he was strange and unpredictable. This resulted in a vague tension in the group akin to fear.

International tension is not an entity peculiar to itself; it is merely the extension of tensions which are normally present in each individual. They occur in fear-provoking situations, so that fear must be regarded in relationship to aggression. Aggressiveness is a normal urge which comes into action as a reaction to interference with the way of life, or as a frustration through inability to obtain the desirable. Such situations create a wide variety of fears. It is significant that when the aggressor finds aggression profitable, there is a tendency for it to become an habitual reaction.

It is our Australian experience that international tension does not arise through an innate incompatibility of race, but from group activities which forcibly impinge upon the economic and ideological ways of living of other groups.

No review of aggression would be complete without reference to the necessity for each person to have what he considers to be a fair share in the good things and necessities of life, whether these be in the nature of essentials, as food, clothing and shelter, or of luxuries and gadgets.

It is not necessary that all people should have the same, but only that each should have an adequate amount. This is illustrated in the matter of group prejudices, since the cardinal factor behind the Australian attitude towards incursion by others is that they are depriving them of something which they consider to be their right. In this connection, it is apparent that there will never be freedom from international tension while there is a great disparity between living standards among peoples, combined with unbalanced exchange of ideas.

In this connection, the average Australian's knowledge of America is from the glamorous films, which show a very high degree of luxury and luxurious living. If America exports them to countries with a low standard of living, she is at the same time exporting the seeds of tension. She is telling them of the inaccessible riches which lie on her side of the garden fence. The psychological result is frustration and jealousy. It can only be offset by films illustrating the other side of reality. They must show that the riches are produced by very hard work, hard thinking and thrift, and, furthermore, that Australia and other nations can acquire them by their own initiative if they so desire. This cannot be accomplished by war or bloody revolution which destroys wealth, but by the same principles of thrift and hard work which have been so successful on so many occasions.

The keys to international harmony undoubtedly include one which unlocks the doors to understanding. Education is most important. In this respect, it is noteworthy that the educated white scientist has no serious international tensions because he is educated to a state of mind in which all scientists are brothers. He sees, beyond race and color, an educated individual with a soul on an equal plane to his own and knows that this brotherhood is irrespective of race.

Such an ideal is difficult to attain for the majority, but all attempts at removing international tension from the masses must depend in part on intensive education of the type which advocates tolerance, gives factual knowledge, and deprecates prejudice.

It is our experience that the tolerance of the Australian prisoner of war to the Japanese is based on his education, which makes him see that the display of brutality was a part of the system and not of the individual. He notes that the Japanese, caught in the military machine, was hard and aggressive. The Australian was able to realize that it was the machine and not the individual which was responsible for the brutality.

Education helps us to sift the chaff from the grain of knowledge. As an example, let us study a number of Australian Aboriginals from different tribes working together. Although they look alike to the casual observer, there are wide differences in their make-up. Each member is suspicious of a member of another tribe to a fantastic degree. They will work in harmony together as in a kitchen or store, however, *because each one knows that the other's eyes are on him.*

This is, of course, to be highly deprecated because the harmony is an illusion. The interracial tensions have not been eliminated. Such suspicions are extremely difficult to eradicate. The only method is by intensive education, so that they begin to comprehend the true manner of the brotherhood of man. Although the prejudices of the average man and woman may be less intense, there is always the need for the continued growth of tolerance through education. We should implement this growth with every means in our power.

In the case of individual nationals settling in another land, they must adopt the ways of the country in which they live and cease to feel strangers. For happy living, every man or woman who emigrates must be prepared to adopt a new citizenship in word and deed. There is no place for the carryover of ultranationalism. They must regard a new citizenship as a pleasant addition and not a painful subtraction. They become richer, not poorer. They have two birthrights in the place of one. It must be clearly recognized that a new and complete loyalty to Australia on the part of a settler does not sever the emotional links with his own country.

Apropos of this, strangers to Australia are often puzzled by the Australian love for England. Although Australia is entirely free from English control to work out its own destiny and the Australian is loyal to his country, he has an additional loyalty to the land of his ancestors. It is a sentiment of sufficient strength to make him go to war in its defense and to give it help in times of distress. The symbol of this loyalty lies in the British throne and the British flag.

When Australians are at home or when gathered together in strange countries, this flag is flown as though it were an embracing mother protecting her children in a period of adversity. In a world of illusion and change, the flag has psychological values which impart a tremendous and perpetual vitality.

History shows that the most effective method in the production of a satisfactory and stable alignment is not one of a mere pact or treaty. Such procedures are based on flimsy psychological relationships and cannot withstand the severe stresses of international aggression. A recent example of this is the League of Nations. Many foresee similar weaknesses in its successor, the United Nations.

It is apparent that in order to provide an overriding sentiment able to withstand internal and external stress, we need a closer union with a greater emotional appeal. Space will not permit discussion of all the possibilities. We must here be content to discuss the broad principles of the most successful method. It is one of Federal Union, already mentioned in the survey of the manner in which the Australian States achieved stability.

Tension ceases when the aggressor and the nation aggressed against become partners in an overriding sentiment. The brotherhood is symbolized by a symbolic object common to the two groups. Means are taken to ensure isolation in order to provide group freedom. The conduct of war between the contracting parties is made impossible. The Australian Aboriginal evolved *ngia ngiampe;* the white Australian adopted Federation on the model of the United States of America.

The average Australian is completely happy in this set-up. There is no noticeable restriction in his individual liberty as a result of Federation. The man in the street would not notice whether the army were controlled by the State or the Commonwealth. The only tangible difference is in the quite irrelevant matter of color and shape of uniforms. As for the postal system, the new design of a postal stamp creates a mild interest which passes after a few days

The most conspicuous mark of Federation is the display of the common symbol. The new flag of union is flown over the continent. It is a perpetual reminder of the essential oneness of all Australians, irrespective of the land of their origin.

Federation permits the maximum of individual and national liberty. It ensures the impossibility of large-scale armed warfare between the groups within the Federal sphere. Within the lifetime of a middle-aged man living today, it would be possible for nations to combine in a Federation of such size that armed warfare would be physically impossible.

The advantages can be readily understood. A strong army gives protection; the abolition of competition in armaments saves enormous sums which can be employed for public works and social services. There is a stable currency and expanding markets, due to the abolition of artificial barriers. Higher standards of living for the people eventuate through greater volume of exports and imports. Livelier trading within the countries themselves results in fuller employment with buoyant markets and better material well-being. Freer movement occurs between the countries of the Union, as with the *ngia ngiampe* passport. Education is assisted through travel. In short, there is a fuller, richer life for the individual, who enjoys not merely his original national life but takes an interesting part in that of other national lives within the Union.

Usually great public benefits are available only at an enormous price. A stupendous dam, a colossal bridge, a mighty ship —all necessitate a great expenditure of time, money, and materials. Federation gives greater benefits. Its price is the mere limitation of the sovereign right to wage war, to have a separate currency, separate customs duties and a separate postal system. They are rights which the average citizen would gladly waive.

And so we close this brief survey of the Australian scene on a high note of good cheer. Although the scene of human endeavors changes with the years, the principles of psychology are unaltered. Tribes and nations can live in harmony if they are prepared to adopt the proven means for creating an effective brotherhood. The simplicity of these means gives hope for the future.

No mention has been made of the atomic bomb, though its grim reality lies close to consciousness in every thinking man and woman. It has a relationship to our problem even in isolated Australia. The countermeasure is not grotesque super-rockets or incredible radar, but mass psychology. The growth of Federal Union will relegate the atom bomb to a shelf in a museum for the curios of war. This is its rightful and predestined resting place in a sane world with normal international tensions.

Tennyson wrote:

"There the common sense of most shall hold a fretful realm
And the kindly earth in awe, shall slumber, lapt in
universal law."

He realized that in the last analysis, international tension will remain high until the average man realizes that the solution lies in his hands. The problem is not one of finding a new solution, but of letting sufficient numbers know that it already exists. When this is accomplished, the statesman will readily create the necessary machinery.

BRAZIL

Antonio Austregesilo, M.D.

Professor Emeritus of Psychiatry at the University
of Brazil; Former President of the National Acad-
emy of Medicine; Honorary Professor at the University of Pernambuco (Recife).

CONTEMPORARY civilized humanity is tormented
by anxiety and doubt. Error of emotions and action have led us
to the evils of world-wide tension. To live means to fight for
personal and collective benefits. Anxiety for want of the biggest
and best, poisons the souls of the nations. The history of civilization is based on this natural consequence of intelligence and egotism, this final and intrinsic formula of the species to which we
belong.

From East to West, from China and Japan to Greece, Italy,
Spain, France, England, Germany, Russia, and the United
States, mankind has been driven by inner psychological and
sociological impulse to win in the unending battle of progress
and civilization. Indeed, mankind has not existed for any thirty
years without war or battles. This driving energy originates from
egotism, from the idea of *mine* and *yours*.

Mine and *yours* were the first concepts which formed the
character and tendency towards the constant struggle of the nations that live on the face of the earth: they are, therefore, the
concrete formulas of our vital selves. There is no progress without egotism and without the obstinate energy which leads nations to a permanent state of tension. The aspiration to better
and bigger things is the basis for the accelerated march of all
nations.

We do not know for sure why there is this ambition for predominance among the races. But the truth of the matter is that
mankind is impelled by ideas of force and triumph, aspirations

to predominate and to be the largest and the best. The large nations of the earth want to be leaders through intelligence, intuition, laws, riches, and religious or political formulas; but they also want social predominance over the weak, small, backward, and undeveloped nations. The fable of the lion is certainly a fable of human pretense.

The organization of all society is built on egotism, a kind of galvanizing conductor, mysterious, rising and continuous. Well-being and duty could be the greatest human aspirations, but they are hidden by the energy that directs and guides nations to rise. The question of egotism presents two aspects: on the one hand it concerns the emotions that look to pleasure and individual happiness; on the other, it concerns the capacity to perform deeds that are useful or profitable to whole groups.

We cannot deny that civilized mankind puts its physical and material personality above all contingencies. Only with great moral, religious, or philosophical effort can man escape from the projections of his conscience. The laws of life determine the beginning of the battle.

Greece and Rome gave way to the Anglo-Saxons in spite of the idealism, intelligence, and formulas of beauty that existed in the mind and spirit of the Greeks and Romans. It is the anxiety for the *bigger* and *better* that leads nations and races to technical as well as social victories. Construction and destruction are camouflaged formulas of human egotism. Morals, religions, and philosophies have not as yet modified the human path. The sociological phenomenon is still a mystery. Religions, philosophies, laws, and ethical conceptions cannot extinguish the moral and social tension of the people of the world.

Humanity is now going through the greatest crisis in history. But the reasons are obscure. Certainly human goodness is imperceptible. The powerful take the maximum for themselves and give the rest to the small and weak; the world is unbalanced by the anxiety for the *bigger* and *better* that poisons nations, races, continents and civilizations. These psychological formulas, especially those concerning the emotions, are the inherited causes of international tension. *Mine* and *yours* cunningly destroy world peace and increase discontent. Humanity therefore suffers from collective madness and dissatisfaction.

Happiness is found in striving toward a useful collective life, for everything that is not useful is regressive. World tension grows from unbalanced fundamental laws of life. And humanity today is such a sick soul that, while it makes an effort towards harmonious thinking, it always errs in its actions.

World tension is born psychologically of emotions and suggestibility. These two faculties become sharp and threatening, and lead humanity to the realm of dreams, probabilities, doubts, and uncertainty. Dominated by evil and pessimism, it is as if false thoughts were realities. Such reactions form false realities in the mind and, as a consequence, this kind of dream-awakening gives rise to the radical psychologies of world tension.

Emotions and suggestibility have led humanity to doubt and to the kind of despair and anxiety that have prepared mankind for the present state of world tension. The contemporary philosophy of existentialism blossomed from international tension; the desire for expansion of thought, emotion, and action follows liberation. After the great war, Kierkegaard, Sartre, Heidegger, Camus, Kafka, and others appeared or were revived to interpret the new spirit. The trend of thought and sentiment and action forces mankind to adopt existentialism as a popular philosophy. The goal of existentialism is to clarify the origin of mankind as a symbol of existence, preparatory to the investigation of thought, sentiment, and action at the international level. Existentialism could be the saving philosophy of humanity, because in the liberation of the hidden complexities of the soul lies the road to the cure of world tension. Humanity is eager and anxious for new moral and social leaders. The analysis of human existence, that is, of the whys and wherefores of social phenomena, forms the background of the psychological cure of international tension. Unfortunately, nations do not understand that to have social and international peace, thoughts and sentiments must be reconciled with the forces of human reality.

The social tragedies of the last thirty years have revealed

how egotism, despair, anxiety, doubt and nervous tension lead us to the death of hope.

Religion, national and international politics, philosophical idealism, rights, justice, morals, and the soaring progress of civilization do not alter the fomenting of human tension. Unfortunately, all the century-old idealistic attempts have failed and have become lost in metaphysics, materialism, sensualism, or pragmatism. The liberation of emotions should cure humanity and thereby escape from the threat of an even more severe form of tension. Political doctrines are not capable of guiding humanity; neither individuality, imperialism, communism, Marxism, positivism, Christianity, or agnosticism has proven to be beneficial. It is regrettable that humanity does what it wants whenever it wants because it believes itself to be master of the earth. Unfortunately for humanity, the more cultured people think only of predominance and triumphs. Shamefully enough, force and power are the only ideals that appeal to mankind.

Sociologists, psychologists, and psychiatrists must cooperate in the analysis of social actions and in the cure of world tension. All sociological problems are psychologic ones, and, as a natural consequence, psychiatric. The social disharmonies of people lead to their undoing and to international tension; their cause lies in maladjustment, ambition, and in the misconception of rights, peace, and liberty. In the psychology of existence there are various problems, the solutions of which depend on time, intuition, and wisdom of political leaders, and especially on the capacity for social adjustment.

Brazil is the largest Latin American country and the second in size on the continent. It occupies the fifth place among the most important nations of the world. As to language, the country differs from the rest of the Americas, for Portuguese is spoken in Brazil. The country lies entirely within the bounds of the tropical zone, except in the parts south of the State of São Paulo down to Rio Grande do Sul, where the temperature is mild. The climate is pleasant, even in the parts crossing the equator. The country is mountainous, with a vast coastline along the Atlantic.

The political history of Brazil is rich and interesting. The country was discovered by Pedro Alvaras Cabral, a Portuguese Admiral, in 1500. It was a Portuguese colony until 1822, at which time Pedro I made it a monarchy and proclaimed himself Emperor.

From 1822 until 1889, it was the only monarchy in America. Pedro II reigned as an emperor for sixty years from the time of his minority until the time of his exile, when the Republic was proclaimed. Slavery was abolished on May 13, 1888, on the eve of the proclamation of the Republic (November 15, 1889).

Three factors have entered into the makeup of the Brazilian: the tropical climate, the easy mixture of the Portuguese with the Indian and the African Negro, and the tolerance of a people who always showed themselves without prejudice toward *mestizos*. Today there are forty-five million inhabitants spread over an area of 8,494,299 square kilometers.

According to the Brazilian sociologists Oliveira Viana, Roquette Pinto, Gilberto Freyre, Artur Ramos, and others, the mixture of races has not prejudiced national evolution because everyone participates in all activities and professions, in intellectual as well as artistic and political circles.

The thinking of the Brazilian cannot be analyzed easily; it must be described in detail in order to be well understood by ethnologists and psychologists. Unfortunately, it is very difficult to establish premises for positive deductions in this connection. Much has been written regarding the intelligence and character of the *mestizo*, mulatto, and the other racial types among us. They are all critical and personal opinions of the authors, who sometimes see things erroneously. We can almost definitely state that the intellectual qualities of the Brazilians are very similar to those of the Latins, who are almost all *mestizos*, with American-Indian blood predominating. In Brazil, however, there is a great mixture of Libyans, Indians, and Africans, with Europeans predominating.

The national spirit is vivacious, providing for easy comprehension and easy assimilation. Perhaps there is no persistence in the continuance of intellectual action. Lack of culture and illiteracy hampers the degree of comprehension and progress of the people in certain ways. Precocity also constitutes a spiritual element worthy of mention. Empiric educational studies, though often badly directed, show that the Brazilian child possesses a high intellectual level. There is unfortunately no family education for the child, and there is noticeable malnutrition through ignorance and lack of resources in the country. Moreover, there is lack of hygiene in the homes as a result of the poverty of the lower classes, especially the *mestizos* known as Afro-Brasileiros, who are absolutely lacking in almost all the elementary precepts concerning the health of children. Illiteracy caused by failure to attend school, difficulties caused by the economic incapacity of the nation to solve such a heavy problem, the neglect of elementary duties imposed by the social principles of civilization, the errors that occur automatically through failure to fulfill certain of these duties, and the resistance to new undertakings and actions are responsible for the fact that the culture and hygiene of the Brazilian child stays on a low level compared with that of the great progressive nations of the world. The physical development of Brazilian children is, as a rule, also deficient. This is especially true in the case of the males.

The Brazilian loves peace. He is not a fighter, nor is he quarrelsome. He is hospitable and without arrogance in his international attitude. He has a natural spirit of justice and tolerance which gives him a sympathetic understanding of world conflict.

In the First World War, Brazil was the first American nation to protest against the invasion of Belgian territory by the Germans; and in the second world conflict Brazil joined the Allies as soon as their sovereignty was threatened. Whenever Brazil is called upon to talk on world peace, she defends the cause of the weak and small nations. The prerogatives of a large nation originate from multiple and complex factors. All the Latin nations of America recognize the essentially moral behavior of Brazil. We realize we have lost many opportunities to overcome various social and other difficulties. There is something of a national complacency toward the great problems indispensable to the furtherance of progress and civilization. Failure to educate our people in reading and writing, the technical elements of agriculture, breeding of animals, industrial and commercial techniques, civic culture, sanitary education, the principles of nutrition, and comprehension of politics and public affairs has caused our national progress to be slow and sometimes not in proportion with that of other nations of the earth.

The example of North America must be imitated. There is in no great northern country our mixture of passiveness and of renunciation. In fact, we will not find it in many nations of the world. All observers say that Brazil is the land of the future and that its natural riches have no limits. Yet nature must be harnessed for the advantage of mankind. In such circumstances, much must be done by the natives to benefit the country. The education of the people is one of the sociological problems that Brazil needs to solve. Comprehension of our surroundings and of mankind as a whole are essential factors toward our progress. All the natural features need remodeling and changing in accordance with meteorologic circumstances. Nature is sometimes ungrateful and very often aggressive. Man must be courageous and self-denying to win. Excessive sun, persistent and killing droughts, river floods, and torrential rains cause man to react with valor, self-denial, and courage. Let us add to all this the abundance of insects that are carriers of diseases and parasites, and we have the dramatic conditions of the Brazilian soil. The history of Brazilian national development is very similar to that of almost all the Latin American nations; the same problems of progress and civilization present themselves for solution. They depend on exploitation of natural resources in the American continent. The only exceptions are the United States of America and Canada.

São Paulo is striving to adopt modern methods in dealing with the difficulties caused by meteorologic and telluric conditions. Our coffee state has given examples of growth and courage to the nation in overcoming the difficulties arising from the cultivation of the earth in the development of existing industries. The Brazilian is capable of conquering all obstacles that may arise in the development of the nation. Racial mixture does not in any way hamper the natural progress, in spite of the disturbances that have arisen over the course of the years.

The Brazilian is no different from other Latin American types. His good and bad qualities are similar to those of other Latin peoples who inhabit the new continent. Intellectual, moral, physical and social capacity are approximately the same. Naturally, we have many biosocial problems to solve; these will require great effort on the part of the Brazilian nation. While the work will be difficult, the social advantages will be enormous. Victory will come, due to our topographic and climatic variations and to the vastness of our country. Yet we cannot hope for the degree of civilization that exists in North America. Undeniably Brazil occupies in Latin America a prominent position. For this reason all pessimism should be abandoned. This is not a question of exaggerated patriotism nor merely of optimistic speculation.

The Brazilian is a contributor to human ideas. A Latin and Catholic country without fighting instincts, prohibiting conquests in its constitution, desiring to solve all its boundary problems by arbitration, Brazil must be placed among those countries which wish peace and happiness for all nations in the world. The nation is politically and socially democratic. And this fact gives strength to the people.

There cannot be peace without morals or without liberation from the accumulated complexities of emotions and anxieties. The existing world tension lies in the maladjustment of the ambitions and of politicians in power. Moreover, the people are politically ignorant and indifferent. The social structure is threatened by a return to barbarism, since men cannot comprehend sociological phenomena. We have to cross a long bridge, and there can be nothing but danger if the travelers cause tumult on their way.

Because Brazil is nationally democratic and there is a continuous battle against communism, the ideology of some fanatics will not have the strength to change the national trend. Throughout the world the desire for change exists. But the tendency of nations is to fight against the communistic idea threatening the world. Everyone desires harmony, liberty, ease, comfort, national contentment, and fraternity among the nations. However, there are powerful countries that wish to guide human destiny. Unfortunately, the soul of the world is ill; sociologists and politicians should employ the greatest efforts to allay world tension and to soothe the anxiety that has befallen the world.

Christianity has not been successful in diminishing moral impetuosity, anguish and despair, nervous tension, or doubt in these troubled times. Scientifically, ours is the era of collective psychopathology. Some nations are anxious to have peace. Others, however, arrogantly desire war. This desire is based on the principle that humanity does what it wants when it wants to. Strength and the instinct for power, along with the promise of victory, stir up and excite the emotions. History unfortunately records these same phases of desire for universal power by powerful nations. Greece, Rome, Spain, France, Germany, Japan, and Russia have already held, or tried to hold, the scepter of authority. Individuals of good will want peace, but no one can control the collective and general crisis of nerves that invades the so-called civilized population of the earth.

Anxiety and anguish go hand in hand; in the shadow there is the tension of despair; above the clouds are hopes that are the dowry of men. Emotion and anguished doubt are the cause of world tension. The whole world feels the mysterious force of the sufferers. The psychological basis of contemporary human tension lies within the conscience of all.

The Republic of Plato constituted the first Utopia of history. Human fraternity was only a myth. And Plato said that only through wisdom could human afflictions be ended. The national sovereignty given to the people is opposed to tyranny, despots, unscrupulous governments, illegitimate possessors of power outside the law, and dictators, of whom ancient Rome was so proud. Social democracy and political democracy must exist in any educated and cultured nation. Their advantages are firm; they afford legal liberty to citizens; stimulate governments in honest and just acts, favor initiative and activities of individuals;

facilitate personal guarantees; and repress abuses originating from favoritism. Communism is expressed in individuals massed together by the State. The purpose is to obtain equality; community of possessions is the doctrine of communism. Socialism, collectivism, and administrative Platonism are political variations of contemporary communism in which the State establishes the formulas of right and possession.

World tension originates from doubt in the choice of governments for the people; we do not know where to find the solid ground on which the code of ethics is based. Doubt, anguish, and despair torment the civilized nations.

How can we combat these evils? The question of nationalities and races is not pertinent because all races are involved in the social phenomena of these trying moments we are experiencing. Culture, and especially education, are elements essential in the solution of the moral crisis which humanity is undergoing. Unfortunately, it is the most cultured and best educated people who suffer most from social tension. Intelligence and culture have sped the explosion of the two world wars.

The principles of mental hygiene and prophylaxis are essential to the cure of world tension. The direction of this prophylaxis lies in home education as well as in schools and in social adjustment. One of the principal points is in sexual education, especially in the early stages of life. A child's character is generally formed between the ages of three and five, when parents and teachers usually do not pay much attention to the youngster. It is important that parents and educators do not forget this early period. Nutrition, action, and duty are the principal factors of mental hygiene. Widespread propaganda should penetrate the mind of the public and the spirit of cultured people. It is essential to teach wholesome adjustment to home and to society. Liberty, work, duty, family, country, laws, politics, beliefs, rights, and human cooperation must be emphasized. In other words, humanitarianism is the best way to eliminate the present tension.

The sound principle of renunciation forms the great essence of humanitarianism. Brutality of ambition makes the leaders and the governors of nations the secretaries of the Latin proverb: *Homo homini lupus*. In all political questions, national and international morals should exist. Ethics can be religious, philosophic, biologic, or scientific—but above all they must be human.

Brazil will always be in agreement with measures for peace among men and nations. The Brazilian is good and honest, an enemy of wars except when the rights of men and nations are threatened. Brazil is a cultivator of international politics and of the good-neighbor policy. She is ready to adhere to the principles of right, justice, and duty when her sister countries are attacked. Brazil embraces those social principles which guide nations to peace and aim to cure the great ills of world tension.

CANADA

George H. Stevenson, M.D.

Professor of Psychiatry at the University of Western
Ontario; Superintendent of the Ontario Hospital;
Chairman of the American Psychiatric Associa-
tion's Committee on International Relationships.
Former President of the American Psychiatric
Association.

EVERY nation has a peculiar pride in its own unique
national development. Its national memories may reach back
into the dawn of history. They may be memories of conquest of
barbarian tribes or of a struggle for emancipation from a more
powerful nation. They may be memories of recurrent struggles
for freedom, with happy periods of successful independence
and unhappy periods of failure and defeat. Whatever the memories, the people of each nation are bound together by them with
a feeling of national uniqueness. Canada, too, shares this sentiment of unique nationalism.

The Dominion of Canada, as we now know it, was formed in
1867 by the British North America Act of the British Parliament.
With a total area larger than the continental United States, but
with only one-tenth of its population, Canada has grown by
natural increase and by immigration to its present numbers.
Approximately 6,000,000 Canadians are of British origin; 3,500,-
000 are of French origin and more than 2,000,000 are of other
racial origins, largely European immigrants who came to
Canada before World War I. Canada's population stretches
from east to west in a narrow band close to the United States
border. The great northern mass of land is very sparsely settled.

For nearly two hundred years English-speaking and French-
speaking Canadians have lived side by side, almost in the same
relationship to each other as France and Germany are to each

other in Europe, but fortunately with a completely different intergroup attitude. Since 1759, neither group in Canada has attacked the other by armed force. Both languages are official. The Province of Quebec, like all the other provinces, is completely autonomous for certain aspects of its government. In the Canadian Parliament it has representation equally with other provinces on a representation-by-population basis.

This does not mean that the English and French in Canada have no differences of opinion, or that there is complete cordiality between these two major population groups. Both groups accept themselves and each other as fellow Canadians. But each seeks to develop its own literature, its own culture, its own way of life; and each does so without interference from the other. While there are elements in the Province of Quebec which would like to secede from Canada and to form a nation of their own, the vast majority of French-Canadians realize they have nothing to gain by such action. The union between Britain and France, as advocated by Winston Churchill in the dark days of World War II, has been a reality for nearly two centuries in Canada between French and English Canadians. This point suggests that there is no essential reason for people of differing national groups to go to war to satisfy nationalistic ambitions. As the two groups in Canada seek to understand each other better, an increasing cordiality is developing. However, neither the French nor the English group cultivates the other's language, interests, or friendship to the degree that would be most desirable.

In effect, Canada has grown by peaceful and civilized methods. It has never been split by civil war and has never attacked another nation. Nor has it ever been attacked on its own soil by another nation. The War of 1815 might be looked upon as a minor exception. But Canada, not yet a nation, consisted of only a few isolated colonies, and the war was really between Great Britain and the United States. The Canadian colonies were in the unenviable role of the innocent bystander. Since 1815 there has been no display of arms between Canada and its great neighbor to the south, nor have there been military defenses on either side of the four thousand miles of the international boundary.

Canada has therefore had peace between the racial groups which compose most of its population. It also has had peace with all other countries, except during those times in which it came to the aid of Great Britain.

Peace with other nations has not been accidental. Nor has it been due to pacts, treaties or negotiations. Canada's peaceful evolution to nationhood has been largely due to its fortunate placement between two of the world's great powers. On the one hand, Canada was established as a potential nation by Great Britain, a world power which developed Canadian resources, supplied it with much of its population, and insured it against attack. On the other hand, Canada is immediately adjacent to another great power, the United States of America, which has never shown the slightest desire to annex or conquer Canada (or any other country in the Americas), although well able to do so if it had expansionist aims. Always has there been the greatest cordiality between the United States and Canada, with free exchange of population for permanent settlement or for transient vacationing. The late President Franklin D. Roosevelt put the matter simply and correctly when he stated that the international boundary line between these two nations does not separate them—it unites them.

Canada has therefore come to nationhood as a child is nurtured and trained by its parents, with one hand in the strong hand of John Bull and the other in the equally strong hand of Uncle Sam. On superficial study, this protected environment might not appear to be a desirable influence in the development of national character and national independence. But the situation can be viewed somewhat differently if one thinks of the Canadian people as a link joining the two more powerful nations together. Canada is a part of each—historically, sentimentally and in actual fact. She is part of the British commonwealth of nations, and just as truly, because of propinquity, trade, travel and language, she is one with the United States of America in her standards of living, world outlook and cultural interests.

Citizens of Canada find it impossible to think of Canada as an aggressor nation. For Canada to voluntarily attack another nation for selfish reasons is inconceivable. Some nations might say that our attitude is so unwarlike because we are one of the "have" nations. With the natural resources of a continent to develop, with railroads and factories and cities to be built, with an open door policy for qualified immigrants from Europe who might wish to share our work and the results of our work, surely these challenges should satisfy our fighting instincts. It would be impossible for Canada to think of waging war for prestige, for trade advantages, for "lebensraum," for "defense," or for domination of other nations for purely selfish nationalistic reasons. War between the peoples of two countries, if both are reasonable, should be just as inconceivable as actual warfare between any two cities of a nation. If intercity rivalries can be solved by negotiation, international rivalries should be equally soluble.

Canada is much more concerned with being international than with being merely national. Just as we prefer to be on friendly terms with one another as individuals, so in a national sense we desire to be on friendly terms with every other nation. When we demonstrate our ability to get along comfortably among our own racial groups, and equally well with national groups elsewhere, we find it difficult to understand why European countries have to be so violently unfriendly with one another, as recent decades have demonstrated. It was this difficulty of comprehension that made us impatient of intra-European quarrels and led so many Canadians to a policy of isolationism. Our attitude to European quarrels might have been worded thus: "If these European peoples haven't any more sense than to fight with one another when there is really no good reason why they should fight, then we don't want to get mixed up in their quarrels." Canada entered the World Wars unwillingly because they seemed so unnecessary.

Canada thinks that nations should live like civilized gentlemen who settle their individual disputes not by force but by means of a generous and sympathetic understanding of each other's problems. Unfortunately, this may appear to be an inept analogy, because the seemingly civilized and cultured individual has often sought to exploit and trample any fellow human being who was in an inferior social or economic position. Underprivileged people have had a difficult time to improve their lot so as to be able to compete on equal terms with the rich and mighty. On a national basis, internal warfare, as in the French Revolution, demonstrated that blood-letting is sometimes necessary to obtain this end. Other instances have been the American Revolutionary War and the revolt of Russia's underprivileged in the Bolshevik uprising of 1917. But within Canada such warfare has not been necessary. By an evolutionary process, by social progress and the rise of labor unions, the same result has been achieved bloodlessly.

Some nations might contend that Canada is a wealthy and selfish country which seeks not only to hold its present wealth, but also seeks to exploit and impoverish still further the economically underprivileged nations.

When did Canada ever seek to exploit any other country or refuse to share her wealth with others? Nations live by trade as people live by exchanging the results of their individual efforts. Canada has lived and worked by the free enterprise system. She has sought a fair price for her products to enable her to live and to develop. Such a program calls for no apology. Moreover, Canada would like to see all other countries equally successful, for profitable trade can only be carried on with countries with adequate standards of living and the means to pay for the products they need to import.

As a comparatively recent newcomer into the family of nations—almost the newest—Canada is grateful for its material blessings and opportunities. It has no traditional hatreds or jealousies. Like a child raised among loving relatives, it wants to be on good terms with everyone. Canada sees no real reason why nations cannot live together harmoniously in one world. Canada is convinced that international difficulties are not due essentially to geography or economics. Because Canadian national development has been by peaceful evolution, we see no reason why international problems cannot be solved by agreement, arbitration, common sense and the application of the golden rule.

There is an impression that in Europe the mere fact that some one speaks a different language or lives on the opposite side of an imaginary line makes such a person an enemy. And if an enemy, therefore he is to be distrusted, kept at bay, conquered or killed. From Canada's viewpoint this is an irrational attitude for civilized, intelligent people to take. Such an attitude is understandable in lower forms of life, but we see no reason for our species to continue such primitive behavior when we all have the same objectives and can solve our problems by intelligence if we will. Our similarities being so much greater than our differences, such similarities should bring us together in cooperative friendship. Our minor differences should not be allowed to cause enmity between us.

Canadians do not want to assume a smug attitude of superior wisdom or higher intelligence than that possessed by European countries. We have led a very sheltered and protected national life in one of the world's most pleasant places. It would ill become us to ask the European countries to make us their example. Nevertheless, if the United States of America and Canada can live amicably side by side for a great many years, with every prospect of permanent friendship, we cannot help but wish the European countries would use good will rather than ill will in their relationships with one another. In the past two or three centuries practically all the larger countries of Europe, alone or in various combinations, have sought to conquer their neighbors. And with what result? Every country in Europe which has participated in such international conflicts is now prostrate and bankrupt. They have lost millions of their finest young men in battle. When one considers the splendid contributions to art, literature, and science that have been made by each of these countries, it is scarcely conceivable that they should have sought to destroy themselves by warfare on the vastest scale ever known. It would be inconceivable if it were not already an accomplished fact.

There are those who claim that all wars are due basically to economic factors. Do economic difficulties need to be solved by force of arms? What is intelligence to be used for? Surely for something better than inventing atom bombs.

The paradoxical fact is that many of the world's economic problems would have been solved if Hitler had won. The German nation, as absolute ruler of the world, would have exacted tribute from all the slave states, and would be wealthy. The slave states (the rest of the world) would have had economic security at a marginal subsistence level. Hitler's war was a war to end all wars for a thousand years. His logic on this point was inexorable. But Hitler did not win his war. He wrecked Europe instead. It appears that Stalin, having won Europe by default, intends to pursue the same logic and is preparing to attack the western nations exactly as Hitler attacked France and Britain. Imitating Hitler, he neutralized the nations close to Russian borders and strengthened Russia for an all-out attack on the western powers. Like Hitler, he prefers to conquer by an ideology—the ideology of communism. Failing that, he is bound to use force of arms.

There are various pretexts for beginning a war—economic need, national security, "lebensraum," welfare of the common man. But these are merely pretexts—they are spurious reasons, or rationalizations. There are deeper psychological reasons for international warfare, reasons or motives which are not understood by the leaders who make war inevitable or by the people who follow the leaders to their doom.

All forms of life are endowed with aggressive qualities to assist them in the search for food and the protection of their lives and the lives of their young. Some forms of life have little of this aggressive drive and depend more on means of escape from potential danger. But the human animal is a fighting animal. He has strong aggressive drives which have led him to first place in the animal kingdom.

In earlier phases of man's development it may have been necessary to kill or be killed. The survival of the fittest is still the law of the jungle. And men have always thrilled to the challenge of a fight. Men still love danger, they still love a fight. Whether it be a modern sublimation of the fighting instinct such as a political campaign, or the actual encounter in warfare, men love to fight. Other popular forms of sublimations of the fighting instinct are the competition between men for financial success, the jealous rivalry between men for the affections of a woman, or the struggles between baseball teams and hockey teams which are shared vicariously by huge crowds of spectators. Even gardening, fishing, hunting or housecleaning can be useful sublimations of the instinct to fight.

In warfare itself few can resist the appeal of military life with its freedom from the daily routine of civilian drudgery, the anticipation of travel, the opportunities of new sexual adventures, economic security and rewards for bravery. Danger itself becomes a joy. And there is always the appeal to patriotism, the protection of one's home and family by the destruction of the threatening enemy.

It appears therefore that most men have an accumulation of energy which they need to release in an aggressive manner. Warfare permits the ethical acceptance of a more attractive mode of life which at one time in our development was normal and mature for those primitive times. Few men would admit that they want to engage in warfare for the enjoyment of it, but there can be no denying that actions speak louder than words. We thrill to the possibilities of war. We become bored and irritated with the inaction of peace.

"A moral equivalent for war," to use the phrase of William James, that will be a satisfactory sublimation of our fighting instincts, is an urgent need. We have many "moral equivalents for war," but the tragedy is that we refuse to be satisfied with them.

In a sense, civilization today has not advanced beyond the schoolboy stage of individual development. Schoolboys are always ready for a fight, no matter how trifling the cause. An adult coming upon two boys in a fight will separate them and urge them to reconcile their differences in a friendly manner. But grown men, millions of them, with much more intelligence than schoolboys, do not take the advice they give to the fighting schoolboys. Instead, they hurl themselves at each other to their mutual destruction. Such mutual murder or mutual suicide (either name will do) does much to support the concept that the wish to die is at least as strong as the wish to live. The need is evident for a maturing of the emotions to strengthen our thin veneer of civilization. People in other countries are people like ourselves. They are our enemies only because we accept that traditional belief, or because their leaders or our leaders force us to be enemies.

We live in a fear-ridden world. The self-preservative and nation-preservative tendencies are usually associated with fear—fear of our own destruction or fear of losing our wealth or freedom. Fear, however it is stimulated, leads us to view with suspicion the nation that appears to threaten our security. Fear does more than that—it may make us believe that the threatening nation is more evil than it actually may be. The threatening nation may be ominous. This may be a wise provision of nature so as to increase our defensive energy. Certainly we do not want to be lulled into underestimating any threat. But when national (or personal) fear is aroused, we cannot view the threat in its correct proportions. An interesting psychological comparison is observed when the emotion of love is aroused. Here we characteristically overvalue the loved object. The young man in love fails to see any faults in his beloved—although other people can see them easily.

It is natural to build up defenses against possible attack by non-aggression pacts, by mutual defense pacts and by the accumulation of armaments. The nation or group of nations which has assumed threatening attitudes observes the defensive actions being taken by other groups of nations and it in turn becomes fearful; it also makes similar pacts and builds up similar armaments. Stockpiles of weapons increase rapidly in the opposite camps, each seeking to increase its own feeling of security and to overcome its feeling of fear. Actually, such augmenting of arms results only in augmented insecurity in each group. The larger our enemy's stockpile becomes, the larger our fear becomes and the greater are our efforts to build

still greater stockpiles of arms. Sooner or later, some overt unfriendly incident is bound to occur, and the stockpiles of arms
are used for our mutual destruction. No man can play with firearms without wanting to use them, whether he holds a small-
caliber rifle or a stockpile of atom bombs.

This does not mean that a growing armament is a direct cause
of international warfare. It merely means that such armament
facilitates war; it makes sure that war is inevitable. The greater
the stockpiles of arms in rival groups, the greater is the assurance
of war.

A reduction in armament by mutual consent might be a helpful procedure. Britain, with Canada's full acquiescence, asked
Germany to agree to such a program in 1912, but Germany refused. And the armaments race went on to its inevitable conclusion in World War I. The race for arms started again in the
Hitler regime only to culminate in World War II. The present
race between the Russian-dominated countries and the North
Atlantic Pact countries can have no other termination than
World War III. Reduction of armament by mutual consent is
at present impossible because of the degree of fear (or greed)
on each side. There can be no military disarmament without
psychological disarmament; i.e. a reduction in fear and an increase in good will.

The most important psychological factor of all is the problem
of leadership and following. Groups must have leaders, and
leaders must have followers. In the western democracies the
people elect their representatives to make laws for the nation
and to deal with representatives of other nations in international
affairs. We select as our representatives those persons who appear to be unusually well-informed, able, and ethical. From
among these specially selected representatives are chosen the
persons of the highest capacity to become presidents, prime
ministers, cabinet members, etc. This is democracy at work at
its idealistic best. But we cannot always be sure we have chosen
wisely. When everyman's vote is as good as anyman's vote, we
may find we have not chosen representatives but rather that
representatives have chosen us.

Many national leaders have strong aggressive drives for dominance over others. They are attractive, magnetic people. They assure us they have no other ambition than to serve us. They appeal to our cupidity by promises to advance our interests. We elect them to power, only to find too often we have elected ourselves into their power. They become our masters. We are hypnotized by them. We believe what they want us to believe. We do what they want us to do. They may be fanatical, paranoidal, selfish and cruel; they may have lower ethical standards than we had thought, and they may have hatreds within them which seek an outlet by aggression. Such aggression may be against minority groups within their own land, or against peace-loving citizens of adjoining lands.

Most people (of any country) are satisfied to have interesting work; the enjoyment of their homes, families and recreational activities are pleasant sublimations of their fighting tendencies. The will to live and develop is quite strong in most people, who desire only life, liberty, and the pursuit of happiness. One who has traveled in countries other than his own is surprised to observe how kind and friendly are the people of other nationalities. They are anything but the violent, evil, or vicious persons he may have expected them to be. Making allowances for minor racial and cultural differences, the traveler realizes that they are much the same as the people of his own country. We have no quarrel with them or they with us. If they have a famine, or a plague or an earthquake, we send them aid; they do the same for us if the situation is reversed.

But let an unprincipled or psychopathic leader sow the seeds of fear or suspicion: then everything changes. Hostility develops, unfriendliness replaces friendliness, tension mounts. The evil leader manipulates his people into a warlike position. Arms are increased. The chain reaction has started which too often ends in the explosion of war.

The problem is how to select leaders who are genuinely ethical, unselfish and capable, and who are broad-minded enough to consider the welfare of all people. National leaders should be required to demonstrate approved qualifications for the tre-

mendous responsibility that goes with high office. It may be premature to urge that candidates for parliament or congress be
given psychological tests, as is done in the case of candidates for
the medical profession and for various other professions, to determine their personality fitness and aptitude for such responsibility. We already insist that barbers, engineers, dentists and
persons in many other occupations and professions hold a cer-
tificate of competency. Should the leaders of great states not
also hold certificates of competency? Is any position more important for the welfare of the citizens generally than a position
of national leadership? Are personal magnetism and a selfish
ambition sufficient credentials for high office? Should not political parties be required to secure the approval of the highest
social science bodies in the nation for candidates for parliament
or congress?

We may not be ready for such radical proposals. But there is
no problem in international relationships so acute or so important for the welfare of the world as the selection of national
leaders who have a conscience for international responsibilities.
Education is the most important word in any language, but it
is not the education of the masses that is needed; it is the education of our leaders. The people of all countries, if offered a ref-
erendum, would vote overwhelmingly in favor of peaceful and
constructive national and international development. But too
often these friendly peaceful aims are thwarted by the rise of
psychopathic leaders. The people need to be educated in better
ways of selecting their leaders, and in the vicious effects of disturbed emotions which may be planted and cultivated in them
by unprincipled leaders.

Leaders should be broadly educated not only in the art of
winning elections but, more important, in the psychology of
international friendship, as well as in political science and economics on a world basis. Leaders should also be broadly trained
in history, and should have a thorough knowledge of world
history not merely from books but from actually living with
peoples of various races and nations.

And if education is the final key to world peace, we should

endeavor to become educated to the necessity for emotional maturity, and the need for advancing far beyond the present stage of international relationships. We need to be educated to recognize that people of a different tongue or a different color who live on the other side of an imaginary line are not enemies, but friends. And they need to be similarly educated about us.

It would be presumptuous and untrue to claim that the Canadian people are all emotionally mature and endowed with an altruistic world outlook. Nevertheless, the Canadian people as a whole, irrespective of their original national origins, have no greater desire than to live on good terms with their fellows in all other countries. We hold no national hatred against any people. We realize that the German people who have settled in Canada are among our very best citizens, and that the German people in Germany who became Nazis were equally good citizens until they fell under the evil influence of evil leaders.

The world's tragedy is the failure of certain countries to find the right type of leaders for their international relationships. It has rightly been said that it takes two countries to agree on peace, but only one country to agree on war. Germany was determined to dominate the world by force and would not recede from this position, forcing other countries to defend themselves. Russia at the present moment resembles the Germany of 1914 and 1939. War is the only end of such warlike preparations. But the Russian farmers no more want war than Canadian farmers want war, nor do Russian factory workers desire war any more than do Canadian factory workers. Therefore it is semantically incorrect to say that Russia wants war. More correctly, it should be said that a small group of Russian leaders, for reasons of their own, perhaps because of internal aggressive drives which they may not understand, are leading millions of good Russian people into a World War III still more devastating than either of its predecessors.

Canada and the other western nations cannot permit themselves to be subjugated by Russian arms; we are therefore forced to arm ourselves for the defense of our homelands. And yet we know that the propaganda of the Russian leaders, directed to their people, would have them believe that the western powers are planning a war against them, thus increasing Russian suspicion and hostility to us. Fear and greed are again leading the world to destruction.

Canada can only plead for psychological disarmament as well as military disarmament, for a broader outlook than a merely national outlook, for the support of law and order through the United Nations and its specialized agencies, the World Health Organization and UNESCO, and for the willing observance of the golden rule. It should be just as easy to maintain friendly relations with people who live outside our national boundaries as it is to maintain friendly relations with people within our national boundaries. This way lies civilization, culture, and progress. The other way lies war, destruction, savagery. All of us are human. Let us show that we are worthy of our humanity.

DENMARK

Hjalmar Helweg, M.D.

Director of the University Psychiatric Clinic, Former Chairman of the Danish Psychiatric Association, and Professor of Psychiatry at the University of Copenhagen.

To understand tension between nations, one must first understand tension between individuals.

Two highly different persons may remain happily married throughout their lifetimes without tension ever arising between them—even though they occasionally disagree fundamentally. Partners of different temperament may work together in business in a perfectly calm and secure manner. If neighbors differ widely in temperament, social position and interests, there need not develop any tension on that account. They may avoid having anything to do with one another. Their feeling for one another may be one of indifference, or even of disgust. While such a condition may sometimes give rise to awkward situations, no tension need arise between them.

The concept of tension implies an element of *active* animosity. Tension appears only if there is reason to believe that one party will grab something at the expense of the other. Tension presupposes a tendency to aggressiveness or at least an assumption of such a tendency. What one wants to grab is quite immaterial. Between individuals, it may take such a paradoxical form as the wish to win the friendship of someone who does not want to give it. The approaches of the first person may even appear benevolent. But the mere offer of favors may be enough to induce tension with its typical stamp of animosity. The feeling of security that prevailed as long as the two parties were indifferent to each other has now disappeared.

Aggressiveness on one side gives rise to fear on the other. This relation may be mutual; both sides may become afraid of each other's aggressiveness. Only when one side is decidedly weaker than the other will the fear be entirely on that side and the aggressiveness on the other. Without aggressiveness and fear there can be no tension, even though mutual sympathy is lacking and the two parties take pains to avoid one another.

However, there is another prerequisite for the development of tension between two persons. They must be in contact. They may be neighbors and owners of adjacent properties, they may be relatives, or they may have business connections. On some point or other they must have to deal with one another. Otherwise they can avoid tension by steering clear of one another.

Are these simple experiences of single persons applicable to nations? Such an assumption cannot be taken for granted. It is not possible to look upon nations as entities in the same way as individual persons are entities. A nation is made up of a great number of persons bound together with ties of varying strength and character. There are geographical borders and political borders, common language, common history, common religion, and cultural habits; there are common government and legislation, common fate under historical upheavals and common industrial interests. Yet all these forms of community need not be present at the same time. Political borders may encompass different nations, as in the case of the Hapsburg monarchy. Switzerland is a nation, even though it is made up of three separate language-groups. Germany was divided into a Protestant Northern Germany and a Catholic Southern and Western Germany. Yet it was one nation. Nor need the ties which hold a nation together necessarily involve all the individuals of the nation. In fact, this practically never happens. But the uniting ties must affect the majority of the community, particularly the independent-thinking majority. Otherwise no nation will result. There would merely be a population, a mob.

Considering the international attitude of a nation and the mutual relations of nations, the matter becomes more complicated. In thoroughly democratic countries, where freedom of speech is completely unhampered, the leaders (political as well as intellectual) represent a considerable segment of the population. From the attitude of these leaders it is possible to draw conclusions about the attitude of the nation. In countries with a dictatorial government, such a parallel cannot be made. The nation *may* agree with the leaders, but nobody can be sure about it. No one would venture to depend upon it. The apparent attitude of the nation may be enforced; but its actual attitude may be altogether different. In countries with this kind of government, we have only the attitude of the leaders to go by. Whether or not this attitude be in agreement with that of the people, it must be taken as reflecting the attitude of the nation. As a result, one often sees a more definite attitude than is found in democratic countries. The latter may sometimes appear so divided that they seem to have no attitude at all. This situation has been particularly true in France during certain periods.

International tension, then, is not as simple as emotional tension between individuals. The century-old tension existing between Denmark and Germany has never prevented many Danes from maintaining close friendship with certain Germans. Lively business connections and cultural associations have been able to blot out tension for long periods. The tension is felt only when the ties uniting individuals into a nation are forcibly brought into the foreground. But even in the most harmonious periods of peace between two nations, there may be large factions maintaining a state of tension with its deep-rooted animosity. At decisive moments the sentiment of these factions may become dominant. The tension between nations, then, is characterized by critical situations. However, it may be present as a latent possibility.

As in the case of tension between individuals, the prerequisites of tension between nations are aggressiveness on one side and fear on the other, with contact as an indispensable condition.

It is obvious that the danger of international tension has increased greatly in the past fifty years. It is also an ordinary but indisputable truth that our present highly developed means of communication have increased the possibility of international intercourse. To an even higher degree, they have increased the danger of international conflict. As late as a few decades ago, no one envied Denmark the colony of Greenland. Today it has become a border post. Until a few years ago the border of England might aptly be said to lie at the Rhine. Today the border of the United States of America is said to be situated at the same place. Air traffic has made neighbors of us all, with the advantages of neighborship, but also with its danger of aggressiveness and tension.

What is it that creates aggressiveness? Some nations live as peaceful neighbors without the least notion of attacking one another. An example of this situation is found in the Scandinavian countries. Through the centuries they waged war on one another. Denmark was once the master of Sweden. Sweden occupied Denmark, seized its capital and deprived it of its provinces. Up to the time of Napoleon, Denmark had to reckon with Sweden as a potential enemy.

But then the Scandinavian countries stopped fighting. They became close neighbors. Yet they still differ in political interests and national temperament. On special occasions, beautiful things are said about the brotherhood of the three peoples, their near-related languages and their historical solidarity. But apart from these festive oratories, in all three countries are heard expressions of ill-will towards our emotionally differing neighbors. If one wishes friendly relations with them, it is advisable not to enter too far into a history filled with war and mutual aggression.

Yet the Scandinavian countries quit fighting. In 1905, Norway separated from the personal union with Sweden. A self-conscious nation will usually not tolerate such action. Some people were afraid it would mean war. But war did not come. Sweden and Norway simply could not go to war against each other. Norway got its new king from Denmark. Yet this did not spoil Denmark's friendly relations with Sweden. Some years ago, Denmark and Norway disagreed over certain rights in Greenland. Some people began to talk about war. But the greater majority of people looked upon these persons as fools. War between Norway and Denmark was impossible. The matter was decided by the

International Court at The Hague. Norway lost the case and
deferred to the decision of the court. It was a bitter cup, but
good neighborship stood the strain.

The World War of 1939–45 put the Scandinavian countries
to a hard task. Norway and Denmark were occupied by the
Germans, while Sweden kept up relations with the enemy. Finland, which makes the fourth link in the Scandinavian ring, went
directly to war on the German side. In spite of everything, it
was realized as an unshakable fact that under no circumstances
would Scandinavian countries wage war against one another.

The only explanation of this phenomenon appears to be that
the Scandinavian people have overcome the tendency to aggression. And this not merely because the countries are small
and weak. Other countries, which militarily are far from being
great powers, enter into war in the hope of being able to seize
territory at the expense of their neighbors. Even today, Sweden
is strong enough to fish in troubled waters by appropriating
parts of Denmark. But Sweden will not do this. Sweden does
not want the enmity of her neighbors.

This absence of aggression persists in spite of many national
contrasts and divergent interests. What has become of the Scandinavian tendency to aggression? Is its disappearance a result
of weakened national feeling, or slackness and lack of character,
of degeneration? Is the tendency to aggression any proof—the
only adequate proof—of the power and viability of the nation?
And when a nation has lost its power as well as the desire to
attack its neighbors, is it then unworthy to live as a free nation?
Is the loss of the aggressive tendency a symptom of national decay, the beginning of the final dissolution?

These are the things that Hitler asserted. They give us food
for thought. Hitler consistently and successfully preached war
as the most sublime manifestation of the individual and of the
nation. He gloried in conquest and the suppression of other nations. He even claimed their annihilation as the mission of Germany and as a task predestined by Providence. Yet Hitler was
mad, not only in the popular sense, but also in the psychiatric
sense. He was a psycopath with strong neurotic and hysterical
elements in his make-up. This fact in itself must necessarily

raise doubt about the gospel he preached, a gospel which the entire German nation accepted and applauded.

Since a nation as a whole cannot become pathologic and neurotic, why did so many Germans enthusiastically embrace the Hitler doctrine of aggression? Only individuals can become neurotic. But a nation may include so many individuals who are susceptible to pathologic thought that they become strong and numerous enough to carry the masses away with them and establish themselves as rulers. That is what happened in Hitler's Germany. After the defeat in 1918, and the following inflation, the Germans were disillusioned, perplexed, and far more susceptible to suggestion than to common sense. Those who tried to arouse the tendency to aggression stood a far better chance to succeed than those who attempted to show the way to rational cultural development. The insecurity of the German population was utilized to produce a regressive feeling, a retrograde development towards a more primitive cultural stage.

Culture is cultivation. And if there is to be any sense in the meaning of the word, the cultural progress of a nation must mean a continuously rising development in the utilization of the materialistic and spiritual resources of the people. A return to aggression in the form of the destruction of others is a breach in cultural development and is in conflict with the normal.

When it was realized that Hitler had aroused the aggression of the German people, neighboring countries began to be afraid. In Denmark, a close neighbor of Germany even before airplanes did away with the significance of political frontiers, it took considerable time before the tension became conspicuous. Much has been said about the carefree way in which Denmark failed to prepare itself defensively and the unconcern with which it was taken for granted that unprovoked attacks were something that might take place elsewhere, but not in Denmark. It was indeed a heedless attitude. But it arose from the circumstance that Denmark had culturally outgrown its aggressive tendencies. Hitler's *Mein Kampf* had been read by relatively few, and hardly anybody had understood it. It was "foreign" talk which no one cared to take seriously.

There is a parallel here with certain phenomena encountered

in psychiatric practice. A man becomes irritable, neurotic, and psychologically unbalanced when previously he had been friendly and considerate. Now he becomes inconsiderate and brutal; in his quarrels with his wife he threatens excitedly to kill her. She does not take this threat seriously, for she knows her husband in his normal state and she knows that he is not a killer. One day, however, he really kills her. It is realized too late that this action might really have been expected.

In Denmark, where all thought of aggression had long been discarded, the people neither could nor would understand that their German neighbor again had become dangerous. The last time Germany had made war on Denmark was in 1864. While this war had not been forgotten, it was a thing of the past for the younger generation. It was long ago, and those parts of the country which were then lost and which had preserved the Danish mind and language had been returned to Denmark, voting themselves back after the First World War. The past had been put aside, just as the old Swedish conquests of Denmark had been wiped off the slate long ago. In brief, the idea of aggression had left the mind of the Danish people.

This carefree, naive, and stubborn aversion to facing squarely the cultural decline of Germany was maintained not only after the attacks on Austria, Czechoslovakia, and Poland, but even after the German occupation of Denmark on April 9, 1940. This act was not misunderstood. Not only did it violate the unwritten laws of civilization, it was an outrage against solemn treaties as well. Yet many Danes were unable to realize what had taken place. Cultural regression was beyond their understanding. They could not imagine themselves falling down, and they could not comprehend such action in their German neighbors. During the German occupation of Denmark, the Danish people slowly became conscious that this was not a bad dream but the real and deadly truth. The people then began to defend themselves —late but earnestly.

The development from lust of power and aggression to peaceful work and achievement thrives better in a small country which, from its very lack of power, is forced to curb its aggressive tendencies. It is difficult to get rid of aggression as long as one is strong enough to be aggressive. Aggression is a sign of immaturity, both in the life of the individual and in the life of the nation.

The tendency towards aggression in itself is not abnormal. In modern child psychology, it is recognized as an indisputable fact that the normal child possesses a clearly-developed aggressive tendency. It is also recognized that if aggression is not released, it may bring about neurosis and serious developmental disorders. One of the chief tasks of education is to direct the aggressive tendencies of the child into the proper paths. It must not be crushed nor should it be improperly encouraged. It must be directed so that its inherent power may be utilized for the free evolution of the full potentialities of the individual. It is not a sign of abnormality when a boy breaks his toys, fights other boys or throws stones at the porcelain insulators of the telegraph poles. But it indicates a faulty development if he continues this practice. As he grows older, his energies must be guided into other channels.

Something similar applies to a nation. Denmark was once a nation in its childhood. The Danes, in the Viking period, conquered England and plundered and sacked towns in France and Italy. Culturally, this was an immature and childish stage. But the people had to go through it, and it would be unjustifiable to take it as evidence of an abnormal mentality of the Vikings. On the contrary, seen from a culture-historical point of view, it would have been abnormal if there had been no such period.

It is quite a different matter when aggression is not led into other channels, or when it suddenly turns up again at a later period in its immature form. Both these things happened in Germany. German culture, which rightly has been highly praised, was uneven. In the old Empire, before 1918, aggression was still alive, in spite of a highly developed material and spiritual culture. It was alive because the German form of government was not democratic. Aggression was able to put its stamp on the entire nation as long as it was present in even a relatively few powerful individuals. When, after the First World War,

Germany turned to a democratic form of government, the mind of the people was still unbalanced. The conditions for cultural evolution were extremely unfavorable. It was then that the regression to cultural immaturity—to aggressiveness—took place. This process developed with a force and violence which astounded the other countries of the world. It staggered them into paralysis. That this process was set into motion by a madman was symbolic. But the real culturally pathologic aspect of the matter was neither the influence of Hitler nor his utilization of the situation; it was the cultural regression to a more primitive developmental stage.

For the present Germany has been forced to put its aggressiveness aside. But how this action will behave in the future, is hard to say. If one can draw inferences by analogy from the developmental forms of the aggression in the individual, the prospects are not particularly good. If an individual falls back to the stage of aggressive immaturity, it is very difficult for him to develop in a healthy human way. It is not altogether unreasonable to fear that nations will behave in the same way. Cultural decay in the form of even more uncontrollable aggressiveness is an obvious possibility. It is to be hoped that mankind will be spared such a calamity.

The damage done thus far is more than enough. The people killed and the countries destroyed constitute the visible and measurable destruction. This damage is inconceivably great, yet it is measurable. But the psychological consequences of cultural regression are beyond measure.

Tension between nations was great before the two World Wars. But in many places it was greater among the governments and diplomats than in the mind of the man in the street. Prior to 1914, there was a widespread feeling that there was a trend away from aggressive wars and conquest among civilized nations. This belief was a matter of blind faith, but it did exist. It suffered a shock during the First World War, and yet it revived here and there. Today tension, with its two usual characteristics, aggression and fear, is present everywhere.

Historically, there is no reason why Denmark should fear

Russia. Russia has never done Denmark any harm, and perhaps has no intention of doing so. But can this be relied upon? The world has regressed to developmental forms that belong to the childhood of culture. It is no longer normal; its further development is incalculable.

The greatest crime of Naziism was that it stopped the evolution away from fear and tension between nations, that it threw the world back into immaturity. The mature man and the mature nation desire order, peace, liberty, and evolution rather than war and revolution. The lust for power belongs to the stage of immaturity. Even the most highly gifted and prominent men, if they have the lust for power, convey a certain impression of immaturity. One cannot help thinking: It is a pity that this gifted man is not a fully grown man. With his great faculty, he would then be able to do all the more good. More important, there would then be no need to fear him. Similarly, mature nations go to war only when they need to defend themselves. It is the immature nation that is the danger to peace.

One might now ask, what is it that promotes maturity in nations? Such maturity grows gradually, as increasing numbers of individuals think independently and allow common sense to prevail over their emotions. When the Scandinavian countries silently agreed not to wage war on one another, it was not because the inhabitants had advanced in virtue and morale; it was because they had become more sensible. They realized that war is foolish. Sigmund Freud asserted that the progress of humanity depends on the extent to which common sense overcomes emotional daydreams. Freud gives a side glance to cultural evolution in general, saying: "Owing to morbid factors or particularly strong desires, a certain percentage of humanity will probably always be asocial. But if we could reduce the anticultural majority to a minority, much would be gained in our own time—possibly as much as might ever be hoped for."

Aggressiveness determined by desire is hostile to culture. It leads to tension and war; and any nation wishing to strengthen itself culturally will have to counteract this tendency.

The objection might be raised that the individuals who govern a country and who decide to wage war are by no means always guided by emotion and desire. At times they are, but often they are hard-calculating intellectuals. But these unfeeling rulers cannot wage war by themselves. They are powerless unless they can carry the nation with them. This can be done only by arousing the emotions. A nation dominated by clear-thinking individuals is difficult to drive to aggression. It must first get excited. Its common sense must be suspended to such an extent that the few persons still guided by their intellect have nothing to say.

A large and powerful nation would not be dangerous to a small and weak nation if common sense were always strong enough to assert itself; especially if culturally mature individuals were able to put a damper on the immature and primitive ones. Danger arises when the latter group gets the upper hand.

The remedy against aggression and war, therefore, consists in culture. And culture is simply the national cultivation of positive values. War has no positive values. The doctrine of Mussolini and Hitler that war is the most valuable and most noble display of the strength of a nation is probably the greatest delusion of modern times. War is destruction and nothing else. It is hostile to culture. The heroic emotions it arouses can, at best, merely establish the fact that culture is rich enough even in its downfall or destruction to display some elements of beauty. But these glimpses of beauty are paid for dearly.

Thus the maturity of nations is promoted by cultural evolution—by education, liberty and independence. Freedom of thought and speech—briefly, democracy—is indispensable. Those who are forced to think only what others dictate can never attain intellectual superiority. They will always be threatened by the danger lurking in primitive desires and passions.

The question now arises: What makes cultured nations fall back on immature and aggressive patterns of behavior? For those acquainted with the glorious cultural past of the German nation—its achievements in music, poetry, philosophy and science—it seems inconceivable that the cultural downfall which began in 1914 and which culminated in 1945 could take place.

This downfall is explained by the fact that what we call

culture is a very complicated evolutionary process. Its development need not necessarily be harmonious, nor does it advance equally in all fields. Certain forms of development, such as the arts and sciences, are so radiant as to make us overlook the lagging development in other areas.

Psychiatrists speak of a form of developmental inhibition called psycho-infantilism. The psycho-infantile person may be highly gifted and capable of intellectual contributions of the first order. Yet he is immature and his mental development is not harmonious. Outside his own profession his thought remains naive; he reacts to the conditions of life as an adolescent.

It might be improper to speak of psycho-infantile nations. But sometimes we meet with features in cultural evolution which remind us of this condition. While the gifted individuals of a nation are capable of high accomplishment, the attitude of the nation and its potential conduct depends on the man in the street. If the masses are untrained in independent thought, are without spiritual freedom and security, and are bound by the second-hand phrases of authority, the day will come when they will fall victims to emotional delusions. Then the more brilliant cultural developments are swept aside, and primitivity reigns supreme. As the strength of a chain is measured by its weakest link, the strength of culture depends on equal and harmonious development in all fields.

A cultured nation, however, while developing mental maturity and adult common sense, may nevertheless be poor in great creative minds. As such, it has no chance of contributing to the spiritual life of the world, and as a cultured nation it will stagnate. But if the large masses of a nation are lacking individually in mental maturity, there is the risk of sudden spiritual retrogression. Such a nation then becomes dangerous.

War and its precursor, international tension, are not diseases. Large masses of people do not become mentally disordered at once. World tension and war depend on the outbreak of a compulsive lust which, at a given stage of culture, should have been suppressed or overcome. Such behavior is a regression to a state which civilized man should long since have outgrown.

ENGLAND

Ernest Jones, M.D.

Honorary President of the International Psycho-
Analytical Association, British Psychoanalytic So-
ciety and the London Institute of Psychoanalysis;
Editor of the International Library of Psycho-
analysis; consulting Physician to the London
Clinic for Psychoanalysis; Co-editor of the British
Journal of Medical Psychology.

A SPECIAL interest attaches to tension between
powerful nations in that the culmination of it may be catastrophic and world-wide. But psychologically the causes and
motivation of such events cannot be fundamentally different
from those of minor conflicts. We shall be well advised, therefore, to consider a broad review of the problem. This has the
further advantage of freeing us from a particular topical tension
where it is hard to avoid the bias of emotional prejudice.

A full discussion of the topic in general could profitably take
place only among a group of those fully informed on various
aspects of it, including the biological nature and development
of human instincts, the psychology of the derivatives of those
instincts, the economic history of man, and the history of national policies and ambitions. Here, however, we are restricted
to one aspect of the whole: namely, the contributions that a
knowledge of psychopathology can make to our understanding
of it.

The first observation that may be made, dating from the time
of Le Bon (during the First World War), is of a purely descriptive nature. It concerns the remarkable contagiousness of certain
emotions, often with corresponding behavior, when a group of
people are closely linked together, either by physical propinquity, as in a crowd, mob, or meeting, or by any other bond of

common interest and means of swift communication. When these conditions are present, the display of an emotional attitude on the part of one or more assertive members of the group may often arouse, in an extraordinary degree, similar ones throughout the group. Fear, anger, hatred, enthusiastic acclamation may in this way, given certain conditions, spread with terrific speed and ever-increasing intensity. The important thing is that other mental attitudes of a more critical nature, which otherwise would check or guide the emotion, are far more easily suspended in a group than in an individual. Hence the notorious fickleness and irrationality of mobs.

The difficult problem at once arises of estimating the relative importance of the instigator of the emotion, one who commonly becomes a leader, and the spontaneous activity of the crowd. At one extreme of the scale, where the external situation speaks for itself, he may be quite insignificant; when a theater is burning it doesn't matter who starts the panic by shouting "Fire!" At the other extreme, a powerful personality may infuse a group with emotion that beforehand would have astonished its individual members.

It is most noteworthy how extraordinarily rare it is for a nation to refuse to follow its leaders into war. The government has to be totally discredited and the army itself faced with overwhelming defeat, as with the Russians in 1917, before insubordination and mutiny occur. This weighty fact must signify either that the commands of leaders are of decisive importance or that they divine the will of the people beforehand with peculiar accuracy. The latter thesis is the harder to maintain. When one thinks of the dynastic wars of the Middle Ages, or the probable outcome of the American Civil War had not the great figure of Lincoln insisted on the relentless pursuit of it despite the apathy and opposition of so many of his people, one must suppose that there is more power behind the leader's voice than is to be explained on purely rational grounds; that there is some deep irrational tendency to support and obey him (or the Government, which may be regarded as one Big Man) irrespective of whether individual members would agree with his policy if they were in a position to estimate it coolly. Even the Communists, who might be supposed to be furthest away from class distinctions and the worship of individuals, however prominent, have deified Lenin to a height perhaps unequaled in history, one which most Roman emperors would have envied.

Subsequent ages, with the opportunity for more detached appraisal, have seldom been able to share entirely the contemporaneous attitude towards these leaders, despite the sporadic appearance of such hero-worshippers as Carlyle. It would therefore seem that the suprarational or magical powers they often display must have some personal origin. The group who responds has to feel that he is "our leader" or "my leader." It was Freud who made this addition to Le Bon's original description, and it was also he who divined the source of the leader's magical powers. This remark takes us at once to the heart of modern psychopathology, and it cannot be expounded without first making clear the essential contributions that this branch of science has made to our knowledge of human nature.

They may be summed up in two words: the "unconscious" and the "infantile," two concepts which are closely related. We mostly live our lives without extreme manifestations of passion. When these occur, in the form of devoted adoration, deadly hostility, bloodthirsty cruelty, and so on, they are apt to be alarming and often dangerous; control and criticism are swept aside. Now, according to psychopathology, all these manifestations are revivals of corresponding, but inexpressible, passionate attitudes experienced in infancy. Freud discovered that the mind of the infant contained asocial wishes, perhaps inborn, whose nature would be described by such words as "savage," or at least "uncivilized." Sexual and murderous impulses, of the utmost significance to the individual, are examples of what had not previously been recognized as part of infantile life. The infant has to effect extensive changes in its mind—taming, renouncing, controlling, etc.—before it consents, so to speak, to become a child at about the age of three or four. Many have great difficulties in doing so and only imperfectly achieve this desirable transformation. The child, from then till puberty, plays at life, tries not to take its passionate irruptions as seriously as formerly, and more or less patiently passes through a period of physical and intellectual growth until at puberty the emotional life once more comes into its own.

Among the truly unconscious attitudes of infancy, an extremely important one is the attitude toward an image, highly charged emotionally, of a powerful Father. This is independent of the actual male parent, often an ineffective enough figure in reality, and indeed independent even of his existence (*e.g.*, orphans). A rich complex of emotions clusters around this image: adoration, hatred, dread and so on. And the interplay of them is fateful for the social (and religious) reactions of later life. An easily intelligible component in this complex is the wish to be protected from danger and the belief that the great Person has absolute power to protect one. Oddly enough, this goes hand in hand with the opposite attitude of protecting Him, presumably because of his being vital to one's own safety or existence. This is often illustrated in warfare, where men will fight with the utmost desperation to protect a leader or king whose life or standard is in jeopardy.

Akin to this theme, but much more connected with the maternal parent, is the alternation in infancy between the extremes of helplessness and omnipotence. The latter attitude normally gets toned down by experience into self-confidence, which in its turn diminishes the dread of helplessness. Nevertheless it is astonishing to find how much of these extreme attitudes may persist in the unconscious mind of adults, and how seldom is a perfect balance struck even in consciousness. A great obstacle to the attainment of this desirable goal is the fact that agencies other than the original one enter into the situation. If strong inferiority feelings develop (these, incidentally, always originate in sentiments of moral unworthiness, *i.e.*, guilt), the individual may react to them by reverting in the direction of one of two early attitudes. On the one hand he may feel unequal to coping with the guilty aggressive impulses that lie behind the inferiority feelings, and so come to depend on some strong being who is supposed to protect him from himself. Or, on the other hand, he may defiantly proclaim himself above any guilt feelings and turn into a bully. Both of these results have profound political effects when they assume a mass form, that is, become part of the reaction of a group. The Germans after the First World War gave an excellent illustration of what is meant. The majority reacted to the "Guilt Clause" of the Treaty of Versailles (and all that went with this) with feelings of inferiority and displayed a lack of self-confidence, and consequently of capacity, in conducting their own affairs, *i.e.*, governing themselves in a democratic fashion. A minority, on the contrary, were defiantly aggressive, and the strength and confidence this stimulated made such an appeal to the majority that for the most part they followed them in a pathetically docile manner, evidently hoping they could regain their self-respect or more by leaning on this great Führer and the small group around him.

This example, presented in a highly condensed fashion, may serve as a bridge between the purely descriptive observation with which we started and the more dynamic considerations that modern psychopathology can contribute to the general problem. The outstanding one is that *any emotional attitude disproportionate to the actual situation is derived from associative stimulation of a corresponding one in infantile life still persisting in the unconscious mind*. With this formula as a basis, one is in a position to investigate more profitably innumerable historical and diplomatic problems where argument often takes the place of illumination.

We meet at once, however, the formidable difficulty of determining what emotional attitude is disproportionate. One may count with near certainty on the person concerned being unable (or unwilling) to cooperate in answering the question. On the contrary, he maintains inflexibly that his emotional attitude is a normal, natural and inevitable response to the situation that has evoked it and is precisely proportionate to its objective significance. This has some truth in it; the reaction may be proportionate to the significance the situation has *for him,* but this still leaves open the difficult matter of ascertaining why it has. Few more important tasks lie before psychology than to provide

objective criteria for answering these two questions. The daily
experience of psychopathologists with individuals, by now very
extensive, has already begun to contribute material for the formulation of such criteria.

In the first place, we may assert that the disproportion in
question is much commoner and more extensive than either the
individual concerned or the general run of people may think.
The world is very lenient towards manifestations of the unconscious; or perhaps it would be nearer the truth to say that it
enters into a general conspiracy to overlook such manifestations.
One of the many characteristic signs of their presence is inability
on the part of the person concerned to discuss the matter, an
outburst of anger often taking the place of a free discussion.
There are many such indications which psychopathologists have
learned to recognize. What is important here is that in certain
circumstances particular situations can acquire an increasing
emotional significance because of their becoming more and
more closely associated with unconscious ideas that they symbolize, until a point is reached where they function as a vital
"test case" where everything of value is felt to be at stake. What
is then happening in the unconscious is that some literally intolerable idea is being stimulated, at first slightly and from afar,
and then more and more poignantly, until some violent defense
mechanism has to be brought into play to prevent—what? Chaos,
collapse, extinction? What lies behind this notion of an intolerable idea? Evidently something dominated by acute and un-
bearable "anxiety," as dread and panic are technically desig-
nated in psychopathology. Certainly one cannot exaggerate the
central part that "anxiety" plays in the unconscious; it is the key
to most problems there.

This picture of man as fundamentally a fearful animal is very
alien to our usual view of him. The reason for this is that only a
very small proportion of the unconscious anxiety, even in the
universal psychoneuroses where it is most often manifest, is allowed to come through to consciousness as such. The greater
part is prevented through the action of various defense mechanisms, which vary in form and intensity from one individual to

another. So important is this matter of protection against anxiety that the greater part of a person's character is made up of the various defenses he has learned to employ in the course of his early development. When one or another of them is so exaggerated as to form a striking characteristic of his personality, it may afford a broad hint of the amount of underlying anxiety and, furthermore, of its particular type.

The contribution made by the unconscious to a person's response to various current situations relates not only to its content, *i.e.*, the type of attitude concerned, but also to various psychological mechanisms characteristic of the unconscious. There are a good many such, and I shall select one or two of them to illustrate what is meant. In the unconscious there is no discrimination, there are no nuances, and attitudes akin to judgment are often of the "all or nothing" type. This often affects consciousness in the way of over-ready generalizations, which play a prominent part in international relationships. Nothing is commoner than remarks like "I hate the French," "all Americans are arrogant," "all Italians are thieves," and the like. Here, reasonable discrimination is completely absent. It is evident that these national prejudices must in their nature be extreme generalizations from very limited data, since few if any people possess a really extensive knowledge of the national group that is being condemned. Moreover, some of the strongest examples of such prejudice may be found among people who have had no experience whatever with the nationals in question. An experimental proof of the truth of this statement was afforded recently by a study in the United States correlating various types of prejudice. The investigators slipped in names of three or four non-existent nations among those about whom inquiry was being made. A certain number of the subjects expressed in their replies a considerable measure of animosity toward these unfortunate ghosts!

Another familiar, and even more important, example of the unconscious mechanisms that often influence conscious attitudes is "projection." By it is meant the ascribing to a person or persons in the environment, ideas, intentions and emotional attitudes that strictly belong to the subject himself, but which have been repudiated—usually unconsciously. He then not only believes intellectually that the other person displays the attitude in question, but feels it in a direct way and responds to it emotionally, often very strongly. It is seen in its grossest forms in various mental disorders, *e.g.*, when a patient believes so firmly that someone has evil intentions on his life that he protects himself by forestalling him and carrying out a prophylactic murder. This very example must remind one of the so-called "preventive wars" and opens up the question of the original source of the aggressive intentions.

One sees this same alternation in many forms. The history of mankind could well be depicted as a struggle between the desire for freedom, self-confidence and self-dependence on the one hand, and the craving for protection and help from stronger beings on the other. Perhaps there are even cyclical periods in history where one or the other of these opposing tendencies gain the upper hand. The nineteenth century was characterized by, among other things, a widespread desire for freedom and self-government. This was manifested not only by the emancipation of many countries from foreign rule, but also inside numerous countries by the increasing revolt against the previously ruling oligarchies or monarchies, by universal suffrage, emancipation of women and many more cognate movements. The cry for freedom was a favorite theme for the poets, who passionately declaimed it as the highest good; and the dramatic cry of Patrick Henry, "Give me liberty or give me death," was echoed and acted on over and over again. The twentieth century, on the other hand, has seen the rise in one country after another of powerful dictatorships whose tyranny has seldom been equaled in history. More significant than the forcible suppression of individual liberty has been the extensively successful denigration of the very concept of freedom, which, far from being the highest virtue, is now widely regarded as an outmoded superstition if not actually an antisocial vice, and is to be replaced by the nobler one of docile "loyalty" to the current regime.

The psychopathologist, being accustomed to view genetically all adult manifestations as derivations of early tendencies and believing to the full that "the child is father to the man," would connect the epoch-making happenings just mentioned with the infantile conflict between dependent helplessness and omnipotent fantasies.

What is in some respects the opposite to this mechanism is the more obscure one called "introjection." Here the observed attitude of another person (or nation) is incorporated within oneself and often becomes a permanent part of the personality. Much of what is regarded as the child's "imitation" of the parents is of this nature. In the unconscious fantasy, however, the process goes further, and the other person is actually imagined and *felt* to be inside one. Naturally much then depends on whether the incorporated person is regarded as friendly, kindly, and helpful, or, on the contrary, unkind, harmful, and evil. Curiously enough, there are motives impelling towards the introjection of both kinds, so that both "good" and "bad" objects, as they are called, live side by side within and may act on each other. Fear lest one's precious objects (together with one's own capacity for love) may be destroyed by the evil influences is common and leads to complex defensive reactions.

In international relations similar processes are at work, and similar variations may be observed. A good example was the attitude of the English (and presumably also the Americans) towards Russians at different periods in recent years. Before World War II, the prevailing attitude was one of aloofness, doubt and suspicion. During the war the Russians were welcomed with open arms and incorporated as "one of us," "one of the Allies," and so on. After the war, resurgent doubt deepened first into suspicion and then into the fear that after all they might turn out to be hostile, and that the United Nations had incorporated a "bad object" into their midst.

After this brief but necessary introduction on the psychology of the individual as seen through the eyes of a psychopathologist who has to investigate the deeper layers of the mind, we have to turn to our theme proper, and the bearing such knowledge may have on the sources and nature of international tension.

It is natural that we should think first of modern conditions, of nations with their popular opinions pervading them, and of **responsible Governments negotiating with other Governments.**

But we should do well to keep in mind a broader historical perspective. For essentially what we are concerned with is the problem of latent hostility between groups, small or large; particularly, of course, when this hostility reaches a dangerous degree of tension. And history is only too replete with instances of this phenomenon in all forms of social organization. When the Mongol hordes swept westward into Europe, it was certainly not because of any unfortunate conflict between their leaders and the leaders of other countries. Naked force was the first indication those unfortunate countries had of any "Mongol problem." Nor were the Jews the first or the last exponents of genocide when three thousand years ago they set out to exterminate the Amalakites, Canaanites, or whoever else stood in the way of their intentions, irrespective of any diplomatic incident or disagreement between Governments. We have, in short, to do with not merely any such recent matters as the mischief of armament makers, the iniquities of secret diplomacy, or the evils inherent in the capitalistic system, but with a far older, deeper and more general tendency of human groups to generate hostility among themselves.

That man can so readily hate and destroy members of his own species is a prerogative that he shares with no other vertebrate animal, though it is displayed by many of the insects. With those insects, man also has shared the propensity to devour his fellow-creatures. And although he has now for the most part (if by no means altogether, as the last war illustrated) learned to refrain from this logical culmination of killing, it is disconcerting to know that cannibalistic impulses are a regular constituent of the infantile mind and remain one of the most common features of the adult unconscious.

All this signifies that there is in man a permanent capacity for hostility, aggression and cruelty towards his fellow creatures; whether this capacity, mostly dormant, is best described as a propensity, a trend, or an innate instinct is a difficult problem about which there is much discussion.

Such statements as those just made are so unpalatable and so hard to accept that one is not surprised at the various attempts that have been made to discount or deny them. Some anthropologists, for instance, have insisted that primitive man is a peaceable creature, living in harmony with his fellows and his environment until artificially stimulated. No doubt it is possible to find isolated communities living in favored circumstances where this description appears to hold good. But it is certainly far easier to find primitive ones where it does not; hence the term "savages." It is also possible to find civilized nations who are exceptionally peace-loving, Scandinavia being at present a notable example. But all these observations simply present us with an important problem: how does it happen that the latent hostility psychopathologists know from their studies of the unconscious to be *always present* sometimes lies dormant in an individual or a community and at other times becomes only too manifest?

Let us consider a few historical examples. A thousand years ago the Danes were to the coastal inhabitants of the British Isles, whether Celts or Saxons, people who looted, raped, and murdered without the slightest provocation. Their incursions culminated in their seizing the throne of England. About the same time, their Norse neighbors became the terror of Europe as far as ships could sail—from France to Sicily and Cyprus; their seizure of the throne of England in 1066 proved more lasting. To Russians with any historical memory, Swedes signified the conquerors of most of their country—and the word "conquest" is generally a euphemism for many things whose activities continued in the seventeenth and eighteenth centuries. In the fifteenth century, the Swiss pikemen were the most dreaded warriors in Europe, as Italy in particular knew to her cost. Yet in the whole world there are no more pacific peoples today than the four just mentioned, nor peoples whose neighbors may feel safer from any aggressive tendencies.

These are very striking examples of a complete reversal of behavior. Other cases of change are not so unambiguous. What the English did to the native inhabitants of America, Australia and Tasmania who objected to their land being seized stands on record. Only in New Zealand did they establish an amicable relationship. Their treatment of the natives of Ireland and India is a more controversial question, but the fact remains that they have peaceably withdrawn from both countries, and there is every sign of their days of aggressive expansion being finally past. The conduct of the Spanish in Central and South America is only too notorious, although perhaps it may be said that their aggressive tendencies were not glutted thereby, as with the other nations we have considered, but continue internally against their own people. The Greeks managed to combine their internal dissensions with external expansion from the seventh to the fourth century B.C., and have never been able to dispense with the former type of hostility. The Germans have lived fairly peaceably for centuries, except when disturbed from without, and even without many internal conflicts (between State and State). But their recent history appears to betoken a reversion to the characteristics ascribed to them by the Romans. Similarly, the Jews, according to their chronicles, must have been among the most ruthless peoples of antiquity. Yet for two thousand years they have been noted for their abhorrence of any kind of violence; it is possible we may now be witnessing a resuscitation of qualities long dormant.

Most striking of all instances of unprovoked aggression is the story of the Mongol incursion. A study of the career of Genghis Khan is indispensable to anyone concerned with the investigation of aggressive impulses. But history is replete with examples in every area of the world, so we need not continue in our relation of them.

We have therefore the picture of periodic surges of aggression on the part of one community after another, whether a nation or not, surges which then equally mysteriously die down and apparently disappear. Here we have the naked form of aggression, but actually these surges constitute only one type of situation, that in which hostility on the part of one side only culminates in war. There are the more complex cases where suspicion, rivalry, and hatred between two nations proceeds until an outbreak comes about. Here it is not a case of an overwhelming aggressiveness against which nothing can prevail except a successful military defense, as when the Huns were checked at Chalons or the Goths at Tours.

It is at this point that we acutely feel the need of cooperation with good historians, trained in both economics and psychology, who might be able to unravel both the underlying and the inciting causes of a series of wars, and in that way to afford some sort of classification from which further investigations could proceed. Two broad kinds have just been singled out, which for the present may be termed "aggressive wars" and "quarrel wars" respectively. But plainly this is a very rough grouping between two types that cannot be sharply divided, and which needs very much refined modification. Nevertheless we may start with it, if only for the practical reason that the treatment of them must differ; the technique of stopping the rush of a mad bull is quite different from that of settling a dispute.

A noteworthy feature of the second group of wars is that so many of them would seem to have been easily avoidable if only a modicum of good will and tolerance had been allowed to operate. Examples of this are the British-American War of 1812, the Crimean War, the Franco-Prussian War, and even the first World War (the second surely belongs to the other group). It is probably true of the American Civil War, and certainly of the English one. The more fortunate outcome was often prevented by suspicion, *i.e.*, the imputing of exaggeratedly bad motives to the other party, with the fears that always underlie such imputations.

There is no more delicate task for the diplomatist than to measure the exact degree of danger in an apparently aggressive neighbor; he could do so much more accurately were he able first to allow for the probable projections from his side. Of course, there are always real issues of a complicated kind, but it is suggested that these are seldom of so acute a nature as to preclude a working compromise. When, however, any compromise is felt to be a surrender which the other party will regard as a weakness and of which he will proceed to take further advantage, the case is difficult and it may need a considerable measure of good will and self-confidence (based on easy conscience) to succeed.

If we ask in what circumstances a government will decide to use force rather than other means we come to an extremely complicated problem, since at first sight the motives appear to be so manifold that one might well despair of reducing them to their fundamentals. Most governments, though not all, are prepared to fight if the alternative is slavery or domination, *i.e.*, to fight for their freedom and independence. It is perhaps the clearest case. But beyond this there are many situations where the importance of the issue is judged very subjectively, where it is estimated quite differently by the parties immediately concerned and by others at a distance either in space or time. Few foreigners, for instance, could understand why Great Britain should have thought it necessary to fight the Boer War, and the number of British who think it was necessary has diminished with the passage of time, although the large marjority thought so at the time. Then we have the question-begging phrase "vital interests," which covers a vast scale of varying degrees of importance from the rare instances where it might be appropriately used (*e.g.*, when the supply of food is imperiled) down to those where only some minor economic interest is concerned. This leads on to the equally ambiguous term "prestige," one that usually applies to strong powers who insist on weak ones paying them due respect, that is, admitting that they have reason to fear them. At one time, if Albania had blown up two British destroyers, Great Britain would certainly have landed troops to demand forcibly that she be accorded due apology and reparation, a course now forbidden by the thought both of Russia and of the United Nations; the insult, *i.e.*, the lack of deference to her strength, would have been felt to be intolerable.

The comments a psychopathologist has to make on these complex matters are as follows. In the first place, when a nation strongly feels a certain interest to be "vital," and when it is plain to other people not concerned that the phrase is very exaggerated, the exaggeration represents an addition of emotion derived from unconscious sources. It is psychologically the same sort of surplus that the neurotic exhibits when he dreads suffocation if he enters a closed place. The interest that is felt to be vital, although not actually so in itself, has come to *symbolize* one of the few unconscious ideas that the unconscious truly regards as vital. Death or castration, for instance, represent attacks on what

the unconscious regards as vital interests. So extensive are the
latent fears in mankind that there is an exaggerated sensitiveness
to any stimulus that may, however, indirectly, stir them. The
conclusion is that many violent decisions which produce an appearance of aggressive assertiveness are much more defensive
in their origin than might be thought; more will be said presently
about the important theme of "aggressive defense." The conclusion just enunciated needs to be confirmed by analyses of
specific instances of "vital interests," "prestige," and so on. It is
highly probable that these concepts would be shown to be unconsciously associated with more fundamental ones characteristic of the unconscious.

Here we have been considering cases where the attitude of the
government is representative of that of the people. There is also
an extensive class of cases where its attitude is more concerned
with its own interests, separate from and often opposed to those
of the people. When this is so, the leader may be concerned with
his own interest only, those behind being either commanded to
follow, or, as with William the Conqueror's invasion of England
or Napoleon's invasion of Italy, induced to do so by promises of
loot. Or again, and this is a much more sinister situation, the
leader may be concerned with the mutual hostility between himself and his nation and decide to deal with them by deflecting
both in the direction of external aggression by proceeding to pick
a quarrel with some neighbor. There is indeed a social theory
according to which foreign wars are characteristically of the
latter nature, being designed to divert the tension between different classes in the community. This theory is connected with
the common suspicion that wars are deliberately brought about
by rulers, capitalists, and "the old men" to further their own
interests only. Such a theory can be sustained only through considerable distortion of both historical events and human motives.
Rulers are seldom so Machiavellian. Oxenstjerna's famous remark to his son, "Quantilla prudentia regitur orbis" ("You do not
know with what little wisdom the world is governed"), is much
nearer the truth.

Although psychopathologists can never forget the permanent
aggressive impulses deep in man's nature, they would probably

agree with the prevailing sociological opinion that in an organized community the impulses of individuals can for the most part be kept within tolerable bounds. There are many outlets available for indirect and relatively harmless expressions of these impulses in the way of rivalry, ambition, sport, competition, the surmounting of difficult tasks and the achieving of emulous aims (exploration, scientific discovery, and so on).

The sporadic exceptions in the form of criminality could be brought within much narrower bounds than at present by an adequate social psychiatric service and advances in police efficiency. The danger of serious outbreaks of hostility, therefore, is confined to mass combinations: internal revolution and international tension, two manifestations which, as were pointed out above, are by no means always disconnected. It is for the sociologist and historian to study the various situations in which these eventualities occur, but the psychopathologist would maintain that in the nature of things the agents bringing them about must ultimately be of the same order as those that evoke an outbreak of hostility (murder, etc.) in the individual, and that they must operate through similar mechanisms.

Psychopathology can show that an uncontrollable outburst of aggression in the individual is always due to frustration or fear (or, of course, both). With the month-old infant, anger is evoked by unavoidable and what may be called "normal" frustration, *e.g.*, the fact that the nipple is not available at every moment. Later, when the child has acquired some capacity for tolerating frustration, it needs a larger amount, one that may be called undue or excessive frustration, though the amount varies greatly with different individuals.

The part played by fear is both less evident and more important. We are familiar with the observation that a cornered rat may, in its desperation, turn savage; and that the ferocity of a tiger increases with its sense of danger. These are reactions of aggression to manifest fear. What we are here concerned with are similar reactions of man to invisible fear, to the unconscious anxiety of which he is not aware, but which is the mainspring of various other emotional attitudes.

Although the instinct of fear appears to be universal throughout the animal kingdom, even among the most powerful animals, with man it has certain unique features. Like other animals, he can be afraid of dangerous aggression spontaneously emerging from the outside. He can also be afraid of external aggression conceived by his conscience as retaliation or punishment for his own aggressive impulses. Moreover, he often projects these on to the outer world and responds with fear to what may in that case be a largely imaginary danger. This is the typical paranoid reaction.

Much more important than all these, however, are the purely *internal* sources of anxiety. It would seem that the primitive mind, that is, the mind of the infant and of the adult unconscious, relatively reacts with anxiety to its own aggressive impulses. This reaction has many fateful consequences. It is important to remember that although some of this anxiety may leak through, especially with neurotics, and although much of it may betray itself through various indirect effects, it is essentially unconscious. There is always far more anxiety present in any individual than is externally manifest to either himself or others. Many elaborate defenses are developed to cope with it. One unfortunate one is a defiant increase of external aggressiveness, as anyone who listened to one of Hitler's characteristic tirades will recognize. In the political sphere it is indifferent whether the aggressive impulses of rulers leading to unconscious anxiety are primarily directed against foreign natives, against their own people or, as in Hitler's case, against both. But when they lead to great anxiety the aggression is often further increased; aggression is then both the cause and the effect of the anxiety.

Another equivocal defense against unconscious anxiety is an increased harshness of the superego, that warning agency of which the conscious manifestation is the sense of conscience. Unconscious guilt plays a most important part in political life. Its presence, for instance, is a typical precondition for the projection that so disturbs any hope for the reasonable discussion of sundering issues. An especially interesting problem in this connection is the case where the pangs of guilt are so intolerably painful that secondary defenses have to be erected against them, or some mysterious transformation of them has to be effected. The colonizers who exterminated native races seem usually to have been successful in that respect, and one would greatly like to know whether William the Conqueror or Genghis Khan ever experienced any such pang. Henry V persuaded himself so thoroughly that he was the rightful King of France that when he invaded Normandy he was preposterously outraged at the "treasonable" behavior of the French in opposing their lawful sovereign; on the other hand, Shakespeare, with his usual insight, saw deeper and credited him with many painful qualms on the night before Agincourt.

It is possible to summarize in one sentence the gist of this brief essay: what the psychopathologist has to contribute to the understanding of international tension is to point out the significance of aggression, guilt, and above all anxiety in the unconscious mind, with the effects of these on behavior.

FRANCE

Angelo Hesnard, M.D.

Director of the Section on Psychoanalytic Therapy
and Psychosomatic Medicine of the 1950 International Congress of Psychiatry; Former Professor at
the Marine Health Service School, Toulon.

T HE threat of a war more terrible than anything yet
encountered has produced an intense anxiety in the world. So
great has been the terror that even psychologists and psychiatrists have been called upon for help. Unfortunately their studies
do not aim so much at the psychological analysis of the international crisis itself, but rather at sociopsychological criticism of
the "good" society (meaning a pacific society). In short, they try
to decree what *should be,* instead of first making an attempt to
understand *existing* conditions.

In the opinion of French psychologists, such studies should be
carried on for the sole purpose of scientific objectivity. As a man
of science, the psychologist must silence his own prejudices,
whether of a patriotic or a religious nature. The scientific
method, if it is to be effective, demands perfect equanimity. It
must rigidly avoid becoming the more or less conscious tool of
political propaganda.

World tension is a disturbance of collective human behavior
which expresses the *threat* of a war and contributes to its outbreak. In some respects, this behavior is comparable to mental
disorder observed in individuals.

During previous wars, French psychologists attempted to
analyze the psychological dynamics of *declared war.* While their
observations help a little to clarify some of the more subtle aspects of international prewar tension, they are not sufficient for
a thorough grasp of the entire problem.

In this connection Gustav Le Bon, who studied the course of

the war of 1914–1918, described its emotional and mystical causes and its collective irrational reasons. He presents the struggle as a conflict of "psychological forces" in the service of such irreconcilable ideals as Individual Freedom versus Tyranny of State. Nevertheless, while Le Bon embraced an abstract conception of psychology which is compatible with a general and metaphoric interpretation of events, this conception is foreign to the deeper significance of these events.

French sociologists, like sociologists of other countries, in their studies of the causes of war allude to a "psychological element" in the war process. The real causes, according to them, are primarily of an economic and demographic nature. However, their "psychological element" seems badly defined and imponderable. What they do not express clearly is that human occurrences, like war and prewar tension, though they do demonstrate the influence of economic factors on the behavior of nations, are but a part of the drama of inter-human relations. This drama is subject to those laws applicable to man, namely, the laws of psychology. Like any event concerning a group, world tension has two aspects, the economic and the dramatic. On the one hand, tension indicates an economic fact; on the other, it influences the course of events and the progress of history by its very existence as a psychological fact. Here lies the reason for our interest in understanding the deep human meaning of the existing tension. Through this understanding, an attempt may be made to act upon the tension in order to avoid its transformation into a mortal peril to civilization.

How does this acute, concrete fact of world tension express itself?

Two general characteristics related to the mental disorder of an individual are immediately noticeable:

First there is the characteristic of *fatality*, bringing to mind the inherent fatality which leads the mentally ill to antisocial acts. For example, it is amazing to find that the idea of an approaching war, however terrifying the massacre of one part of the world by another may be, is being accepted by many people with even more resignation than was expressed in the face of conflicts in the past. This is a fatality of a mystical kind against which the psychologist revolts. He can see in it only the capitulation of reason, the inability to get to the bottom of the acute world problem, or else a pathological tendency to avoid it.

Second, we have the characteristic of *determinism*. In order to define determinism, the true significance of this amazing phenomenon must be grasped. According to the two hostile attitudes which all the nations of the world are progressively adopting, the advancing division of humanity presents a kind of reciprocal double obligation. Rational thought refuses to concede this obligation as mysterious and irresistible, but the ideological aspirations on which these various nations rely are far from explaining it.

French psychologists are in a good position to observe and analyze this acute global fear, as their country is subject to it more directly than many others. Before the last war, France was a center for intellectual audacity and offered an open forum for the presentation of ideas. During the war, she became a hotbed of hateful discord among citizens. Today she is suffering painfully from the collision of conflicting ideologies. On the one hand she sympathizes, through her own revolutionary tradition, with Russia, where the Socialist revolution triumphed over the tyranny and economic atavism of the Tsarist regime; but on the other hand she loves (as does any Occidental nation) human dignity and the cult of private property, free criticism, and cultural traditionalism. She is located between the irrational thrust of totalitarian governments—of whom she is afraid—and the irrational thrust of anti-communist reaction. She rejects the latter as a contagious and dangerous phobia more detrimental to its advocates than to others. Moreover, the terrible humiliation France suffered under Nazi occupation, more painful to her than financial ruin (and a humiliation which non-invaded nations can hardly imagine) has plunged her youth and her leaders into a state of mental confusion that will be difficult to cure. France has been experiencing a depressing sense of inferiority and economic, military, and particularly moral dependence on other great nations. Yet this accumulation of misery has produced one

advantage: It has given French thinkers a clarity that arises from
material weakness. Moreover, it is painfully clear to them that
they are witnessing events which are passing them by, and of
which France once again risks being the victim.

Therefore French observers feel crushed by the power and
concentration of aggressive threats. The acute world tension
derives its formidable power from the terror arising from the
destructive capacity of atomic warfare, and from the extreme
polarization of contradictory tensions. These tensions are centers of attraction and repulsion. Due to the fact that inter-human
connections over great distances are being multiplied (an
achievement increasingly necessitated by modern economic
conditions), and also to the fearful perfection of technical means
of propaganda and aggression, the world of tomorrow appears
extremely small to the small nations. They fear the possibility
that the planet will be conquered by *one* of the great powers that
are aligned against each other, and that their own small territories will be sacrificed. Therefore they feel that humanity is
being swept with irresistible force towards abysmal suffering.
Later we shall attribute this state of mind to the "bad conscience" of the actors in the world drama. Innocent onlookers
as they are, the French do not intend to share it.

Before we go into more detail regarding the latent phenomenon of "bad conscience," two apparent consequences resulting
from world anxiety should be noted: its extraordinary contagion
and the primitive or regressive mentality it induces.

The blind terror characterizing world tension is revealed,
without exception, by countless disconcerting symptoms in all
fields of human thought. In France, a nation with particular
susceptibility to such anxiety, the terror manifests itself not only
in diplomatic and military activities (where it would be logical),
but even in the conscious mind of individuals; in their attitude
toward morals, religion, art, education, philosophy, and especially—on a more concrete level—in the reactions of public opinion. In Paris every informative publication discusses this obsess-
ing drama. Every editorial, on whatever subject, however remote from politics, refers to it and adopts some attitude towards

it. The world problem is reflected in theatrical and cinema productions; it is flaunted by the titles of books. Salon conversations center on Christianity and Communism, on Existentialism and Marxism. Even science, the most objective discipline of man, becomes involved in this process, and methodology—from mathematics to genetics and from physics to biology—is influenced. The dialectic of Marx and Engels, extolled and attacked, haunts the university students of France.

As to the primitive behavior of crowds, this phenomenon in France as elsewhere is seen on a large scale and in modernized form. The same irrational, archaic thought and actions that have been previously described by such observers of war as Sighele, MacDougall, G. Le Bon, and Freud are present.

It is important to remember that regressive behavior is related to such elementary phases of mental activity—evolutive or involutive—as precivilized thinking, childlike thinking, and the thinking of persons with mental disorders.

This behavior lends its imprint of affective, "prelogical" conduct to the precivilized mentality. Its animistic concept consists of a universe populated by heroes or traitors, angels of peace or aggressive and malevolent spirits. This world is presided over by a Providence that is supposedly divine. Each group claims the Divine Power for its own good purposes. Its mystical participation in one's own ideological entity is presumed, and its magical conduct utilizes the technical sorcery of our scientific era: mass hypnosis, administered in spectacular ceremonies (no more under the aegis of the Germanic racial ideal, but under that of a benevolent and prosperous democracy, or else under that of a humane and righteous revolution).

The influence of regressive behavior on infantile mentality consists of its naive dependence on authority. The position of the parents is replaced by political and social personalities of international importance. These personalities become objects of exalted love or aggressive hatred, with which each man identifies himself in renouncing self-criticism. Gigantic human groups (now reducible to two), which Freud called "the grand individuals of humanity," range themselves around the leaders. Each group makes up a synthetic personality integrating concrete individual peculiarities and behaving in an infantile fashion. They manifest the all-embracing power of thought which serves to put into effect, by symbolic action, embellished collective desires. After symbolism follows violence. Here belongs the ritual of cursing or excommunicating the opposing group, or that of narcissistic assertion of their own value and right. At the same time, any mention of possible disaster to the group itself is considered sacrilegious and is completely suppressed.

To the psychopathic mentality, regression lends the instinctive attitudes of sadism and masochism. The risk of innumerable lives among the innocent civil population excites the perverted imagination enough by its very horror to make it appear justified or at least inevitable. Of particular interest here is the unconscious projection of the group's own inherent conflicts on the opponent—conflicts of "unconscious guilt," as we shall see later. Here originate powerful and fictitious emotional drives. They are hostile and of a persecuting nature for the adversary, and favorable and benevolent for the ally. They bring forth detestable human prototypes like Capitalists, Cagoulards (historical organization in France comparable to the Ku Klux Klan), "Fifth Columns" organized by the enemy, the Soviet Robot, the "Monster" of the State, or populations tainted with "totalitarian infection." These entities may be abstract and quasi-divine, or they may be rationalized for the purpose of justifying hidden tendencies that are less noble. On the other hand, there are the prototypes of Liberty, Human Personality, and Rights of Man, embodied by leaders who appear providential and highly virtuous. It is now necessary to define the more concrete problems arising from the intervention of these irrational, regressive psychological forces in the present world conflict.

Psychological inferiority is a hidden and sometimes highly symbolic regression to lower forms of emotional life. It characterizes world tension and is expressed objectively in an inherent contradiction (discernible to the impartial observer) within each of the two gigantic forces in existence. For both of them conform to the sentimental logic of the masses. While this situation results in amazing justifications for either adversary, it entails a contradiction between theory and practice or between end and means.

The Western democracies claim to offer truth, legality, ideological tolerance, the spiritual values of humanism (whether Christian or liberal), and economic assistance to nations menaced by hunger and starvation. But their opponents detect behind this solemn and complex superstructure the policy of exploitation of man by man, of plutocratic or colonizing greed based on military repression, of extortion perpetuated by misery, of the cultivation of pauperism and the fetishism of the dollar. Accordingly, such a policy would result in class hatred and in the material and moral dependence of a great majority of workers on a small minority of owners determined to defend their hierarchic, outdated, and unjust material privileges.

On the other hand, Russia sets forth its striving for purity and severity of conduct and for the equality of human beings whatever may be their culture, religion, ethnic origin, or color of skin —all this within the disciplined loyalty of the Common Good, the ennobling mysticism of work, and in accordance with a rational and concrete plan of social action. Its opponents, however, point out the alleged cruelty of a tyrannic state control, sectarianism, unavowed nationalism in the pan-Slavic sense, inhuman procedures of police supervision, and the impudent propaganda infiltrating the consciousness of nations for the purpose of undermining spiritual ideals.

It must be noted that both positions are greatly interested in science: the Western bloc proclaims the increased technical perfection of its scientific research, confirmed each day by sensational discoveries. At the same time, the Oriental bloc proudly boasts that its laborious fervor is inspired by the only authentic modern philosophy of science—dialectic materialism. Thus we are witnessing this striking contradiction: while the Soviets are spreading across the world the implacable "truth" of Marxism, the Occidental political leader wants to pierce the iron curtain in order to introduce behind it a bit of "truth." Certainly the truth concerned is not the same!

In order to realize true humanism in a new form of society, the U.S.S.R. is practicing a tough policy which she justifies by the tactical obligation of postponing the advent of true liberty; the concrete freedom of Socialism appears to her achievable only by terror and social contest. On the other hand, while America is following a sinister policy of conserving social inequality, she justifies the inhumanity of this principle, its sacred egotism, by practicing charitable liberalism and by proclaiming the virtue of international prosperity which she proposes to bring about by way of economic development. On one side there is a generous purpose imposed on any occasion without compromise or pity by use of revolutionary violence. On the other, an egotistical purpose is being maintained in conscious respect through beneficence.

Economists have taught us how this double contradiction came about historically. Today numerous political, philosophical and social movements, notably in France, are trying to dismiss it, though without apparent success. It finds expression in the double political current of modern times. On the one hand we have the attachment to the past, a reactionary factor of prudence and social misoneism, a relic of the ancestral cult developed from the belief in "eternal values." On the other hand we find the drive toward the future as an efficient incentive of social action and of audacious aspiration toward an ideal society (or one that is at least improvable) based on cultural progress.

However, the acceleration of industrial progress has distorted this scheme, on which the first Socialist theory of class struggle was based. The most disturbing incident was furnished by the menace of Hitler's hegemony, against which both the conservative and progressive elements of the world united. But once the European peril arose, new aspects of the international problem appeared. Capitalism, which was already fortified by the prosperity of the New World, and which, by improving the conditions of its workers, had progressively demonstrated to the proletariat of the world that its class consciousness had been sacrificed, came out of the war concentrated and powerful in an untouched continent. It was capitalism which, from now on, seemed to represent the spirit of enterprise, and capitalism was ready to radiate on the universe. At the same time, the communism of a nation frightfully mutilated by invasion had to brace itself in order to subsist and to resume its ideal of action by forced labor. A new wave of distrust, due to the resistance incurred from the capitalistic nations to her ideological conquest of the world, accompanied Russia's efforts.

This difference of fortune between the two groups of victorious nations appeared in a different light to each group. For America, her victory confirmed the irresistible and enviable efficiency of a remodeled capitalism that had saved the world. To Russia, American prosperity, though increased during the war, meant only an episode in the flux and reflux of an economically condemned system. It was viewed merely as a particularly strong swing in the dialectic movement of history. The fatal consequence of such a swing was, for the capitalistic economy of America (which sooner or later would be threatened by catastrophic depression), the obligation imposed on this nation to defend itself not only by conceding its material aid to all nations of the world successively, but also by the need for unlimited and therefore impossible expansionism. According to the doctrine of the self-destruction of capital, this expansion will be deadly, though only after a delay.

But whatever the historical and economic truth of either of the two interpretations may be (and no judgment of values is attempted here), their opposition exists and constitutes a menace to humanity. The concrete psychological fact of world tension expresses the stalemate of human behavior in trying to overcome this obstacle.

The world hopes that the present stalemate is only a critical moment in history and not the first phase of general armed conflict. In any case, the situation results from a morbid impotency of collective thought. However, in spite of an inevitable irrational quality, the thinking of civilized peoples tends toward practical knowledge, rational action, and the exclusion of violence. In fact, logical consideration is inclined to predict that a new war on a planetary scale would surely fail to be worth the massive destruction inflicted on humanity. Neither could it realize any of the progressive aims (authentic or otherwise) of either adversary.

The irrational, generalized, and accelerated tendency that world tension imposes on collective human behavior at this moment is actually, in a contradictory and absurd manner, one of suicide and social self-mutilation. At present civilization is at the point of stagnation in its march toward progress. It is ruining itself by preparing for war. Perhaps tomorrow it will exterminate itself. At the same time, civilization cites human progress in its effort to justify this conduct on an ideological level.

Today humanity is racing towards self-destruction by radical genocide, just as the mental patient is driven to suicide when he is confronted with an incomprehensible and insurmountable conflict in his personal life.

However, the trend of collective behavior in the direction of a stalemate illuminates only superficially the psychological problem it raises. The meaning of this irrational factor is outlined more clearly if viewed from a profound and concrete knowledge of human behavior. In the light of modern psychological experience, the factor of extraordinary importance to the unconscious life of the individual and his group is called *guilt*.

Observation of individuals indicates that results alone appear to them as a reward, even as a proof of merit. Do not riches in themselves, even though gained dishonestly, acquire them the consideration of others; and does not poverty, even though honest, appear to the successful as a breach of manners?

This guilt as a collective experience, and felt as a threat to human value, is revealed in various disguises in each crisis of history. While economic and military success has always been considered a virtue, deadlock—whether economic crisis or military disaster—has been considered as a retribution for a mistake. When this happens, those who are responsible must be found.

Among the invaded countries France has succumbed in a particularly poignant and catastrophic manner to this law of a mystical and superstitious ethic. During World War II she split into two camps. On the one hand, we had the limited camp of expiation, which submitted to the odious yoke of the aggressor. On the other hand there was the progressively growing camp of virtuous protestation, which, while denying its own guilt, transferred it to others in order to relieve its own obscure restlessness of conscience. The scapegoat that was found was not so much the aggressor himself (whose triumphant tenacity kept off military retribution) but compatriots who were the "traitors of their country." At the end of the conflict the far-sighted, fortified by victory, proceeded righteously with the undertaking called by the moralizing name "epuration." At this stage citizens denounced each other and each pure soul found a less pure one to accuse. This was an abominable turn of false public morality in which personal hatreds were satisfied and perpetuated to the point where the moral and civic unity of France was lastingly impaired.

The acute world drama consists, on an enlarged scale, in such an accusation of one party by the other. This means the transfer of the subconscious guilt of one group to an opposed group. After having experienced common victory as proof of their own virtue, the two great powers could have eliminated on a rational basis their political differences and their respective possibility of destroying each other on a profound and irrational basis. Unfortunately the appearance of atomic weapons has visibly aggravated the conflict by aggravating the responsibility involved.

Freud's philosophy, outdated today in certain ways, dealt with the anxiety of man in connection with his mastery of the forces of nature. Freud, who was the first to analyze this anxiety, spoke of an opposition between a destructive force driving toward return to disorganized matter, and a creative force which maintains life. Today, beneath this metaphysical myth, scientific observation of man reveals the reality of a secret primitive behavior which drives the individual and his group to react to happenings in conformance with a pseudo-morale that is totally unreal but of a fundamentally aggressive nature.

If actually the most primitive or undifferentiated human behavior is anxiety—distress of the individual when confronting the world and its threats—and if this anxiety crystallizes on one present terror and becomes fear and eventually (by way of reaction) an indomitable object hatred, then guilt is the most complex behavior resulting from the prohibition opposing the tensions of human needs and desires. Moreover, prohibition is the very condition of all inter-human relations; first in the pre-social setting represented for the child in the family, and later on by social organization. In revolting against the individuals personifying this prohibition, man accepts it for himself. Yet this new prohibition imposed on oneself is nothing but inverted aggressiveness always ready to revert to aggression against others. As a personalized human menace, the guilt dormant in every person is much less the result of conscious temptation to indulge in acts forbidden by the codes than the *ignored* tension of profound, inherent inclinations toward self-assertion.

Collective guilt functions according to a comparable psychological mechanism. Just as intensified individual guilt provokes defensive reactions against its intolerable menace in the form of neuroses or mental illness, it may, translated into the common phenomenon of a cosmic anxiety, result in a kind of collective psychosis. Knowing its own power to annihilate others, a group denies all conscious intent of aggression and relieves the obscure anxiety of its own growing guilt by projecting on the hostile group this same anxiety in the guise of accusation.

Thus Russia and the United States distrust each other and attribute to one another aggressive intentions. Because of this state, either one of them may arrive at provoking the *real* aggression of the other. In this manner the most pacifist group may prepare for war most feverishly and attempt to encircle the other militarily in punishment for their defense—anything in order to insure peace!

This unsuspected conception of collective moral life exists in the present world conflict. America, as a "great individual of humanity," does not admit to herself the survival of her cult of privileged classes. She accuses the hostile coalition of making an attempt on the dignity of man through the tyranny of the state: the *sin of communism.*

And Russia accepts as inevitable (at the present stage of her history) the abdication of the individual in favor of the anonymous mass. She is accusing the leaders of the hostile group of encroaching egotism: the *sin of individuality*. Undoubtedly the degree of superstition and even of tactical efficiency of either accusation might be argued.

Thus the discord in the modern world is based essentially on the transfer from one group of nations to another of their own ethical superstitions. Archaic and irrational guilt is dormant beneath collective consciousness. In the form of a menace to normal inter-human relations, this attitude contains a formidable reserve of aggressiveness, the anachronism and sterilizing power of which lend it the pathological significance of an arrestment of cultural thought. Guilt prevents, in effect, the truth of liberalism—constituting the possibility to realize human solidarity *as of now*—from appearing in the light of a rational ethic; it also prevents the same for the truth of the communist intention—namely, *scientific socialism,* an inevitable and logical outcome of technical progress, of genuine rationalization, and of the modern evolution toward unification.

Perhaps psychologists, like the intellectuals whom the French philosopher Merleau-Ponty mentions, have only a small part to play in this tragic conflict. But they do have the duty to define "the true terms of the human problem . . . and to maintain intact, in spite of propaganda, the chances that history may still have to clarify itself."

The man of science cannot, in truth, resign himself to the inevitability of a new war. Therefore he must conjure up rational and concrete means to render it impossible.

These means are being advocated every day by many statesmen, thinkers, and even men in the street. But in order to influence the public opinion of the world, they refer, especially in France, to the traditional prestige of "spiritual values." By affirming their necessity they claim to push the human being in the direction of goodness and sacrifice. This mysticism, partly religious and partly secular, reiterates respect for the human personality and the cult of brotherhood. It characterizes especially the virtuous "occidental world" today.

Yet this venerable propaganda by abstract values (which basically is only a rejuvenated form of magic) has proved its total inefficiency; the atrocities of all wars, and especially those monstrous abominations perpetrated on "subhumanity" during the course of the latest, are incontestable demonstrations of this truth.

We think that only in the misunderstood procedure of scientific world organization can effective means for a change possibly be found. Such an enterprise would attack the prime factors of the drama but not its idealistic justifications, its concrete human determinism, or the mystifications distorting its true meaning.

We are not concerned here with the construction of a scientific myth, which, like the ideological ones, would enter into the service of politics. Nor do we propose a return to the dream of the triumph of Reason which haunts the philosophers, and particularly (by some irony of fate) the German philosophers. The kind of reason whose application would be desirable is not abstract Reason—a metaphysical idea of general or idealistic Hegelian dialectic—but simply the same rational thought that has led modern man to his mastery of nature in the field of technic.

Two specialized branches of science should be consulted to elucidate the data of the problem: first and immediately *psychosociology* whose qualified representatives in all countries should be called for discussion at once. Secondly, and as a project of much longer range, *psychopedagogy* is needed. The latter would furnish the means to create veritable "citizens of the world," *i.e.*, persons who would be practically suited to keep up a normal inter-human relationship and capable of resolving in a peaceful manner the conflicts arising between human groups.

A common psychosociological study should be promoted by all governments. The leaders of nations, even if well-meaning, are not the true representatives of national groups. The latter are deeply pacifist. Their leaders, however, are in a state of emotional dependence due to their political role and the responsibility imposed thereby. Therefore it is very doubtful if they ever could—either by means of interpretation through their diplomats or personally—construct a friendly organization between opposing national coalitions. Collective action against war, an action which could not very well be pursued *against* them without anarchy, could be taken, however, *without* them. This could be done subject to the condition that the consistent pressure of a well-informed and alert international public opinion would be exercised on them, demanding the collaboration of economists, sociologists, and psychologists without any sentimental or so-called political (in the common sense of the word) consideration.

The nation should arrive at a previous agreement, in view of the co-existence of the two social systems of the capitalist and the socialist type. This should be done under one express condition: that all military aggression—primarily atomic genocide—be excluded, as well as any armed interior revolutionary action under the aegis of a foreign nation.

Finally, this intermission should be taken advantage of by studying the possibilities of establishing a general agreement of socioeconomic principles of organization among nations. Actual cooperation would be impossible during the present economic confusion resulting from the present radical war of currencies. Under the heading of reciprocal adjustment of concrete national needs—whether by accelerated reform or by pacifist revolutions—the principle of limiting capitalistic expansionism would be decreed. Simultaneously, and in balance thereof, communist propaganda should be limited. It could be restricted to critical information in cultured popular media and universities.

There would be reason to expect that little by little the utopia of international goodwill, so far counteracted by political superstition, would be embodied in history at this level of scientific organization in society. Many French thinkers believe that the small European nations, where the spirit of balance and free criticism exists, would quite easily adopt scientific information thus received. Their adjustment could furnish an element of world stability and make these nations not a political "third force" but a crossroads of interpenetration between two antagonistic currents of world thought.

As to the ethical and social formation of the individual of to-morrow, we must turn to the primary principles obtained from the research of child psychologists, psychoanalysts, and behaviorists.

Surroundings free from ethical superstitions and from all unfavorable influences affecting the development of their personalities should be created for the children of all countries. Their universe should include only a purely social prohibition no longer personified by parents who are ignorant of their child's soul. From the child's life would be banished the sexual tabu and retribution by the "withdrawal of love." This means that the young individual would grow up as free personally as would be fully consistent with the lives of others. Individual sexual morality would be replaced by mental hygiene, and the natural need for violent action absorbed by the stabilizing practice of sport.

From the moment the child acquires the first two tools of knowledge, memory and speech, he should be taught the equally obscure but necessary conditions of normal inter-human relations—sense of community, joy of helping each other, and the horror felt toward any attack on the lives of others. This means that his social conduct will be fashioned for him before he is permitted to construct for himself a moral conduct that would be truly personal or autonomous. His conduct would then no longer be an outside threat imposed on him by force. Consequently there would not be the germ of aggressive danger to society. This status would reduce the moral imperative to nothing but social adjustment: the prohibition of the realized act.

The collective ethic arising from a humanity composed of individuals thus freed since early childhood from all inner moral superstition and brought up in the innocent spontaneity of their normal desires and in abhorrence of any personal violence perpetrated against others would be concrete, efficient, universal, and, in this case, truly humanistic.

This collective ethic would help greatly in making our world more than a vast jungle inhabited by ethically primitive tribes, secret slaves of the aggressive superstition of barbaric centuries, and refugees from the world of the unconscious. It would create a planet that is organized efficiently for harmonious and laborious community life: a planet that is truly *habitable*. Finally, this adjustment would render the outburst of war not only shameful but unthinkable.

GERMANY

Klaus Conrad, M.D.

Professor of Psychiatry and Neurology, Director of
the Neuropsychiatric Clinic at the International
University of Homburg-Saar.

A BRIEF answer to the question as to why people
cannot live peaceably on earth is not easily given. Every individual must admit that it would be much more pleasant to live
quietly and in peace. We shape our life on earth. Why do we
not provide for peace and unity just as we provide for electric
light, gas, and water? Peace would be assured if every individual would sacrifice annually only a small part of his ego-
position, in the same way that he is willing to pay out of his
material possessions for the installation of light, gas and water.
But we do not do this. Nothing is more difficult than to descend
just one step from the throne which our ego occupies, or to give
up voluntarily the power level which we have gained.

We need power in order to exist. The abandonment of a
power-position entails the increase of someone else's power with
a consequent threat to one's own existence. We would have to
renounce power for the sake of peace, but in doing this we might
jeopardize our own existence. Therefore I can only obtain peace
by jeopardizing my own existence. But should I decide upon
security of my existence by increasing my power-position, I
would then reduce the power-position of others, and at the same
time I would be deciding against peace. War signals an even
greater threat to my existence. My existence is therefore always
threatened, regardless of what decision I might make. It is this
very conflict which constitutes the cardinal problem of the era
in which we live.

Let us first consider an elementary example. What would
happen if twelve clever men were stranded on a desert island

where the necessities of life were so scanty or where conditions were so poor that only five would have sufficient food and the other seven would have to starve? Would these twelve clever men come to an agreement according to which every one would be given the same, though inadequate, amount of food? Or would the five strongest and cleverest get all the food at the expense of the other seven, who would be left to die of starvation? Neither one nor the other is likely, according to our experience with similar conditions in prisoner-of-war camps. In all probability, a compromise would be found. The five strongest and cleverest men would fare better than the other seven, but the big five would bend every effort to maintain the fiction that the agreement was being enforced and that the distribution was "equitable."

Undoubtedly tension would ensue on the island. Inasmuch as the distribution was never equitable, and due to individual differences in intellectual and physical power, we would soon observe the formation of different groups. Weaker ones would attach themselves to stronger ones, whereby the latter might also profit in some respects, and others might isolate themselves and join the opposition. As soon as imbalance of power is manifest, *i.e.*, as soon as stronger and weaker groups emerge, we would find an increasing disparity between the groups. The stronger group becomes stronger at the expense of the weaker one. All the while the fiction is maintained that the sparse goods of the island are being distributed in a fair and just fashion, and the stronger group will more and more dictate the rules by which further distribution is to be made.

Should the tension between the two unequal groups result in aggressive action, we would find that the aggression would originate with the weaker group, which, after all, is fighting for equality. The outcome of this open conflict resulting from tension could hardly be questioned, in view of the uneven distribution of strength. The weaker group would be defeated. It is expected that moral condemnations would follow because the fiction in regard to the just distribution of goods was maintained until the end. The vanquished, having been the aggressor, must also appear as the guilty party. Guilt and innocence—the moralistic dichotomy—becomes superimposed upon the dynamic dichotomy of stronger and weaker. Both sides used force during the course of the conflict. However, a careful distinction is made between the deeds of the innocent and the misdeeds of the guilty, despite the fact that there is no overt difference between them. Only the latter are punished.

Our example demonstrates that might and right, violence and lawfulness, egocentricity and objectivity, self-assertion and self-denial are peculiarly and inseparably intertwined in the communal life of individuals. We are sensitive to the other person's insistence upon his right to live and consider it a violation of our own life interest. However, we consider the drive toward the expansion of our own power as quite proper. What is advantageous to us we are prone to consider as just; whatever might be harmful, as unjust. Too often we forget that we can neither be the prosecutors of our judges nor play the part of judge where we are the defendants.

Another useful concept is illustrated in our example, namely the fundamental psychological "Law of the Circle." Wherever tension arises in interpersonal relationships, we find that this tension has a self-perpetuating potential towards increase, according to the "Principle of Circulus Vitiosus." This principle is at work in every realm of psychic life. A slight altercation between a friend and myself will result in a change of my attitude towards him. This in turn will induce him to act more coolly towards me, which again will aggravate my own ill-humor. This diabolical circle can only be broken by a new and opposing principle. This new principle is quite alien to the primordial, naive, instinctual, unconscious, and infantile psychical realm. It originates in an entirely different universe, namely the universe of spirituality.

This principle rests upon the divestiture of the ego, upon the conscious triumph over instinctual drives; it rests upon renunciation. As soon as I abandon the idea to make my friend suffer for my upset, he will see his way clear to approach me with greater cordiality; in turn it will be possible for me to take a more conciliatory attitude. The "circulus vitiosus" becomes a "circulus virtuosus."

No matter in what direction we may look, we observe these "circles." Whoever has insulted me, I shall insult, giving him more cause to insult me further. Should I appear distrustful, I invite those around me to concern themselves with my affairs, giving rise to greater distrust on my part. If I am curious, people will withdraw, which will increase my curiosity. Should I attempt to control people, they rise up against me, which induces me all the more to control them for the sake of my own security. In trying to impress others they will avoid me, making me more bombastic in order to impress them. We continuously react in this fashion without really knowing it. We appear secure to those who feel insecure, thus increasing their feelings of insecurity. The self-assured make us feel insecure. Whoever shows an inimical attitude toward me, will also find me hostile. Wherever anyone has obtained even a trace of power over others, he has sold his soul to the devil. His power will increase and the devil will not release him from his claws. A diabolical circular motion starts.

* * *

Let us turn now to our real objective, the investigation of the psychological causes of international tension in the world of today.

If one were to conduct in Germany today a poll according to the Gallup method, one would obtain a great diversity of answers to the inquiry into the causes of international tension. The majority would probably believe that all tensions are the result of the political tension between the western and eastern hemispheres. They would consider the differences between these two worlds to be so antithetical that they must remain irreconcilable and insoluble. By necessity, a settlement, one way or another, will have to come. This collision must be a violent one; a peaceful solution is not possible.

On the other hand, a smaller but not inconsiderable group of Germans would not consider the causes for international tension to be as irreversible or as inevitable. They would more likely believe that these tension are arbitrarily and artificially created by large and powerful groups for purely economic reasons. With the aid of the press and other agencies that influence public opinion, one nation is played against the other to raise nationalistic emotion to the boiling point. Such action is of course necessary for the creation of a military conflict. This state of affairs is often preceded by a brilliant demagogic prelude designed to fan public opinion. Those who share this belief are not too much concerned with demonstrating whether oil, arms, banking, or press interests are at the bottom of it. They merely suppose that it is some anonymous, sinister, and invisible power that holds the reins and controls the politicians of most countries just like marionettes. This same power supposedly plays one group against another and has already inscribed upon its calendar the start of a world war at a time when the innocent man on the street still harbors the illusion of a hundred years of peace.

A third group, probably smaller than the preceding one, represents the belief that international tension is fundamentally based upon biological factors that differentiate between various human races. These races would be comparable to large biological organisms which would settle their differences in the same fashion that individuals would. The race with the greater biological vitality would irresistibly absorb the weaker one, or else would force it into extinction. Biologists have studied in detail how certain animal forms have disappeared, and how the fittest have displaced the weaker ones. Therefore, those who profess this belief would ask why the development of human races would not follow similar lines. After all, we see that the white race, in astonishing fashion, has not only maintained itself but has swept ahead of all others. Among these large groups one would find similarly that the more vital sub-groups would forge ahead of others. Accordingly, it would appear Utopian to assume that war would ever end, because racial vitality is not constant, and one kind which will take the lead until it is replaced by another will always emerge.

A fourth group, presumably the smallest, would hold that international tension originates in a certain peculiarity of contemporary mankind, namely, the secularization of the occident. Despite the fact that we continuously pretend that the occident is the epitome of Christian culture, that we are living in a Christian world, and that we are Christians ourselves, we must nonetheless admit that we are true Christians only very remotely. Were we really Christians, neither discord nor tension could exist in the world. If we would apply the Commandments of Christ to such essential aspects as loving our neighbors as ourselves, pardoning the guilty, and turning the left cheek if the right one were struck, we would not run the risk of stimulating discord between individuals or tension among nations. But we do *not* live in Christ-like fashion, although we continuously pretend, full of hypocrisy, to be doing so. In reality we love ourselves above all else, just as pagans would. We seek revenge and retribution, we yearn for worldly power and try to satisfy our sensual urges. Dancing around the golden calf, we offer daily sacrifices to the idols of our passions. We want to strangle our neighbors just as soon as our own sphere of interest is touched upon. At the same time we indignantly decry the menace to our own security. Therefore peace cannot come to mankind. War among nations is merely the present-day expression of the pagan and cannibalistic culture in which we live.

A great variety of answers to the problem of international tension has been presented. Political, economic, biological, and religious differences are considered the cardinal factors. However, these differing concepts are not mutually exclusive. On the contrary, they could easily be interrelated. East and West are fighting for economic power, but simultaneously it is a fight between two different human races for the supremacy of the fittest. This fight is possible because both groups are fundamentally and thoroughly un-Christian. They are locked in combat like pagan tribes. The choice of whether the causes for tension are political, economic, biological, or religious is in the final analysis merely a matter of taste and character.

As psychiatrists, however, we must regard these matters from a different point of view, though we must be conscious of the one-sidedness of our own considerations. It is the psychological aspect that concerns us. International tension—and we have to make this point clear from the start—is not tension between nations, but tension between nationalisms. The problem of the origin of international tension then becomes the problem of the origin of nationalisms. Nationalism is a form of collective egotism. Therefore one has to inquire into the origin and the conditions that bring about collective egotism. This problem involves us immediately with the deep layers of human psyche. It focuses upon the assertion of our own ego as opposed to the non-ego; upon the development of the superego, upon self-assertion and self-surrender, as well as upon the fundamentals of subjectivity and objectivity.

The laws of the human soul have been intensively studied since Nietzsche and Scheler. Freud, Adler, Jung and their disciples have given a half-century of subtle and circumspect labor. On the basis of their discoveries, we have labeled as "neurotic" those mechanisms that lead to exaggerated defenses. They are the very mechanisms that produce ego-inflation and self-assertiveness, and their roots are buried in the despondency of man and the anxiety that springs from it. The origin of collective egotism, or nationalism, as we call it, also stems from this neurotic mechanism. The tremendous spreading of nationalism in the occidental world of today is a result of the increasing neurosis of the occidental world. The psychiatrist and the psychotherapist are therefore charged with the investigation of the cause for international tension. Psychiatric examination and treatment are required.

* * *

Tension between Germans and Frenchmen, Englishmen and Irishmen, Italians and Yugoslavs, Greeks and Bulgarians, Jews and Arabs, Russians and Turks, as well as the tension between certain South American countries, should by no means be confused with tension of the individuals of these different countries. Germans and Frenchmen can get along with one another most cordially. They experience a certain kinship and are much more desirous to compliment one another than to fight one another. Similar dynamics underlie the relationships of all the other nations. Even today neighborship need not entail enmity; it can equally well result in friendship. The individuals of these nations do not feel hostile toward their neighbors. Nonetheless the existence of tension cannot be doubted. How can we explain it? That is the problem which faces the psychologist today. If the tension between two groups is not predicated upon the tension between the individuals of these two groups, then we cannot equate the group tension with the tension between the group members. Despite the fact that the group is composed of individuals, it comports itself differently from the way its members behave.

It is questionable whether revenge, ambition or competitiveness of a group, a clan, a society, a party or a nation can be directly compared with individual dynamics. The desire for revenge on the part of all the group members becomes consolidated into a collective desire for revenge which forms the basis for the collective spirit. But, strangely enough, experience shows that only a few personal characteristics become part of the group character, while some never do. The collective spirit need not be distinguished solely by negative characteristics, inasmuch as one may talk of a country's courage, a group's loyalty, or a nation's industrial skill. On the other hand, one will rarely, if ever, have the opportunity to talk of a country's self-denial, objectivity, justice, piety, honesty, or incorruptibility.

One cannot talk of the wisdom of a human group. The individual may be distinguished by these characteristics; in the group, however, they cannot become a dominant feature. On the contrary, they generally disappear altogether. A group composed exclusively of wise people would not behave wisely, but would behave just like any other group.

To equate the group with the individual is not always possible. In searching for a distinguishing mark between the two, we come upon a remarkable result. Under certain conditions, we are able to ascribe to a whole group all those characteristics that we can isolate in an adolescent. But those traits that set the adult apart from the adolescent are never found in the group. Neither the child nor the group can be considered wise and just.

In the final analysis, neither one of them can act in a rational fashion.

What is it then that distinguishes adult traits from juvenile traits? It is the control of the intellect over the instinctive urges of youth. It is the mastery over one's own urges, the renunciation of ego-impulses and the triumph over self.

Group relationships are childlike, and that is the way nations act. Exactly as Adler demonstrated, they are bent upon increase of their power, unlimited authority and self-assertiveness. Completely lacking is the voluntary renunciation of power-aspirations in favor of an all-encompassing ideology, which of course includes the ego. Indeed, one may say that groups behave like primitives. Self-assertiveness is law also among South Sea Islanders, though it is tied to an orthdox ritual. The laws of blood-feud and power aggrandizement at the expense of one's neighbor are in full force and unlimited. Therefore one can formulate this conclusion: Groups react to one another like animals of the jungle. It is the law of might that counts. Only the efforts of the individual ever reach a level of humane conduct. Though the individual believes himself to be the leader of the group, it is the group that nearly always forces him back into a course of infantile, primitive and animal-like egotism and assertiveness.

Here we are confronted with the difficult sociological problem that deals with the relationships of individual and group. The relationship is a reciprocal one. The group produces the individual, who in turn elevates himself to its leader. At the same time, however, the group decides upon the leader, who can never lead at will. The group prescribes his decisions without his being consciously aware of it.

It has often been debated whether "men make history" or whether "history makes men." In authoritarian eras, the former belief would be prevalent; and democratic eras, the latter. In reality both are right. The reciprocal interrelationship between individual and group is evident in every epoch. It is in just those apparently authoritarian eras that the group is the more powerful and the leader is merely the exponent of the collective will of the group. In non-authoritarian epochs, the group very often does not know the individual who by virtue of the anonymity of his will becomes the deciding factor.

Functionally we see in this cyclical relationship that the law of the circle is in force. The group that is embarking upon a neurotic development will select a certain type of leader. Most likely a leader will be chosen who is a self-assertive neurotic himself. Inasmuch as this particular leader was chosen by this particular group, he will continue to lead the group in such a fashion that more and more severely neurotic elements will emerge from the group as new leaders who in turn will continue this fatal and diabolical cycle.

We are here concerned with the problem of the elite group. The fate of a group depends upon its ability to form an elite. There are groups among which only people with high intellect are able to maintain a leading position. In those groups it would be impossible for a psychopath or a neurotic to remain in power, even if he were swept into office by a series of adventitious circumstances. In those cases there is a consistent and healthy process of structurization, during which the best are elevated and the inferior cast aside. Such a group is healthy and adaptable and able to maintain itself for long periods of time.

On the other hand, there are groups in which just the opposite occurs; the superior individual steps aside and resigns from leadership. Even if requested to take a leading position, he will probably refuse. If he accepts, he cannot maintain himself. Those who succeed are the psychopaths, the shouters, sneaks, demagogues, windbags, moral scum-bums, and the unscrupulous and corrupt show-offs. This destructive process continuously undermines the healthy structure. The organism of this group is sick and diseased.

While the health of nations depends upon the wisdom of their representatives, the wisdom of statesmen depends upon the health of the nation they represent. A sick nation chooses psychopathic and neurotic leaders instead of intellectual and judicious men. The longer these psychopaths are in power, the more psychopathic will the national conduct be. It is quite possible that such a nation has in its midst some highly intelligent and ingenious men. But they are not being utilized. The situation is similar to that of the individual psychopath, who may possess some brilliant potential without being able to put it to constructive use.

We could come considerably closer to the solution of our problem if we were in a position to conduct an intensive psychopathological study of the leading statesmen of all occidental nations. We would be taking a large step forward if we could form in Europe an international council of psychiatrists whose duty it would be to evaluate and appraise the qualifications of every leading diplomat. Probably very few men of today could stand the test. Upon close scrutiny many would look like hollow shells and claptraps of dubious background. It is merely the turbulence of our times that has elevated them to the positions they are now occupying, positions for which they have neither the ability, the education, nor the character.

It was said in Nazi Germany that the only profession for which one needed no education whatever, and not even a character, was that of a "gauleiter" (district chief). Curiously enough, one can say the same thing about a number of leading personalities in Germany today.

It cannot be expected that leading statesmen would submit to an investigation by a psychiatric council. One generally calls the psychiatrist when it is too late. But it is evident that national morbidity is reflected in the personality structure of a nation's self-appointed leaders. The structure of a group becomes manifest if one allows it to organize itself spontaneously and to choose its leadership (as in the case of such groups as prisoners of war, college classes or athletic organizations). Sociologically, essential factors are demonstrated when elections are analyzed. It is revealing to know whether individuals with high intellect, power-mad individuals, pretentious windbags, swindlers or insignificant zealots are elected.

Here we may observe a certain lawfulness in the development of public opinion. Public opinion is created by demagogues; conversely, demagogues are created by public opinion. Why does public opinion listen to demagogues? Because demagogues listen to public opinion. And demagogues say what the public wishes them to say. That again shows the principle of the circle at work.

Turning to the more specific problems as they concern conditions in Germany, it cannot be denied that the Germans have made a considerable contribution toward the development of international tension through the history of the last hundred years. In the society of nations, they have played the part of a not untalented but unpredictable psychopath. On the one hand, the German is ambitious and self-assertive; on the other, he is insecure and shows a labile emotional structure. The German continually believes that others discriminate against him. He became insulting and aggressive toward neighbors and relatives so that they had to make energetic plans for their own defense. This conduct of the Germans has all the earmarks of neurotic behavior, and one is forced to view it from the standpoint of psychopathology. As in all neurotic development, one must investigate the childhood experiences, in this case the childhood of an entire nation. Analysis of a neurosis always requires some historical investigation designed to highlight the historical circumstances that led to the disorientation.

The German nation had a very unhappy infancy and youth. All kinds of wars in the interest of might or ideology have been fought on soil occupied by Germans ever since the time of Charlemagne. The most diversified interests were involved, and it is not a coincidence that even today the boundary between the western and eastern hemispheres runs through the heart of Germany. The geographical area that until recently was Germany showed, one hundred and sixty years ago, an utterly confusing criss-cross of boundaries between small and tiny districts, each under a different sovereign. An area equal to the size of New York was made up of a jumble of domains owned by the Duke of Wuerttemberg, the Emperor of Austria, the Catholic clergy, the knighthood of the empire, various secular governments, as well as some free imperial cities. Each little spot was not only fenced off, but was fortified against attack. An atmosphere of keen tension prevailed in that small area. This tension was brought about by the confluence of a variety of powerful interests. A trip from Biberach to Ulm (23 miles), about the distance from Staten Island to the Bronx, necessitated the crossing of ten frontiers, each one equipped with gate and guardhouse. The establishment of the zonal boundaries in 1945 is reminiscent of former conditions in Germany.

The sovereignty frequently changed hands and the German population had to accustom itself to a concurrent change in religion and way of life whenever a new ruler took over their territory. Similar conditions would exist today, were American and Russian occupation forces to exchange zones. Yet one thing is certain: the early dismemberment did not impede the emergence of some outstanding and brilliant men. At the same time (in 1790), the following men lived on German and Austrian soil: the poets Goethe, Schiller, Hoelderlin, Herder, Wieland, E. Th. Hoffman, Uhland; the philosophers Kant, Mendelssohn, v. Lichtenberg, Hegel, Fichte, Schelling, Brentano, Schlegel; the musicians Haydn, Mozart, Beethoven; and the painters Runge and C. D. Friedrich.

The century-old dismemberment of the German nation is a unique phenomenon in all of Europe. That this fact is the reason for the neurotic structure of the nation appears quite obvious.

In order to make this clear, we will have to draw upon the experience of Individual Psychology (Adler, Kuenkel). If many heterogeneous influences act upon a child during the very important infantile period of ego-organization and ego-structurization, it can easily happen that this developmental process becomes extended or contracted. The concurrent discouragement leads to an overvaluation of the Ego and ultimately results in an egocentric disposition. A child will become spoiled by too lenient an education. If it is sheltered from the problems of life for too long, it will avoid them and continue to avoid them. This spoiled child will become hypersensitive to the influences of his environment. He cannot muster the courage to deal adequately with problematic situations. On the other hand, a child will never gain confidence in authoritarian figures if his education is too strict. This child will become stubborn and suspicious; he will take on an inimical attitude toward the environment which he believes is out to harm him. He will try to fight and possibly control this hostile environment. The hypersensitive person tends to become more and more sensitive by continued pain-avoidance; the insensitive person tends to become more and more thick-skinned by continued exposure to the rigors of life.

The process of discouragement is common to both types of people. The spoiled child does not dare walk the hard road of life. He lives constantly in fear of suffering. The tough child, on the other hand, has lost confidence in his environment and he, too, leads a safeguarded existence. The greatest catastrophe, however, that could befall the child is when pampering and discipline are applied concurrently. Such inconsistency can often be observed in educational methods, particularly when parents are unhappily married.

This condition prevailed in the German nation's youth. The struggle between Emperor and Pope resulted in the unfortunate victory of particularism. Germany is the product of the unhappy marriage of different social structures, the West and South on the one hand, and the East and North on the other. This was already obvious early in the cruel Christianizing of the Saxonians by Charlemagne, and continued through all German history until the Thirty Years War of the Reformation. For centuries torn between the struggle of these two powers, the nation could never develop a normal national attitude. From the beginning, Germany was tempted to give up its own self, and to become Swedish, French, Austrian, Roman, or English. On the other hand, it was also prone to show boundless conceit and to experience a pathological degree of ecstasy when exhorted by a leader who appealed to its neurotic and hypersensitive nationalistic sentiment. So Germany has always vacillated between degrading self-denial and exaggerated nationalism. The cause for all of this was a feeling of discouragement, as in the case of every neurotic who is afraid to face life in a natural and not self-conscious fashion.

Deep down, every German is afraid that he will not gain full recognition, just because he is a German. This feeling is often unconscious and well repressed. Being a German is not a self-understood characteristic as far as he is concerned. He cannot reconcile himself to that fact in the same fashion as he accepts the fact that he has two hands and a nose. He either has to be proud to be a German, or else ashamed; and sometimes he is both. Therefore, he will always emphasize that he is a German poet, a German professor, a German merchant, and not just a poet, a professor, or a merchant. A critical remark such as this one, coming from a German, will never be judged objectively and will therefore not be accepted or rejected on the basis of its intrinsic value. It will be considered treasonous, I am quite certain.

A German will always compare himself with others, he will always try to impress himself and others with the idea that nothing can exceed German efficiency. He thereby proves his deep-seated feelings of insecurity. It is quite characteristically German that I gave you a list of "great Germans," just a little while ago, when I discussed the contributions of those who lived on German soil in 1790. Of course, I was then not conscious of this typically German tendency of self-aggrandizement at the expense of those who cannot produce a comparable impressive list of names. But for the sake of this doubly illustrative value I shall let it stand as it is.

Some knowledge of history will make us realize that the many small districts in early Germany were shut off from one another through turnstiles and custom barriers; these districts were comparable to small countries of different nationalities. The peasant or artisan who lived in a village that was under the domination of a secular prince would resist turning "Austrian" or "clerical" or "ducal." Many small nationalistic cells and boroughs came into existence. Later, when larger units were established, and still later, when the great unification under Bismarck took place, the neurotic-nationalistic spirit was so deeply imbedded in each individual that it could not be exterminated. Rather, it became more firmly established. The perpetuation of this spirit through many generations has nothing to do with heredity. It demonstrates a much stronger law: the law of continuous transmission and development of mental and spiritual structures, such as language, belief, and knowledge.

One can sense this tremendous German nationalism in every

German club, council meeting and political faction, even in matters of ecclesiastic or religious importance. It is always the problem of prestige, power and assertiveness that plays the deciding part; it is seldom the subject-matter itself. Everyone is primarily concerned with his own personal interests. The alleged consideration for the common welfare is merely a pretense to cover up and camouflage these personal aims.

Such conditions can never improve spontaneously; quite to the contrary, they deteriorate and become aggravated. A discouraged, neurotic, and insecure person forces the people around him to take an egocentric attitude. He forces others to be aggressive if he himself is aggressive. If he isolates himself, others detach themselves from him. Both reactions accentuate his peculiarity, either his aggressiveness or his desire for isolation. Such a trend, once started, perpetuates itself irreversibly. Nationalistic and collective inferiority cannot produce anything but exaggerated nationalism. Nationalism, in turn, leads to an exorbitant need to display autocratic behavior. It furthermore makes for unfairness and subjectivity in demands, and in the end it leads to violence. Violence induces a counteraction on the part of the oppressor's victim and a rejection of demands. What follows thereafter is a renewed and intensified demand. And so the cycle continues. Every type of nationalism—collective egoism—creates new and opposing types of nationalism. Defensive forces are not mobilized until the attack is imminent, and the inception of new kinds of nationalism produces new types of aggression and new collective egoisms.

It is this law of the circle that is the essential psychological root of the peculiar motive power of international tension in the world of today. Now the question arises: How can we break this vicious, diabolical circle?

*   *   *

We have seen that no tension exists between the individual German and the individual Frenchman, though tension has existed between the German and French collectives for many centuries. We also know why this is the case. It is only the individual who possesses the divine quality to forgive and to abandon his desire for revenge; to reduce tension by giving up part of his ego-position. The group is not capable of doing this. A group is able to fight for its rights, but it cannot forfeit its rights, just as an animal can fight for its existence, but is unable to sacrifice it voluntarily. The individual stands on a lower level of individuation when judged in reference to the group than when viewed merely as an individual. The group is more closely tied to the rigid laws of nature and is not able to make use of the specifically human principle of freedom. But this is the only possibility of freeing oneself from the eternal circle into which man was drawn and always shall be drawn by the strange integration of unconsciousness (bios) and consciousness (logos).

Individually, we can clearly see the road that would lead out of the turmoil of eternal strife and war. It is the belief in reason and the necessity of self-renunciation. But as members of groups with which we are inseparably bound, we are not able to follow such a course. No individual German harbors a grievance toward an individual Frenchman, but he will unhesitatingly take up arms against France. As a member of the collective he will fight against Frenchmen, who in turn as members of their own group will fight against him. Yet the individual would like to shake hands with his adversary and tell him that he is his brother. Whereas it is true that the individual of today has achieved a greater degree of freedom than anyone ever before, it is also true that his ties with nature are still very strong when we look at him as a member of the group. It is quite certain that mankind will continue with ever-increasing tempo on the road to self-destruction until eventually it has exterminated itself, unless the same mechanism that is activated in preventing the individual who is faced with a crisis from committing suicide can be activated within the various groups. There is a need for insight, followed by a reduction of tension.

This principle was proclaimed two thousand years ago as a new gospel and provided a great surprise for the people of that time. The demand was made that we substitute gentleness for force, love for hatred, forgiveness for revenge, asceticism for lust and self-denial for possessiveness. Ever since then, this gospel has guided our epoch, has lent its name to our living, has been taught us in school and has been drilled into us in our religious training. But apparently it is only valid for people as individuals; as soon as man acts on behalf of the group, the principle is no longer binding. The life of nations is regulated according to principles of opportunism, utility, economy and might. A country which would not act according to these principles, but in accordance with those which were mentioned before, could not continue to exist. A stronger neighbor would soon devour it. Any country that would preach passivity to others, and practice it with all of its ramifications, would most likely be forced to make the ultimate sacrifice. Christianity and politics are disparate concepts. Politics are aimed at achieving, securing and increasing might; Christianity starts with the first attempt at giving up the desire for might.

We have seen that the Germany of 160 years ago was the battleground of feuding power interests. Today we find that it is not only the whole continent of Europe but the entire occidental civilization, in slightly different attire, that is in a boiling state. It matters not whether we are dealing with commercial interests, industrial trusts, private enterprises, newspaper or banking interests, political parties, churches, private clubs, trade unions, minorities or pluralities, natives or DP's, large or small nations; wherever we look, we find one group trying to subject another group, attempting to bring it under its complete domination. In the end there is nothing else involved but the lust for power.

Let us recall the result of our fictitious Gallup Poll investigating the problem of international tension. We shall then find that it is truly immaterial whether we emphasize ideological, social, economic, or biological factors as the determinants of tension. The important thing is that groups are always involved in a fight with other groups for domination and supremacy. This struggle is fought on ideological, social, economic, and biological grounds, and the form it takes depends largely upon adventitious events. Does it matter whether one group is strangled by economic measures, maligned and beaten to death in public opinion, liquidated through diplomatic moves, subjugated through sanctions, or exterminated by atom bombs? All we see is the fight of jungle animals for the survival of the fittest, even though the most ingenious methods and highly-developed techniques are used.

Slowly, however, it is dawning upon us where this road leads. A tremendous crisis has befallen civilized mankind. People are beginning to realize the direction in which they are headed, but they cannot turn back. The diabolical wheel is turning ever faster. Those who had just been the plaintiffs have now become defendants. The victors must now rush to the assistance of the vanquished in order to avoid being conquered themselves. Who is guilty and who is innocent? Who is the outsider and who is the participant? Who can claim that he, personally, is not involved?

Somewhere court is in session, like a phantom theatre without an audience. Everyone knows that he is guilty himself, regardless of what language he may be speaking or on which side he might have been standing when his guilt was established. The greater the number of people sacrificed on the pagan altar in worship of a revengeful justice, the more will this heathenish deity crave for blood. The more he drinks, the greater becomes his thirst.

The neurosis of occidental mankind is now in the critical state. There are only two possible ways out. The one is suicide, a path upon which the world has apparently decided. The other would be a renunciation of the ego-position by means of reason. This would become possible if the large nations would voluntarily begin to curtail their demands for might, or if the large nations would honestly and persistently begin to demobilize.

This latter course can hardly be imagined. The tiger does not cut his claws, nor does the wolf blunt his teeth. But then again, groups are made up of individuals who are endowed with reason and capable of insight and resignation. The miracle may yet come, because man is not only of bestial but also of divine origin. Perhaps man, after all, will come to his senses and realize that love is stronger than hatred, forgiveness stronger than revenge; that life is stronger than death, but sacrifice of life stronger than life.

GUATEMALA

Carlos Federica Mora, M.D.

Professor of Medical Psychology, Mental Hygiene
and Legal Medicine at the University of San
Carlos de Guatemala; Former President of the
University of San Carlos; Former Minister of Edu-
cation and Public Health of Guatemala; Technical
Advisor to the National Institute of Social Security.

L OCATED in the heart of the Western Hemisphere
only a few hours away from the nearest North American city,
Guatemala is not a great power. Moreover, it does not have a
civilization that can be called its own; its national characteristics are identical in many ways with those considered typical of
all the nations in Spanish America. Nevertheless, its political-
social problems, especially its difficulty in gaining a more secure
position in the world and in establishing more satisfactory relations with other countries, undeniably have an influence on
world tension. Perhaps this influence comes about in an insidious
and unexpected manner, but it is certainly worthy of being taken
into consideration. One must correct the disorder of the smallest
organ if the entire organism is to function effectively. If we do
not wish to overlook anything in our diagnosis of the ills that
afflict humanity today, we must examine the factors that contribute to the misfortune of the smaller countries.

The problems of Guatemala are quantitatively and qualita-
tively quite different from those affecting larger nations. They
must be examined individually in order to reveal their true
weight as factors contributing to the abnormality of the present
day. To make them clear we shall also state the case of other
countries of similar origin in the Caribbean region.

The historical background and present structure of Guatemala are so different from those of the larger countries which

make up Western civilization that a brief examination of these factors is necessary. Otherwise it would be impossible to understand the true nature of our conflicts and limitations.

The present population of Guatemala had its origin in the union of two races: the Mayan-Quiche and the Spanish. Being entirely unknown to each other, their fusion created a stock uniting the most disparate genetic factors.

When the Conquistadors arrived at the beginning of the sixteenth century, Guatemala had for centuries been the center of an extraordinary culture whose permanent records remain to this day. A series of vicissitudes suffered by tribes belonging to the ancient Toltec empire (which covered most of what is now Mexico) and the Mayan empire (which settled most of the Yucatan peninsula) sent migratory waves to the south. As they spread, the Toltecs on the Pacific slopes and the Mayans on the Atlantic watershed, they founded a civilization that was in many respects superior to the contemporary civilizations in the Old World.

As it has happened so many times in other epochs, the two mother races of Indians joined; they had fused in the best moments of their history, increasing the sum of their scientific knowledge and of their intellectual attainment. For the formation of the national character, the contact between the two civilizations was a fertile one. As J. Antonio Villacorta says: "The materialism of the Mayans was imposed on the spirituality of the Shoshone-Toltecs, and to the latter's contemplative mind was added the former's eminently practical nature. From the mixture of the tribes and from the mutual acceptance of each other's religions and customs was formed the new Mayan-Quiche race, called upon to play such an important role in the history of human civilization."

At the time of the Spaniards' arrival, this civilization, whose origins coincided with those of the Christian era, had decayed greatly. The division of the primitive empire, the secular conflicts between the different groups, and the destructive influence of climate and epidemics undermined the vitality of the great kingdoms to the point where conquest was made much easier for the invader. Nevertheless, the subjugation, colonization, and the arrival of a new culture did not succeed in exterminating the native races. Even as their material work remains in the earth, the descendants of these prodigious artisans can still be found—the purity of his ethnic type intact, his traditions still alive, and his language preserved.

The conquest imposed on the conquered races, as far as possible, the religion, language, customs, and the particular concept of life held by the conquerors. However, an essential difference should be noted between the systems of domination followed by the Spaniards and the Anglo-Saxons. Whereas the latter repulsed the Indian and almost exterminated him, the Spanish Conquistadores mixed freely with the natives and produced a sub-race of *mestizos*, who are improperly called the Latin American race. This difference in attitude toward the primitive people had—and still has—a great deal to do with the historical development of every one of the American countries. We can call it a divergency, for in the passage of centuries their respective politico-social and economic characters have divided them and created in their separation a real state of tension, even though it is generally concealed and well-controlled.

The *mestizo* and the pure descendant of the Conquistador, the creole, form the upper (if not the largest) stratum of the new nationality which has been forging itself since colonial times. Another result of Spanish-Indian mating was the founding of communities which, in each of the dependencies of the Spanish crown, quickly acquired an individual character, an autocratic tendency, and a feeling of belonging more to America than to Europe. These attitudes stimulated the formation of new nationalities. The many Indians who did not fuse with the whites remained to form the largest section, if not the most superior, of these embryonic countries; and they continued to be the objects of stubborn missionary and civilizing efforts by the Europeans. As day laborers, they were frequently badly treated by the land agents. While they were defended by papal bulls and protecting laws, nothing practical was done to raise their moral and economic condition. Three hundred years of submission during the colonization and one hundred and twenty-five years during the regime of independence have been enough to entirely erase in millions of Indians the good qualities of their antecedents. They have been converted into an enormous mass of passive beings who live on the edge of modern life, alien to the anxieties of the ruling class and incapable of being interested spectators of the drama of humanity.

Independence was obtained without war and without major effort. That which had cost other countries of Spanish American blood, heroism and long years of struggle was nothing more for Central America than a meeting of neighbors and authorities. The Act of Independence was accepted by everyone without difficulty or opposition. The mother country did not send soldiers nor make the slightest attempt to regain its lost dominions.

Central Americans saw themselves freed in this fashion overnight. But they were without the maturity required to govern themselves. From then on, cultural and political progress were disturbed by disorders, disorientation, administrative incompetency, lack of group ideals and united public opinion, and lack of respect for institutions and laws. Then came the time when the Central American Federation broke up, giving rise to five tiny countries in the place of one. These countries dedicated their energies to fighting each other and destroying their strength, their scanty economic resources, and their possibilities of progress. Their suicidal agitation gave them the reputation throughout the world of being backward and turbulent. Their constant uprisings were given the unmerited name of "revolutions," and there was a continual oscillation between long periods of dictatorship and short intervals of anarchy. These were the disadvantages of being formed of such heterogeneous human groups, and these disorders consumed long years of the autonomous life of these nations, with a minority of whites and *mestizos* dominating and oppressing a majority of *mestizos* and Indians. The leaders were intent only on satisfying their own appetites and desires. They were completely unprepared for anything else.

In spite of such huge obstacles, Guatemala has been consolidating and advancing in an evolutionary rhythm which has increased as the nation has approached maturity. Material progress, slow at the beginning and faster after communication with more advanced countries became easier, has been considerable. Spiritual progress has been less noticeable because of the discrepancy between the aptitude of the cultured classes to conceive it and the incapacity of the illiterate mass to assimilate it. However, the moment is already in sight when the masses will have absorbed enough to take an active part in the raising of their own cultural level.

Two revolutions, those of 1871 and 1944, and the only ones really worth the name, were responsible for the greatest good to come out of the Republic's development. The first brought a vigorous stimulus to public education, destroyed some aristocratic abuses, and promoted material advances. It was a democratic and liberal revolution. The revolution of 1944 opened the way to social justice, which had been violently attacked by the dictatorships of the century. It suddenly opened the doors of Guatemala to the humanitarian currents which had already prevailed for many years in the civilized world outside. Unfortunately, the revolution of 1871 failed to reach its goal of spreading education throughout the nation. The number of illiterates has remained virtually unchanged during the seventy-five years of the post-revolutionary era. Will the revolution of 1944 also fail to reach its objective of bettering the conditions of the workers? Its defeat would mean the continuation of an absurd and intolerable state that would contribute to the continuation of world tension.

The national character, acquired through the centuries, presents a series of psychological traits which are distinct in each of the social strata. It is obvious that these traits have a decisive influence on our reactions as a human mixture and on our adaptation to the exceedingly difficult conditions of the modern world. Because of the heterogeneity of our social elements, the Indians, *mestizos*, and creoles must be considered separately.

Undermined by the endemics of the tropics, bad habits, and by inadequate and badly balanced diet, the Indians are a burden and a negative force in many aspects of the life we are striving for; and they will continue to be so as long as there is no deep change in their present social and cultural status. They are lagging many years behind the times, vegetating in their mountains and villages, entirely indifferent to the spiritual anxieties of the average man or of the world in general—for our anxieties and struggles for the realization of collective ideals are none other than the local reflection of those that concern all humanity. The personal habits and ways of living of the Indians are completely inadequate for adaptation to the norms and necessities of life in civilized environments. In their way of thinking and feeling, in their religious rites and beliefs, in their family life, sexual relations, and recreation there prevails a conservative, traditionalistic, impractical spirit which blocks the normal evolution of the mixed Guatemalan population. In the economic field they are of little value with reference to production and consumption. They are hindered by their antiquated and rudimentary methods, and by the absolute lack of fulfillment of material needs. Sunk in the deepest ignorance, they contribute in no way to intellectual or artistic production. Their participation in politics is neither spontaneous nor thoughtful, but rather controlled by others for the sake of party interests. Their share in the tax burden is negligible, for they own very little and produce less. Unfortunately, their greatest contribution to the nation's coffers comes from the liberal consumption of spirits. Their collaboration in all that tends to assure the well-being of the community is nil, or, at least, neither voluntary nor conscious. Consequently they constitute a dead weight, a negative value, and create a systematic disorder in the Guatemalan organism.

It would be unjust not to admit that in Guatemala, whose economy is based on farming, the Indians represent cheap labor, easy to control and relatively capable in the type of work assigned to them. But their reluctance to learn new methods puts a heavy burden on the agricultural economy. It is true that their tendency to quiet and order, their docility and peacefulness, the moderation of their appetites and the horror of violent change or of hurried transformation make the Indians balance, by the strength of their inertia, the frequently irrational or uncontrolled tendencies of the *mestizos*. Nor should it be forgotten that without the frugality, conservatism, and fatalism of the Indian, who reconciles himself to any salary and is consequently outrageously exploited, our one-crop country would suffer economic catastrophe when the price of coffee goes down. But the Indians, in exchange for these virtues, instead of being a factor for wealth, progress and power, are a parasitic and alien element which blocks Guatemala's progress and hinders its international role. How can a country succeed when two-thirds of the inhabitants are not effectively incorporated into the culture surrounding them? Though the thinking minority in Guatemala looks to the future, the majority passively clings to the past and is little concerned with the problems and crises of civilization as a whole.

The pathological attitude of the Indian toward international life is explained when we take into consideration the principal psychological traits of the individual and the group. Global attitudes are but the result of individual modes of conduct. From this point of view, the outstanding and deplorable factor in the psychological constitution of the Indian is the effect of the changes brought about by oppression and feudalism. As I said in one of my earlier books: "The fact of belonging to a class apart, subjugated and mistreated by the ruling class, and of having been in this inferior state for the past four centuries, brought with it the systematic suppression of some mental activities of the highest value, and the deterioration of certain sources of biological action by their abandonment and nonuse. . . . Relegated to the role of mere spectators in the drama of progress going on in our country—if not spectacularly, or brilliantly, then at least with persistence and sound intentions —our aborgines do not use their higher-level intellectual functions enough. Their methods of thinking are rudimentary, their reasoning obtuse and over-ingenuous, their critical ability most limited, and their intellectual judgment very poor. Their thinking is based more on principles of magic than on logic."

Among the major disadvantages caused by this troubled social situation are the great number of repressions, inhibitions, defeats and failures, smothered protests and aggressive attempts which could not be carried out. So many frustrated acts, which hinder the free expression of personality, create a mass feeling of fear and insecurity, consternation and mistrust, and introversion and pessimism. All of this creates an emotional condition and an exaggerated fatalism which undermine initiative, constructive effort, and the desire to do something to change the situation. Another effect is the profound disinterest in the fate of all who do not belong to the same group; there is, indeed, a concealed rancor which is sometimes expressed by mob attacks, by slaughterings in which free reign is given to the cruelty, rage, and desire for vengeance which have been nourished quietly for so many years.

This microcosm found in the heart of a country which aspires to form part of the so-called Western civilization is composed of millions of individuals with every sort of personal difficulty. They practice neither physical nor spiritual hygiene; they do absolutely nothing to better their material condition. When they work for themselves, they do so on a small scale and cling to the oldest of methods. When they work for others, their performance is inferior because, having neither ambition nor great energy, they do only what is strictly required in order to earn the day's pay; when the necessary minimum has been accomplished they abandon the job. Money does not interest them; they do not save it, and they do not dream of rising on the social ladder. Moreover, they drink too much, first, because their religious and other festivals have been bacchanalian since before the time of Columbus, second, because they acquire the habit of alcohol in the early years of their life. Fathers even give spirits to nursing children. Finally, the Indians drink because intoxication makes them forget temporarily their hard lot; it gives them momentary courage, boldness, and freedom from sexual inhibitions and complexes.

But the personality of the Indian does not only contain defects. If the value of his virtues, which are generally fundamental, can be weighed against his failings, which are usually superficial, the balance may result in his favor. Although a psychometric estimate of his intellectual capacity has never been made, simple observation of his conduct in situations new to him shows that basically he is intelligent, adaptable, and able in all things requiring spatial intelligence. However, he is neither original nor adept at abstraction or creative action. He is obedient and mild of nature, with a sound moral foundation. He does not steal, offend, nor slander, nor does he have a tendency to hate. As he becomes civilized, he shows an inclination toward cooperation and human sympathy, tendencies which are not found in the *mestizo*. All in all, he has a good mixture of qualities and abilities, especially those leading to sociability. To enumerate them would be superfluous; but even without doing so one can be sanguine about the possibilities of converting him into a good human element, especially if we give him an adequate education.

Between the pure Indian and the *creole*—or the direct product of the immigration—is the *mestizo*, who occupies a series of gradations which make it impossible to classify typical examples; the differences are frequently more economic, social, and cultural than ethnic. The psychological characteristics resemble those of the Indian or those of the white according to the case. But when the racial mixture is complete, there appears a hybrid type with a character of its own (and hardly a commendable one), which combines on occasions the traits of each of the original races. Under the biological laws that govern union of the races, the mixed breeding which took place in America turned out products of inferior quality to that of the forebears; so much so that it would be useless to seek in these fruits the competitive energy, tenacity, persistence, heroism, creative genius, strong ambition, liveliness, and high tension of the Spanish soldier; or the artistic abilities, moral greatness, power of observation, tendency to order and harmony, foresight, calculation, and industry of the ancient Mayan. Something of all this remains, it is true, in certain outstanding personalities. But this is not the common inheritance of the great majority. On the contrary, in the *mestizo*, we generally find either none of these fine qualities or else their opposites.

Possibly biological causes are not the only factors responsible for the devaluation of the *mestizo*. The rigors of the conquest, three centuries of colonial rule, premature emancipation and unbalance while the nation was being formed, and also the climatic conditions, tropical diseases, inadequate diet, and alcoholism must have contributed very heavily to the loss of the inherent qualities that dignified the two mother races. Whatever the cause, it must be recognized that the social conduct of the Guatemalan and the progress of the country suffer because of a lack of practical sense, an excess of imagination, and a scanty creative ability and foresight; because of apathy, depression, sadness and dismay in the sphere of emotional reactions; and because of indecision, vacillation, lack of firmness and continued effort in the face of difficulties, and the easy abandonment of work that was to be eternal.

The whites, forming a select minority, generally direct and dominate. Mixing with immigrants on the one hand, and on the other with the *mestizos* of predominantly Caucasian origin, they are the owners of the land, the industrialists, the intellectuals, the men of the world, the middle class. But though they are better off, it is not they who give the nation its special character, nor have they succeeded in changing it, outnumbered as they are by the larger racial groups and by the drag caused by the latter's cultural backwardness.

Guatemala has had to overcome difficulties caused by the diversity of its people, lack of public education, obstacles placed in the way of progress by political instability—or the over-stability found under the long periods of dictatorship—and many other difficult factors. But at the present time the country has reached a level which, though not the highest possible, is satisfactory and promising.

After having gone through the first century of its independent life in a series of ups and downs caused by political vicissitudes, varying economic production, oscillations of the consumers' markets, and even catastrophes of nature, Guatemala is now at the agricultural stage of its development. Here it will probably stay, because the conditions of the soil and the variety of climate are particularly favorable for agriculture. Moreover, if a special effort were made in industry, the formidable competition of the nearby United States would easily prove annihilating. The financial condition of Guatemala is excellent and sound; it has not been a country of loans and commercial ventures. But the capital which helped develop its resources has largely been foreign: German at first, for the exploitation of coffee, and then North American, for the growth of plantains (bananas). The great poverty of the working classes is due to this state of affairs and to the kind of feudalism in which the people have lived for so many years. Finally, our agricultural wealth is still potential rather than developed; the full resources have not been tapped because Indians and *mestizos* have little ability in production, in organizing details, or in making themselves self-sufficient. Hence the shocking example of a fertile and promising country having to import even its most necessary foods.

From the political point of view, the "republican, democratic, and representative" regime mentioned in the Constitution has been reached after a long chain of dictatorships that have gone on throughout the history of the country. A flagrant contradiction has existed between the democratic ideal and the specific social structure of the Republic. This contradiction explains the dictatorships, and would even absolve them if any one of them had had the vision to use its power for a firm attack on social evils, instead of making them worse. In our time, beginning with the Revolution of 1944, there have been liberty and respect for the dignity of man. But in order to have the great inert mass formed by the Indians use these privileges and take an active and conscientious part in national life, this mass must be raised from the depths where it now lies, and transformed into a living force. As long as this is not done, the Indians will remain—thanks to the democratic lie—an election instrument in the hands of *mestizo* politicians who, with sentimental excuses, refuse to admit the truth of the causal condition.

From the social point of view, pronounced inequality has arisen from the disparity of social groups. However, there is an excellent opportunity to correct the present situation now that the dominant idea in the world has been accepted in Guatemala. The worker and the farmhand were deprived for many years of all assistance and all justice. They were mere instruments of production. As recently as 1940, it was considered a crime of "threatening the institutions of the State" to declare a strike, establish a union, or challenge the semi-feudal regime in any way. As though the exploitation of man were an institution of the State! In the past five years the situation has changed rapidly and radically: already there is labor legislation, the workers are organized, a prudent system of social security guarantees their present and future, and for the first time in the history of Guatemala, the working classes have found a voice.

From the cultural point of view, if we consider attainment on the higher intellectual levels, there is some satisfaction in knowing that enough is being done to keep us from cutting too poor a figure in the civilized world. But if you consider the level at which the mass of the population rests, our level is admittedly very low. The number of illiterates is overwhelming, and the probabilities of curing this condition in short order are very few and doubtful. Schools and teachers are needed, but most of all we need students. No one is fighting hard enough to rid the country folk of their actual ills, their superstitions, vices, and mental apathy. This neglect checks cultural progress, and our intellectual production is thus very limited. The almost universal lack of preparation reflects in an unfavorable and disconcerting manner on all phases of national life, and puts a tremendous responsibility on each of them.

And now let us analyze the result of these conditions, individual and collective, in the field of international relations. What is the attitude and what is the conduct of the Guatemalan with respect to the other races? What is their attitude toward him? How do these reciprocal attitudes and essential differences makes themselves felt in the field of inter-human relations?

The very exaggerated consciousness of our limitations in the competitive field gave us a feeling of inferiority a long time ago. Although it is disappearing gradually, it still remains quite strong at this time. This situation has brought us into a state of submission to people of other countries, and we have been giving them better facilities and greater social consideration than we give to the sons of our own nation. The superiority of the foreigner in all ways, no matter what his personal quality, was dogma for many Guatemalans for years and years. It led them to grant him preferences and opportunities that were frequently given at the expense of the nation's interests. This same admiration induced the Guatemalan to imitate, as far as possible, what was done elsewhere, without question as to whether it might or might not be suitable to his own environment. This tendency towards imitation and spontaneous submission causes nothing more or less than an absolute surrender of the national ego in the face of the superiority of the foreigner. Having arrived at this form of renunciation, it is not strange that all the interests of our country, even the most vital, have at one time or another been in the hands of powerful foreign groups.

Being essentially an agricultural country *par excellence* and by necessity, Guatemala supports its whole economy on the exportation of its major local products, coffee and bananas. However, in spite of the fact that we are the producers and domestic production by those who buy from us (and, of course, we are referring to the United States) is an impossibility, we are not powerful enough to put fair prices on the products of our soil, as should be done in common accord by the buyer and the seller in any equitable commercial transaction. In our case it is the buyer who, exercising a veritable dictatorship from which we cannot escape, establishes the limits of production by his purchases and controls the transportation and the distribution thus putting us in the position of an "economic colony" into which he enters and where he makes his power felt, much as in a political colony.

This condition is excessively contrary to the interests of a country aspiring to free its laborers. It naturally creates in the world an element of tension to which proper attention must be given. How can we develop the force necessary to advance the welfare of our workers if price dictatorship restricts our economic facilities?

But to add insult to injury, it is not only the fixing of prices which is at the mercy of the foreigner, but also to a large extent production itself. Strong North American companies with magnificent installations and great capital, employing several thousand laborers, devote themselves to the banana crop. They thus have a business which benefits the entire world. But a Guatemalan, poor and ill-prepared, unable by nature to undertake business on this scale and subject to his own limitations and the dictatorial domination of his bad governments, is unable to do the same thing with anything like the efficiency which characterizes the foreign companies. These companies, unfortunately, have been primarily concerned with the idea of doing big business; they thus neglect the interests of their workers and even the interests of their nation. There was a time when the best system was to support and be supported by tyranny. There also was an intimate collaboration with ambitious and unscrupulous politicians who were helped to power by these foreign companies in exchange for concessions and prerogatives frequently inconvenient for the country. Then, too, there was the era of the "Big Stick," now fortunately over, when armed forces intervened to protect the North American interests at the expense of Central America.

It is clear that this manner of exploiting the riches of our land gave rise to an attitude of dislike and antipathy on the part of those directly offended, and later of the sister republics, against a feudalism which, without seeking territorial expansion or direct political control, still continued a form of economic imperialism. The Good Neighbor Policy, fortunately established by President Franklin D. Roosevelt, succeeded in great part in obliterating these defensive feelings. But there is still a long way to go beyond the phase of benevolence and interested help before a truly democratic understanding can be found, with the great and prosperous nation sacrificing ever so little of its pride in favor of the small nations who seek modest security and well-being. Only in this way can cordiality and harmony firmly and truly reign.

Up to now it has been the anti-democratic governments and

not the oppressed people under them who have counted on the support of the powerful neighbor. And even when we were at war to defend democratic ideals, we had to present the absurd contradiction that in order to defend these ideals in our own countries, alliances were made with governments of pure Hitlerian type, to whom even arms were given so that they could crush all democratic aspirations inside the country. How could the Guatemalans believe in the sincerity of the great national government that here, in front of their eyes, created this tragic paradox?

The time for fighting the enemies of democracy on the battlefields is already past, but now the moment is coming for the Guatemalans to reap the benefits of their democratic revolution. A deep politicosocial change has taken place in the Republic; but that change, though awkwardly and brusquely made, has not exceeded its abilities and goals by boldness. Yet it has naturally hurt the interests of the foreign companies who felt quite at ease in a regime where no one demanded better economic treatment for the natives. These companies, however, showing themselves to be understanding and well-disposed to accept the new order of things, immediately made the concessions required by the terms of the most elementary justice. However, following the natural course of agreements between capital and labor, as the demands kept increasing and threatened to have a deep effect on the interests of foreign capital, the conflict grew and greatly influenced the state of our national economy.

The repercussions of this dispute can have two equally lamentable effects on international relations: they may create the suspicion that the just claims of the Guatemalan peasant have a communist stimulus; and they may damage the confidence and warm friendship created by intelligent efforts. When the threatened interests saw that the claims of workers were viewed with a benevolent eye by the government, they became alarmed and transmitted their concern to the political spheres of Washington, with such power of persuasion that even in the United States Senate there is thrown against our government the crushing epithet of "Communist!" Does communism, then, consist of supporting the demands of one's fellow nationals for better working conditions under the foreigners? Anyone can see that the accusation is unjustified; but in the realm of human relations and in that of the hope for peace and harmony among mankind, reactions of this type invariably have a deplorable effect.

Proceeding like doctors, we could close this analysis with a few remarks about the suggested treatment. But fortunately, our task is more pleasant than that: it is not of possibilities we must speak, but of proceedings already under way. In the interchange of actions with the United States—the only great shadow cast over our destiny—work is being carried on which is well-directed and will surely be successful.

For the past few years an endless human flow has been going and coming between Guatemala and the United States. Students, tourists, investigators, businessmen, investors, scientific explorers, experts in every line, artists in love with our landscapes and our aboriginal element, and admirers of North American progress and greatness—these and many other emissaries of good will have contributed much and will continue to help in wiping out the prejudices and correcting the errors through personal contact and direct observation. But going much further ahead in their intelligent planning, organizations dedicated to international cooperation are doing admirable work in Guatemala. From the standpoint of education and public health, they are remedying precisely the ills that are the intrinsic factors in our difficulty of adaptation: the biological deficiencies, errors of nutrition, and cultural backwardness of the Indians; the need for better leaders; and the lack of large centers for public welfare. Improvements in these directions are the best remedies for everything that might constitute a danger or a state of tension in good human relations between Guatemala and the rest of the world.

ICELAND

Helgi Tomasson, M.D.

Medical Superintendent, State Hospital for Nervous and Mental Diseases, Reykjavik.

THE psychopathology of international tension presents two aspects: first, the local conditions which are conducive to such tension or help to create it; secondly, the local social conditions evoked by it.

To understand either aspect in the case of any nation, it is necessary to have some preliminary knowledge of the geographical, political, social and cultural history of the nation, as well as of present-day conditions. The roots of international tension are principally to be sought in the fields of culture, ideology, economics and politics. Insofar as these roots are in the minds of certain leaders of nations, they will not be discussed here.

The contribution of a small nation to the illumination of the question of international tension may, to a certain degree, be compared to the laboratory experiment. It is justified by the fact that ability to think is not a prerogative of the physically powerful or the numerically superior.

Iceland is situated high up in the North Atlantic, occupying a periscopal position separated by some six hundred miles from the Scandinavian peninsula, by five hundred miles from Great Britain, fifteen hundred miles from the North American continent, and two hundred miles from the east coast of Greenland. In ancient times it was a stepping-stone on the route from Europe leading to the discovery of North America. In subsequent centuries, it lay off the beaten track of communication between the Old and the New World. It enjoyed an era of isolation, so that few people knew of its existence, and others attached fabulous meaning to the very name of the country. In recent years, through modern advances in means of transport and communication, its isolation has gone. It has again assumed to some extent the old role of stepping-stone between northwestern Europe and North America.

The present Icelanders are descendants of the ancient settlers of the country in the tenth and eleventh centuries. These settlers, usually considered to have come from Norway, and to a smaller extent from the British Isles, brought with them their habits of life. They were not prepared for the naturally-occurring catastrophes of their new fatherland. These catastrophes therefore took a heavier toll of the population than was the case after centuries of acclimatization. Being without modern knowledge of geography, geology, meteorology, and various factors conditioning soil fertility, the possibilities of adequate food, housing and clothing were greatly restricted. All this tended to the depletion of natural resources, with subsequent destruction of woodlands, soil erosion, deterioration of the land, poverty, malnutrition and retardation of the population.

To these factors were added, as in other European countries, the various severe epidemics of the Middle Ages. In 1703, the first general census (the complete records of which have been preserved) showed that the population was about the same as it had been in the eleventh and twelfth centuries. Subsequent censuses showed considerable fluctuations in the population. A permanent increase began in Iceland about the same time as in many other European countries with the advent of antiseptics, the beginning of bacteriology through the use of the microscope, technical advances of all kinds, and the general appreciation of the psychology of the individual as well as of the community. Perhaps a more general acceptance of spiritual values and intellectual achievement has been characteristic of the Icelanders than of many other peoples. These qualities constituted the backbone of the nation through the ages and were the mainstay of the individual in the dark hours of northern winter, the fight against earthquakes, volcanic eruptions, ice-encirclement, famine, epidemics, and last but not least the sea, that constant foe as well as friend which has taken a heavier toll of the Icelandic people than many wars have done in other countries.

Even in ancient times the settlers decided to meet such

natural disasters collectively. A codification of social insurance is to be found in the ancient Icelandic Codices as far back as a thousand years. It has been retained until the present day, modified to meet greatly extended needs. A vast machinery of social institutions, characteristic of the Scandinavian countries, has arisen in Iceland parallel with those of other northern European countries.

Icelanders very early accepted arbitration as the means of settling important questions. The original settlers were heathens, and when the march of Christianity threatened to split the country, the question of religion was settled by arbitration. Although the arbiter was himself a heathen, he resolved that the religion of the country should be the Christian one.

Feudal disputes in ancient times, although often solved by arms, were also solved by arbitration. However, the ancient republic succumbed after three hundred years to the aggressiveness of the Norwegian kings; the infiltrative technique of modern fifth columnists was used on a people accustomed to negotiation and arbitration.

Through the union of the kingdoms of Norway and Denmark, Iceland came under the Danish kings. In due course the country accepted the autarchy of the Danish kings. This situation lasted until the middle of the nineteenth century. In previous centuries the Danish kings allotted or sold the monopoly of trade with Iceland to Danish firms, which maltreated the population and operated in an almost vampire-like way. They created such a tension that for years the word "Danish" in Iceland was almost synonymous with some of the most despised human qualities. A feeling of animosity was created against the Danish which did not really subside until all political ties between the countries were severed and Iceland was made an independent republic again in 1944. The road was long and arduous, but Danish businessmen contributed their share to what we consider a happy fate. They were an impetus to national aggressiveness and to the nation's struggle for life, even in days of despair and times of extreme economic and spiritual depression.

Parallel with the gradual achievement of complete political

independence, with the better utilization of the riches of the sea, with cold and hot water power, modernization of agriculture, the beginning of industrialization, improved housing, more adequate clothing and food—in short, with improved economic conditions, higher standards of living, and better hygiene —a rebirth of the nation's mental and physical qualities has begun.

The mental life of Iceland as a whole, roughly estimated on the basis of yearly production of books, printed papers and artistic achievements, is intense. It is comparatively much more intense than in many other modern communities, although peaks on an international scale must be rare in such a limited number of individuals.

The thinly populated, often difficult country seems primarily to create an individualistic attitude of mind, and of necessity a certain polypragmatism. On the other hand, the historical fact of the ever-imminent common dangers make people—with the exception of some psychopathic personalities—face in common what may be coming. There is a feeling of equality, a cooperative spirit, and a community-mindedness for the cultivation and defense of the rights of free men and women. There is probably a more intensive "nationalization" in many fields than is the case in many other countries. Religion, education and health services are all "nationalized"; means of communication and transport, industrial and other power plants, and several lines of business are either wholly or in part conducted or controlled by the public for the public. The standard of life is high, the export–import averages about five hundred dollars per head, and the production of goods consumed at home approximates the same amount.

Tension between nations may often be rooted in business competition. About ten years ago, Iceland and Norway competed for the dried cod market in Spain, Italy and Portugal. This competition compelled the Icelanders to harness their brains to improve methods of catching and curing, conservation and distribution. There developed a certain tension between these two countries, sometimes disguised under the mask of mutual flattery. However, even this quite "friendly" tension often appealed to less desirable qualities in some members of the third nation —the nation for whose favor the competition ran. Nevertheless, such qualities are considered compatible with good business ethics.

This quite innocent-looking tension between nations living in seemingly wholehearted friendship, rooted in common kinship and common cultural attitudes, could be multiplied endlessly by analogous *chroniques scandaleuses* on an international scale. The starting points of international tension in the field of economics are the outposts of business and commerce, especially foreign trade.

Culturally, the old Icelandic sagas are the same as those forming the historical background for each of the northern European countries. They contributed to the feeling of self-esteem and national unity, and thus led to the struggle for independence. Early differences were often solved by wars, but in more recent years they have always been settled by arbitration. Actually, there have been no ideological or social trends in Iceland that can be assumed to have had a permanent influence on neighboring countries.

Politically, the geographical position of Iceland is of strategic importance. In previous ages, the country was of importance to the ruler of the seas. It was entirely dependent on the attitude of Great Britain during the Napoleonic Wars and World War I. In World War II, it was an important link in the Allied chain of the North Atlantic, especially as an air base. The future attitude of Iceland certainly will be a matter of concern to the powers bordering on the North Atlantic. At present, the attitude of the people of Iceland is a preeminently western democratic one. Adherence to the Atlantic Pact will in all probability be taken for granted by all except the Communists and a few other leftist people.

Strategically, the position of the country is certainly more important than the number of its inhabitants. But after centuries of acclimatization, their innate knowledge of the country and the fishing waters around it may be an asset which even numerically superior powers will have to recognize.

Given international tension in fields of economics, culture, ideology and politics, what local social conditions are, or have been, created by it in Iceland?

The country, being primarily a food-producing country, is to a large extent dependent for other amenities on its imports. The world market, by dictating the prices of these amenities, greatly affects the cost of living and the economy of the individual as well as of the nation.

The standard of living, which was formerly adjusted to that of other northern European countries and Great Britain, though somewhat below that of those countries, has of recent years surpassed them, and nearly equals the North American standard. This is a probable consequence of the recent war, when comparatively large numbers of American soldiers were stationed in the country. All imports came from America, and Iceland became a sort of distribution center for American goods to other Allied countries. Exports from Iceland during these years went entirely to Great Britain. Eighty per cent of the fish supplied to the British market came from Icelandic fishing vessels. Since the war, exports have had to be distributed to as many other European countries as possible, as British fishing vessels now largely supply their own home market. The postwar standard of living of most of the European countries to which our products are exported is as yet below prewar standards, and especially below the North American, which our own standard has approached as a result of the fortunes of the war years.

It is a problem for our country's politicians to find ways and means of adjusting our standard of living to that of the outer world with which we have to trade. They must also find a way of maintaining it as far as possible while the buying and productive power of our customers is rising. We must hope that, in the meantime, internal conditions will approach a standard compatible with the level to come.

Owing to the conditions of international trade, it has been thought feasible or necessary for our government, like so many others, to enter into a number of trade agreements and to exercise intensive control of all imports and exports. The consequences of this have been a greatly restricted freedom of the individual businessman and the ordinary citizen to do trade where they would like. There is a bureaucracy which some people dislike. It shifts the feeling of responsibility from the individual to the authorities, and causes a sense of frustration in many otherwise capable people. Below a relatively quiet surface, one is aware of a general turbulence. Political extremists operate advantageously in such waters, creating an atmosphere of insecurity and tension, resulting in certain circles in increasing demands for higher wages in spite of decreasing output. This growing individual tension is reflected in an increase in the consumption of alcoholic drinks and in juvenile delinquency, although the growth of urbanization may also have its influence in this respect. There is an acceleration of urbanization and an increase of indoor workers, along with a diminishing number of persons available for the basically productive work of agriculture and fisheries.

To my mind, the general difficulties of international trade at present are mainly responsible for the trends which I have indicated as examples of the effects on the mass and on the individual of international tension.

Tension rooted in cultural disharmony has not had much appreciable direct effect in Iceland. The ruggedness of the country, the strain of maintaining even the minimum means necessary for life, and the heavy toll of physical and mental acclimatization are certainly not tempting to emigrants from warmer climates. The question of assimilating immigrant culture has not therefore arisen except in a few cases. On the other hand, many foreigners who have lived in Iceland for even a considerable part of their lifetime leave the country again when they can. This might be taken as a sign of the difficulty of assimilating foreign cultural elements.

However, Icelanders themselves are a well-traveled people. A number of them go abroad and become subjected to various cultural trends. Such people, however, are mostly mature men and women beyond the main periods of plasticity. They are, therefore, not so susceptible to unconditional acceptance of foreign culture or radically new thought. Rather, they are more liable to adapt what they can to local conditions. On returning home, it is a natural thing to relate what one has seen and heard. In this way a popular knowledge of the cultural characteristics of other countries is extensively spread, although this knowledge is unevenly stressed according to the education and interests of the individual in question. Therefore, one may easily run across prejudices regarding other countries.

Although Iceland has never been directly exposed to severe cultural pressure from any other country, the repercussions of the cultural streams of the middle centuries (18th, 19th, and 20th) have indirectly reached our shores. The effect has, however, been a quiet, almost evolutionary contribution to the rebirth of the nation. The general stir-up in twentieth century Europe seems to have had a mentally fertilizing effect on the nation. Of course, we have not been spared the frustrating effects of the general and mutual misunderstanding of each other's terminology, and to a smaller extent of each other's mentality, between the east and west. Owing to the lack of communication in previous centuries, news of all events reached Iceland only after they could be seen in perspective and in their relative setting. The revolutionary influences of 1789, 1830, 1848, and 1871 had therefore considerably cooled off while crossing the North Atlantic before reaching Iceland. Nevertheless, they all left their mark among a people who were awakening to literature and politics. But the process here was slower and more temperate than abroad.

In the twentieth century, increased means of communication and transport facilities, increased production of books and periodicals, and increased imports have all contributed to an entirely different effect. Now news of all events reaches everybody instantaneously without any possibility of being digested or seen in perspective.

Practically every home in the country has a radio set. Certainly every family reads at least one daily paper or weekly edition of a daily paper, and one or more weekly and monthly periodicals. Probably a large part of the population reads two or more newspapers. The number of newspapers is about one per two thousand of the population, yet the biggest are read by about sixty to seventy per cent of the population. The number of books published exceeds per capita that of many countries, and the publishing business is one of the most lucrative in the country.

All these sources of information on the international situation —the radio, newspapers, periodicals, books—are extremely common. Different and often conflicting ideologies are therefore widely presented to the public, each of them having its propagandists. This may be in art (expressionism, impressionism, cubism, futurism), or religion (orthodox versus free theology), in sociology (socialism, communism, fascism, nazism, individualism, internationalism, United Nations-ism), in philosophical psychology (Individual Psychology, reflexology, behaviorism, psychoanalysis, Gestalt psychology), in parapsychology (spiritualism, occultism, yoga, theosophy), in pure superstition, and in all other phases of life.

The effectiveness of the propagandists depends largely on their personal qualities and positions, but often also on the forces backing them and pushing them forward. Samples of all these conflicting ideas may be had in the radio programs, daily press and a disproportionate number of journals dedicated to the most diversified specialized fields and often enjoying an amazing relative circulation.

It may be fairly well assumed that it is a strain on the minds of men and women, young and old, to be exposed to so many different ideologies, through the various means of mass communication. The eagerness with which the lions of each of the ideologies propound their ideas creates more or less of a tension in the individual. Yet so far as the effect on the nation as a whole is concerned, it has been a generally vitalizing one.

That a small community is able to withstand such an ideological turmoil is probably only to be explained by a century of general education, in which everybody has been taught to read and write and is accustomed to having the freedom of faith, thought, and expression.

International tension rooted in politics per se did not much affect conditions in Iceland until World War I and especially World War II, when the country was occupied first by British and later by American troops. After the war, owing to the American occupation in Germany, it was thought feasible by the American authorities for the U.S.A. to have a contract with the Icelandic Government regarding a certain priority to use one airfield in the country. In some quarters (especially leftist ones), this situation has been a matter of considerable concern and the starting point for an anti-American campaign under a more or less patriotic disguise. A similar agitation was made with regard to Iceland's joining the Atlantic Pact, a move agreed upon by an overwhelming majority of the country's politicians. Probably the simplest explanation of these reactions, as well as of other "wars of nerves," seems to be that of projected aggression.

The international political situation outside the country's boundaries does not directly affect the mind of the man in the street. Only a few per cent of the more reflective people take some interest in these questions. But such people are to be found everywhere.

The geographic situation of Iceland, the multi-national outlook of its leaders in politics, science, art, education, industry and business, and last but not least the press, radio and cinema, go to guarantee a presentation of both pro and con in the majority of relevant questions. The average reader or radio listener is a remarkably intellectually independent individual. In the most unexpected places you may expect to meet a serious and keen thinker on international questions of today and tomorrow, a thinker whose judgment is based on a thorough knowledge of the problems of yesterday.

The historical sense of the people helps to minimize the happenings of the moment. The tendencies to compare the present with the past (though not necessarily to extol the past), and to draw historical analogies between our own history and that of the world, all work in the same direction.

The national characteristic of first asking "who are you, what is your family, who were your ancestors," and, in discussing a

third person, "is he (or she) an intelligent person," makes the
Icelanders form an opinion of the man handling a question or a
problem as well as of the matter with which he is dealing. Many
people who see the problem in the light of the man often like to
contemplate how someone else would have handled the matter.
Problems of dispute are very much seen as the point of view of
the men taking part.

The apparent tension between the U.S.A. and Russia, as presented in situations like the Berlin crisis, the division of Germany, the Palestine question, and the use or abuse of the rights
of veto, does not make any lasting impression. It is much more
often considered as an expression of the mood of the main personalities representing each side than of a serious dissension
over principles. It is also taken by some as a welcome incident
to divert the attention of the public from other strategically more
important maneuvers. An Icelandic farmer was more upset by
the news of the dismissal of the Russian representative from the
World Health Organization, and the reluctance of the Russians
to supply W.H.O. with information, than by the widely discussed veto right.

As in the case of all other countries, there are a few fanatics
and psychological monoculists who see only one side of a question and do not acknowledge any other. Often they may be
screaming aloud, but they are only taken notice of by their
spiritual mates, never by their opponents.

On the whole it may be fairly maintained that the political
form of international tension, as it now exists, does not affect the
ordinary man in Iceland. People do not take the dissensions
seriously enough. Whatever the momentary phraseology, the
thinking citizen of a small nation cannot as yet believe in any
motive of the great powers other than power politics.

INDONESIA

Jan Ferguson, M.D.

Director of the Buitengewoon Ziekenhuis Grogol
(Psychiatric Clinic); Lecturer in psychiatry at the
University of Indonesia, Batavia.

COLUMBUS has always been regarded as the origi-
nal discoverer of the American Continent, the northern part of
which has since become one of the greatest states in the world.
In retrospect, however, it is noteworthy that Columbus set out
with another intention, that of reaching the Spice Islands by a
westerly route. With a little imagination, this fact might be described as the first bond between America and that equatorial
island group on the other side of the world, now known as Indonesia. In actual fact, Vasco da Gama in 1498 was the first
European to visit India by sea, and this eventually led to the
exploration of Malacca and Indonesia.

If we look back on the history of these two widely divided
parts of the world, which were respectively discovered by Europeans in approximately the same period, we find that their subsequent development ran along completely antithetical lines.
In North America there was extensive immigration by colonizers
from many different nations. Heavy resistance was encountered
from the original inhabitants, the American Indians, who either
fought to the death or withdrew to the hills. Consequently, the
immigrants became the progenitors of the present population.
And now Independence Day is celebrated each year as a re-
membrance of the independence obtained by the colonists on
July 4, 1776. So it was that the great American nation came into
being.

Entirely different was the course of events in Indonesia. There
the arrival of the European did not bring any of the changes

that it brought to North America. The native inhabitants had already experienced for centuries the incursions of foreigners, and these had influence on their cultural habits. However, despite these various contacts, the original inhabitants themselves remained the same. Completely different in character from the American Indians, peace-loving and more placid, they allowed the storms to pass over them.

Moreover, the distance separating these islands from Europe was much greater than the distance from Europe to America. In addition, the dangers of the tropical climate, with its as yet uncombated tropical sicknesses, also acted as a deterrent against mass immigration.

According to some authorities, the original inhabitants of the Indian Archipelago came from China, via the top of India, to Malacca, and from there dispersed through Indonesia, pushing out almost completely the few pygmy inhabitants who were already present (1500 B.C.). It is probable that they originally formed one people, but there is little evidence of that now. At the present day it is estimated that there are in Indonesia about two hundred languages, apart from the dialects, while each population group has its own usages, customs, and characteristics. The reasons for the present differences, therefore, will not be found in the origin of the people, but rather in the impact of the outside influences which have affected and imprinted themselves on the different groups. Great cultural changes were brought about by the impact of Hinduism, Islamism, and finally by Christianity and Western culture.

In endeavoring to understand the deep-rooted nationalistic aspirations of the intellectual class, the answer to the question as to whether there was any system of domination during the earlier periods of their national history is of paramount importance. The Hindu influence made itself felt for the first time about the beginning of the Christian era. This Hindu influence reached its zenith and came to its end with the great kingdom of Madjapait in Java (15th century). But it is nearly certain that while it existed, the native-born Hindu sovereign ruled over a kingdom that was constantly extending to embrace more islands.

The same was also true of the Islamic infiltration, which had already begun in the tenth century. After their arrival, the Islamic merchants from Arabia took in marriage daughters of the country, but not before their selected brides had been converted to the Islam faith. Thus the faith was spread, but the Moslem missionary never became the ruler of the country. Nevertheless, in the course of time, local customs and usages became greatly influenced by the Islamic precepts. Quite logically, the coastal strips were those most affected by the new culture, and most of all the larger islands of Java and Sumatra came under its influence. In Borneo and Celebes the effects during the initial period were not very great. In the interior of these islands, traces of the original animistic beliefs, which date back to the period before the Hindu influence, have survived. Traces of this animism are found in many places throughout Indonesia. In Bali, the Hindu conception of life still prevails.

While the conversion of Indonesia to the Islamic faith was slowly progressing, the initial penetration of Westerners began. In 1510 the first Portuguese landed in Malacca, and in 1596 the first Netherlands ship dropped anchor off the coast of Bantam (West Java). Space forbids a detailed account of the history of the East India Company (Oost Indische Compagnie), a monopolistic chartered trading concern, and the wars which it brought in its wake. The record of the conquest of the various islands, the subjection of the many rulers, the elimination of the competition of Portuguese and Spanish nationals and the struggle with the English for the hegemony of the Spice Islands, forms a history in itself. But if a proper understanding of the psychology of the present period is to be obtained, it is necessary that the historical changes should be thoughtfully reviewed. Just as the diagnosing psychiatrist or psychologist attaches at least as much importance to the background of the individual as to his existing environment, so must we analyze the historical background in this case before we can obtain a balanced insight into the present problems in Indonesia. In the beginning, the basis of the relations with the inhabitants was purely commercial; settlements were established at suitable points by the incentive of commercial interests. It was inevitable that this should result in strife, conquest, and subjection. The success of the Westerners, at this stage, has been attributed to the fact that their arrival coincided with the collapse of the greatest of the Hindu empires in the archipelago. Consequently, they came to be looked upon by the native populations as the rightful successors to the throne of Madjapait and, as such, entitled to command subjection and obedience.

The great changes which took place in Europe about 1800 also had repercussions which brought alterations in the administration of the colony. Up to then the East India Trading Company had looked after trading interests only. But on April 27, 1816, a Commission General arrived in Batavia to take over the administration from the temporary British Government that had been installed when Napoleon occupied the Netherlands. They were charged with the dual task of taking over the administration and of carrying out necessary reforms. The status of the colonies was now incorporated in the constitution and an authorized government was established. Slowly the Netherlands began to take more and more interest in her colonies. The market for spices diminished, but it was superseded by a demand for other products. It was being increasingly realized that nature had endowed Java with great riches. With the urge to produce the new products asked for by the changing markets, knowledge of how to grow the products and the provision of a sufficiency of healthy laborers became a necessity. Inseparably bound up with this was the urgency for order and security. These changing circumstances also coincided with an immigration of Netherlanders on a greater scale than had formerly been the case. But despite this, the total number of immigrants remained very small and negligible when compared with the millions of natives who comprised the population of the Indies. The colonial empire was so much greater in comparison with the size of the mother country and its population that it was never possible for the homeland to supply a sufficient core of white colonists. Moreover, as has been previously mentioned, the climate was unsuitable for permanent residence by white people. Many young colonists died from malaria, typhoid fever, and dysentery. An examination of the tombstones in the old Netherlands cemeteries shows that mortality mostly took place before the age of thirty years was reached. Before they could attain that age, many of the colonists died or were invalided to the motherland because of tropical sicknesses.

As the years have gone by, however, the population of Indo-Europeans has increased. Whenever two people live in close contact, there are always sexual consequences. The Netherlands Government has never had in force any regulations forbidding sexual contact between the white and the colored races. In the time of the East India Company, it was, in some cases, actually encouraged. This population group has naturally produced a very great variety, from those who fill the highest positions and are fully educated according to Western standards and accepted by the Netherlands community to the illegitimate child of a soldier and an Indonesian mother who has been brought up with the Indonesian village community. Ten years ago the total Indo-European population was estimated at between eight and nine millions. Not unnaturally, this group of citizens falls between the European on one hand and the Indonesian on the other. In the past they have mostly formed an indefinite section and have had little influence on the working of the state. It is only in this century that they have become united enough to form a federation and thus make their influence felt.

In the beginning of this century the Indonesians, under the influence of Western civilization, became more and more conscious and independent. They demanded Dutch education and schools. They organized themselves in political parties and obtained seats in the Volksraad (People's Council and Advisory Board).

Meanwhile the general welfare in Indonesia increased. There was peace and security everywhere. Agriculture was put upon a modern footing. Great irrigation works were laid down, public health was improved and safeguarded by intensive anti-malarial measures. The local government and police forces worked efficiently and reliably. Social and educational services were

improved and enlarged. Reproaches were sometimes leveled at
the Netherlanders that they kept the population too dependent
and were not working towards their independence. It is doubtful, however, whether this situation has influenced the conflict
of today. Once aggression and its emotional effects have broken
loose, former promises or actions no longer help. Did not one
of the modern Indonesian leaders write before the war, "We
have not the same aversion to the activities of the whites that
some of the other Asiatic peoples have"?

When, on December 7, 1942, H. M. Queen Wilhelmina made
a speech over the radio, promising that independence would be
given, it is unlikely that this speech ever reached the great mass
of the Indonesians or their leaders. But even if it had reached
them, it is doubtful, in view of what happened after the Japanese
capitulation, whether the results would have been materially
different.

When the conflict broke out in Europe, Indonesia in the beginning remained an onlooker. But when the Netherlands fell,
it might be said that the first step towards independence was
made. Perhaps not so much for the Indonesian people themselves as it was for those Netherlanders who were in the Indies.
The Netherlands Indies and her Government had always been
in the past dependent on Holland. The Volksraad, as previously
stated, functioned only as an advisory council. So now after the
motherland had fallen, the colony felt itself becoming independent. True, there was a Dutch government functioning in exile
in London, but between Indonesia and England lay a battlefield
which embraced a continent. Difficulties of communication had
become increasingly great and transport now mostly took place
via America. As the supply of all kinds of materials was affected,
it became necessary to overcome shortages by local effort. This
also became psychologically important for the Indonesians, because they became more recognized and were admitted to the
highest offices in the land. Above all, it was being increasingly
brought home to them that their white dominators were not unassailable, all-powerful, or invincible. They saw the Japanese
moving ever nearer and nearer. They heard of the battles in

Europe, of the advance of what seemed an invincible army which had marched in a short time almost the length of Europe and subdued it. Moreover, they heard that this army had conquered Holland, the land of the white people (negeri blanda), in five days!

Nevertheless the position in Indonesia at that time remained virtually unchanged, with the same system of civil service and the same form of police force. New drafts of Dutchmen were called and reinforcements were built up. But through all this turmoil the Indonesians remained onlookers; they were not drawn into it, nor did they play any active part in the happenings.

Then came the war in Indonesia, revealing how little resistance the Netherlanders were really able to put up. The country was occupied with lightning speed; no important battles were fought. Great disorganization and disorder followed. Institutions which in the minds of the people had appeared as unassailable and invincible for many years were brought to nothing in a few short weeks; those who had upheld these institutions were arrested and imprisoned. The resistance that was put up on the sea and in the air was beyond the orbit of the Indonesians. Now the people were no longer confronted with the white race. This was important because many Indonesians, despite all that had been done in the past, had a feeling of inferiority. The country now had as its masters an Asiatic race that had already won a reputation for its great victories and conquests. And for the mass of the population this army spoke a language that they clearly understood. Theft was punished by the amputation of the hands of the culprit, and the resistance of an individual by the massacre of a whole village. This primitive method of administering the law impressed itself on a people, the majority of whom were primitive in their thinking. Any attempts at uprising or outbreaks of disorder were therefore effectively suppressed. Many of the people bowed to the inevitable and life again resumed a more or less normal routine. The population once more tilled the land, sold their produce in the markets and carried out their work as in former years. In some cases, con-

firmation of this has come to light since the war in a remarkable
way; statistics were kept up to date in their original form and
carefully preserved, even though it was not possible to send
them to their prewar destinations.

Another aspect of the problem which is of importance is the
feeling of their own enhanced worth that the people acquired.
When the Netherlanders were interned, many positions became
available to those who had possibly fostered a secret desire to
attain them for years previously. Simple clerks were promoted
to the management of a whole office, and estate assistants were
promoted to the position of manager. But these promotions,
which were obtained because of the internment of the former
occupier of the position, were not felt as a complete vindication
of their ambitions. The Japanese conquerors were now turning
more and more to the policy of filling the vacant positions with
their own countrymen. It was the youth of the country that was
the most affected by the Japanese influence. The saying "Who
controls the youth controls the future" was also known to the
Japanese. Just as the Germans did, they brought the youth together in organizations. Slogans such as "Asia for the Asiatics"
were very readily adopted in this awakening to freedom. Hard
training and drilling, with strict discipline, toughened the young
recruits to a degree of toughness that the people during the
Netherlands regime had never attained. Well-organized propaganda, based on one-sided information, blinded them temporarily. Nor was this a time of freedom and independence for the
nationalistic leaders, though many of them had been placed in
responsible office. When the might of the Japanese conqueror
began to wane, the cry for freedom waxed stronger and stronger.
The Japanese defeats, which had been carefully hidden by shut-
ting out all communication with the outer world, now began to
disclose themselves. Toward the end of the war, the Japanese
gave the leaders the promise of freedom; but it was allegedly
the youth who, on the 17th of August, 1945, forced the nationalistic leaders to declare independence. From this time the destiny
of the Indonesians has been favorable.

A large number of factors, some of psychological and some of political significance, have come into play, but some factors that were incalculable have also served to strengthen their cause. One can say that they have gone through their teething period with a minimum of trouble and now they are slowly gaining power and outside consideration. After the proclamation, a period of expectant inaction followed. Everyone expected that the former dominators, who had come victoriously out of the strife, would come back immediately. People watched every act for the reaction that they expected would follow. But there was no reaction, at least no noticeable one in Indonesia. There could not be any reaction, and therefore it was an anticlimax.

This absence of reaction was of great psychological importance. The feeling of relief when the Japanese yoke was broken brought to light a long-slumbering hatred, not only against the Japanese, but also against their former dominators. The people wished to be free, had even declared their independence; but nothing happened. People could say what they wanted and do what they wanted; they became intoxicated with their victory. The national movement which began first in a small circle broadened out like an oil slick on water. The call found response, not only in Indonesia but also from Indonesians abroad, and, as it appeared later, not only from the Indonesians but also from other groups of nationals in foreign countries. Had not other peoples themselves fought against domination and oppression, in order to uphold human rights, freedom and the right of self-determination? And here was a land, Indonesia, that had also suffered under colonial oppression, as people all too easily called it at this stage. This land had just broken the yoke of the Japanese oppression; this land was now free and ready for self-government, and it had actually made a declaration to that effect.

This line of thought is logical and understandable. But is there not another motive that plays a major role? Did not some nations resent the fact that a small country the size of Holland should control such rich and extensive colonies? Did not some countries anticipate the possibility of great economic advantages from this rich archipelago, because in its new independence it would need help from outside sources? From the other

side, it is understandable that the Netherlands did not sympa-
thize with this outlook. This country, which had invested in
Indonesian interests an amount equivalent to a quarter of the
Netherlands national capital, could not relinquish it without
due compensation.

Although the Japanese Field Marshal Terauchi had been officially charged by Admiral Mountbatten with the full responsibility of preserving law and order pending the arrival of the
Allied troops and also with the retraction of the Republican
proclamation, nothing was done. In fact, it is noteworthy that
the Japanese had encouraged the Republicans to make their
proclamation and therefore had no wish to precipitate its withdrawal. Here they saw that at least a part of their plans had been
realized. They felt that they were extracting some small compensation from the ignominy of their total defeat, and, amplify-
ing this line of thought, they assisted the Republicans by
surrendering to them arms and ammunition, and later by surrendering themselves for internment. Moreover, a number of
Japanese were left behind for the purpose of instructing the
Republican army.

Meanwhile, as the struggle for freedom increased, the cry for
independence became more intense, especially when the first
Netherlands and Allied troops arrived in Java, and when the
Dutch nationals, who had been imprisoned in the Japanese internment camps, were released. It was like an old inactive volcano, apparently quiet and harmless, suddenly bursting into
eruption. Something from deep inside boiled and bubbled and
suddenly found an outlet. First a small plume of smoke, then a
light shock, and then a slight release of pressure. And so a part
of the mass has found its way to the top, but more and more will
follow, to be forced up and up, making the crater ever bigger
and bigger. Later the white plume of smoke will become black
and threatening, stones and ash will be thrown out, and last of
all the lava will boil out of the crater. This lava will not be
thrown on high, but will flow along the ground, an inexorable
force that kills, destroys and burns.

So the struggle for freedom resembles the eruption of a volcano that has been inactive for centuries. We have seen the lava flowing, that moving mass that has brought with it murder, incendiarism and destruction. The forces of the young republic were too small and inadequate to hold in check the lawless gangs that had banded themselves together. The results of what happened in the "Bersiap Period" (the period of lawless, destructive savagery that took place after the Japanese surrender in August, 1945) caused a serious deterioration in the relations between the Netherlanders and the Indonesians. Murders, robberies and plundering have been the order of the day. It is sad that this should fall on the head of those who for years have suffered the miseries of the internment camp and have sat wearily waiting for their freedom.

The Chinese population has also been a very heavy sufferer. This group of about one million has through the years fulfilled the role of merchant and moneylender throughout the Archipelago. Their religious beliefs are different from those of the other population groups of Indonesia. They display great business acumen and frequently are among the richest members of the community in the towns and villages where they reside. In addition to rapacity, some elements of suppressed hatred have been responsible for the attacks that have been made on them, because in the past their business and moneylending dealings have frequently been too sharp and shrewd for the simple Indonesian.

The plunderings and murders were as often as not of an insane, primitive and sadistic nature—houses were looted and small costly objects that could be removed were taken away, while larger objects of value were smashed or made unsalable. Warehouses, storage buildings and shops were usually destroyed by fire. It is understandable that the Dutch should oppose these acts of wanton destruction as strongly as they were able. The British, however, who were in power during the early stages, held themselves apart from the struggle for freedom. Their position with the small number of troops available was difficult, if not precarious. In a number of instances they sought interviews with the Republican leaders. It is not possible in the present discussion to go too deeply into the motives for the behavior of the British at this juncture. It is certain that the storm of misery through which that country had just passed had some influence. The new Labor Government, with its great difficulties, already had enough to do with its own colonies. It is understandable that they were not willing to bring more trouble on their heads. England was to give freedom to India. Holland must do the same for Indonesia.

What was the feeling in Holland during these events? The greatest fault of the Netherlands and the Netherlanders has been that no matter how great the interest in Indonesia has been in certain circles, the nation as a whole has been too little interested in the Indies. "That hot country, full of snakes and brown people!" "Do you come from the Indies? Where did you learn to speak Dutch?" Such feelings and expressions give every indication of a complete lack of knowledge and interest. The people who went to the Indies were mostly those who had ties there (birth, family, or friends). In history, and also in the telephone book, the same names constantly recur. Sometimes members of these families, who had been in the Indies for generations and remained European, would send their children to be educated in Holland, but these mostly returned to the Indies. But, as has been previously mentioned, immigration on a great scale never occurred. It was not until the arrival of the Expeditionary Force, which was sent after the war, that an entirely new class of people was brought into contact with Indonesia.

Another factor in the problem was that the Netherlands had an entirely different government. For the first time there was a Socialistic-Catholic cabinet, and it seemed as if the socialistic part of the cabinet controlled the policy regarding the Indies. Concurrent with this, there was much, on account of the wartime occupation of Holland, that had to be organized and rebuilt. Above all, it was important because of the fall of Germany that the whole economy of the Netherlands should be reviewed and reoriented. Multitudinous problems therefore were awaiting solution at home.

It also must be mentioned that even before the war voices

from the socialistic party were saying "Free the Indies from Holland." These strongly progressive opinions were very much in agreement with the freedom impulses of the Indonesians. The more conservative groups did not associate themselves with this outlook. Possibly they were too much influenced by the old-fashioned standpoint which refuses to acknowledge the maturity of a son because it means that the parent himself has grown old. From the other side there were many, better acquainted with the Indies, who were of the opinion that the country was not yet ripe for freedom. They forecast chaos, a retrogression of fifty years, followed by a new domination by some other great power. They considered this battle for freedom as similar to a rebellious expression of early puberty, and consequently they wished the parental authority to remain. But such wishes were useless. The boy had tasted freedom. The child felt himself to have become a man, saw independence in the near distance and would, at all costs, become independent. Already the courtship had passed outside the parental control. They felt the support of their companions who were in the same situation, and knew that they had the support of many others. There have undoubtedly been those who have understood the psychological import of the development and who would, had they been in the position to do so, have succeeded in leading this normal movement for freedom along its rightful path.

In Indonesia the following groups were present: the Republicans, who included in their ranks both the extremists and the more moderate Indonesians who desired a close cooperation with the Dutch; the Progressive Netherlanders in varying gradations; and, in contrast, the Colonial Netherlanders. Between these various groups came the British, who completed their task as speedily as possible and then withdrew entirely. The Netherlanders in the Indies felt themselves sold out, betrayed and left in the lurch. The general instruction in Indonesia, when war broke out with the Japanese, had been that everyone must remain at his post, and that the women and children could not be evacuated. The thousands who had known the miseries of the Japanese camps now felt that their lives were again endangered,

this time from internment by the Republicans. The few possessions which they had been able to retain or preserve were now
subjected to wanton destruction. It would not be reasonable to
expect these people, after what they had suffered, to have the
same insight and outlook that one might have expected had the
circumstances been different. In the camp they had made plans
and borne suffering in the hopes of a better future. Family and
home ties had been idealized. They had told themselves that
after the war everything would be different. And then none of
their dreams had come true. No relieving armies marched tri-
umphantly in. No possibility of family reunion, no chance of
repatriation or opportunity to take up their former work. Instead, an order to remain in the camp.

The Japanese continued to be responsible for law and order.
In many cases, there was even a new internment, this time by
the Indonesians. In these circumstances, it is not surprising if
the understanding and cooperation necessary for the rehabilitation which the Government had planned from outside was
not forthcoming. The hate which was felt for the Japanese was
now turned against the Indonesians. All the prejudices and the
feelings of superiority returned and resulted in reactions from
the Indonesian side. Had it been possible to evacuate immediately to Holland all the Netherlanders who were interned in the
camps, and to have replaced them with substitutes from Holland, the problem would have been partially solved. But such a
solution would have been dependent on having available substitutes with a comprehensive knowledge of Indonesia and its
inhabitants. It has been a continuous difficulty that the work
had to be carried out by men who were weary and exhausted;
above all, by men who saw everything coming to a standstill with
no hope for their future. To the present day there are still some
Netherlanders who have not yet been on evacuation leave working in Indonesia. A great contrast was visible when the new-
comers from Holland arrived. Unfortunately not all were competent, and many held extremely radical views. These latest
arrivals included those who held the most extreme views and
were prepared to explain away every atrocity as a passing event.

The arrival of more moderate thinkers led, as might be expected, to controversy.

The great group of Indo-Europeans, or Indonesian Netherlanders, as they are now termed, were faced with a problem that was as great as that which faced the Netherlanders. Apart from a few exceptions, no evacuation leave for this group was possible. Their roots and home ties were in the Indies, and therefore the majority of them had to find their future in Indonesia. They had also suffered immensely during the Japanese occupation because, although they were mostly free from internment, they had had to pass through times of difficulty during those years. During the "Bersiap Period" they found themselves opposed by the Indonesians. A large group of them were housed in the Republican camps; some took up Republican citizenship; and the major part of them, having already assimilated the Indonesian way of life, were hardly conscious of their European blood. The Indo-Chinese and Chinese also ran into trouble and found themselves in the dilemma of choosing which party it was politic to side with. However, in their customary manner they usually managed to take a middle path.

What we see in Indonesia is not so exceptional when we consult the history. The struggle for freedom which is centered around Java has sometimes been wholly attributed to the activities of the Javanese. Nothing could be more false. The Minang Kabaus, the Betaks, and the Sudanese, to give a few examples, have certainly played a large part in the struggle. Indonesian areas other than Java and Sumatra were more quickly occupied, so fewer arms were allowed to fall into unauthorized hands. Though in these other areas the struggle and the urge for independence were also active, the process moved through quite different and more gradual channels. In these areas there was a spirit of cooperation with the Netherlanders. The political groups who originally stood for Federalism as against Republicanism had already received, while the struggle in Java was in progress, far-reaching powers in anticipation of the total independence of Indonesia. In the selection of their president and the form of government to be used they had complete freedom of choice. And so the area of West Java, which was declared free after the first police action, was able to choose as its own president the president of the Republican High Advisory Council.

The recognition of the Republic by foreign countries, although it was a "de facto" recognition, gave prestige and made the Federal States which are situated in the Netherlands-controlled areas more and more inclined to join the Republic. Both groups had the same ultimate goal of reaching independence, but the Federals wanted to attain it in a different way. Because of their common objective, the Inter-Indonesian Conference, which took place in Indonesia on the eve of the Round Table Conference, brought them very close together.

In seeking a psychological explanation of this struggle, the obvious presentation in a psychoanalytical sense is that of the Netherlander as the "father-image"—that fearful, secretly admired, awe-inspiring, terrifying paternal figure. It is interesting to enlarge on this thought, although the complete correctness of the conclusions might be open to doubt. It is questionable whether we can assume that the psychology of the individual is applicable to the mass. During the twentieth century, the paternal image, until then unassailable and invincible, began to appear in another light. People saw how another Asiatic race had defeated the white people, had defeated and humiliated them without incurring punishment. The events in Manchuria and China lay fresh in the memory of everyone. After that came the great march forward and the initial conclusive success. The Netherlanders were completely defeated. The paternal figure was thrown out and a new father-image took its place. To some extent the new paternity-figure was easier to accept because it was Asiatic, although for some years the Japanese in the Indies had the same legal status as Netherlanders.

The awe which the white father for centuries had inspired in the natives, and their feelings of ineffectiveness and impotence, were transferred to a new image which, because of what had happened, had proved itself to be all-powerful. The feelings of hate that broke loose were immediately fixed on the new father. This new paternal figure, however, did not last long. During the military phase it had been strong, but afterwards it proved to be sly and unfair and not so wise as the former father. Consequently this figure was discarded after a few years and this time not replaced. When this happened, all the innate feelings of pent-up hatred and wrath were released.

Meanwhile, the desire for national freedom was steadily extending. The people saw a new father-image in the distance—the Indonesian father who, by a bond with the Indonesian mother, the native soil, brought them a truly acceptable image. The former figure had to be discarded from the mind and thrown out at all costs. The people still feared that it might come back at any minute. In the beginning it did not come back; afterwards, when it did return, it was too weak, exhausted, and impotent to be effective.

A mass occupation of the country was not possible; it was only here and there that some troops could be landed. The acquisition of firearms had made the people feel strong, and they threw themselves with renewed feelings of hatred toward the old image. One must see the mutilations and murders, the incendiarism and the destruction of property, as an attempt to emasculate the father and thereby realize their own maturity. The violation of women can be taken as an indication that the patricide was complete and that they were now their own masters. But the national father-image was not yet permanent. From a psychological point of view both the police actions and the occupation of Djocja resuscitated the former father-image.

The assistance given by such foreign countries as Australia and America has increased the Indonesian's valuation of his own worth. The bond with India is that of a common destiny with another Asiatic race which has also obtained freedom from a Western race. From a psychological point of view, the problem of Indonesia's relations with the Netherlands is as yet unsolved. The Netherlanders have been compelled to give up a struggle which from the military side they could have won. The Netherlands has thus been compelled to relinquish the father-role, while Indonesia is still unsettled of mind with regard to this father-image. By this means the two countries have been brought more to the same level, while their relations have become more neurotic in nature, which has resulted in mutual distrust. There is, however, the danger that the national father may prove too immature and consequently too inexperienced to cope with the great internal difficulties that present themselves. If national independence is not coupled with individual freedom, it will lead only to a tyranny exercised by a national government over its people.

With the situation as it is at present, the people's leaders would rather risk exploitation and despotism than listen further to the Netherlanders. They consider themselves capable of overcoming the difficulties. Because of the neurotic relationship that exists, two countries that have worked together for centuries are now unable to reach a normal settlement. And there is another great danger. It is possible that the young country is too immature to stand on its own feet. If this is so, very radical elements might come to the helm and bring about an unbalanced situation which, because of the present psychological conditions, could result in a quest for a new father-image. What might happen then would depend on the international situation in the Pacific area. In the great chaos that would ensue if these possibilities came about, a complete impoverishment might pave the way for communism. Conflicting feelings are always present in neurosis. The dislike of the old father-image might bring about a desire for a totally opposite type to replace it.

The settlement of the future relations between Indonesia and the Netherlands will certainly cause many of the troubles and frictions which are characteristic of neurosis. Future conferences may be capable of analyzing the intentions of both parties so as to overcome the neurotic attitude and bring about a satisfactory solution and a sound future outlook. Only in this way can Indonesia be fully independent and able to maintain normal relationships with other countries.

IRELAND

Patrick Moran, M.D.

President of the Irish Medical Association; Medical Superintendent of the Mental Hospital, Ardee.

THE task set out here is to reflect the social, political, and psychological climate of my country with a view to assessing factors in it which make for international tension. No reflection of the Irish scene would be adequate without giving due place to the religious factor which is of such importance in our social set-up. Our attitude to external problems is so conditioned by our internal situation that it will be necessary to take a good look at the home front before discussing our attitudes at the European or world levels.

Until 1921, this country formed part of the United Kingdom of Great Britain and Ireland. Our economy was an integral part of the British economy, directed and controlled from London, and was mainly agricultural, producing food for the highly industrialized and urbanized English population. It was geared to produce the kinds of food most needed in England and became largely pastoral, producing and sending to England meat, milk products, and eggs in exchange for industrial products, at prices and exchange rates which were naturally determined by the stronger party. A large part of Ireland now has political independence, but the economy is still largely hitched to and dependent on the English economy. We have drifted into a position in which we are dependent on foreign sources for more than half our bread grains; we also import large quantities of coarse grains for animal fodder. In a country so fertile as Ireland, with an equable climate, there is no justification for such a dangerous dependence on foreign sources for a vital article of diet like bread. The consumption per capita of wheaten bread in this country has doubled in the last century.

Our population per arable acre, actually on the land, is relatively low, and is denser on the poorer soils than on the fertile central plains. Our output, per man and per arable acre, is the lowest in Western Europe. In Denmark, with poorer soil and a harsher climate, the agricultural output per man and per acre is more than twice that of Ireland.

The Irish emigration rate during the last century has never been equalled anywhere in the world, and we are the only white people with a persistently dwindling population. Almost half our native-born Irish live abroad. Moreover, we have the highest proportion of unmarried people in Europe and the highest average marrying age; sixty per cent of our women who remain in this country are unmarried at thirty-five years. The proportion of our people in the higher age groups is also the highest in Europe.

Ireland has the lowest proportion of woodland in Europe, and in a country admirably suitable for forest, we have to import the major portion of our timber requirements. Our arable lands are neglected and deteriorating; a recent commission reported that "tens of thousands of our farms are in such a low state of fertility that they can be classed as derelict." Ideally situated as a center for a fishing industry, we have practically no fisheries, and our coastal waters are fished by foreigners. There is an acute housing shortage, both in town and country districts. The proportion of our earnings spent on luxuries and amusements is abnormally high.

One-fifth of the people of Ireland are concentrated in our capital city, which is not highly industrialized. There is no sound or adequate reason for such disproportionate concentration. The Irish currency is linked to, and interchangeable with, the British (Sterling). Many claim that such a link is an insurmountable barrier to independent economic development, and that we are still just a trailer hitched to England's business wagon.

Prior to 1921, industrial development in the twenty-six counties now forming the Republic of Ireland was negligible; but there was considerable industrial enterprise in the six counties which are still part of the United Kingdom.

There is little coal, no oil, and very few mineral deposits of any kind in Ireland; industrial development must be based on imported fuel and raw materials. However, our considerable peat deposits are now being developed for fuel, and there has been a great extension in hydroelectric enterprises. Since 1921 there has been an organized government-assisted drive for industrial expansion behind tariff walls. Home markets are easily saturated, and low output, together with other handicaps, makes our home products relatively dear to the consumer. Wages in industry are on the English scale, while output per labor unit is much below English levels, which in turn are much below American standards. Income per head of those engaged in industry and commerce is twice that prevailing in agriculture, and this is a potent factor in causing the flight from the land which has been such a feature in this country for the last century. Agriculture will decay in any country in which it is relegated to the position of the least favored occupation. Statesmen with social vision should put first things first and see to it that the producers of the most essential requirements should be the most favored section of the community.

Our leading sociologists tell us that we are a dying nation, and that if our downward vicious spiral of increased emigration and decreased production is not soon reversed we can be written off as a negligible factor in the European set-up. Our low output, coupled with excessive spending on non-essentials, gives us a low standard of living; there is too little thrift, not enough investment of capital in our agriculture, too much emigration, and too high a proportion of non-productive old people in the population.

There is no dearth of teaching in the field of social principles. We all believe in the Universal Spiritual Law which should govern all peoples in all their relations, internal and external. The Papal Social Encyclicals are preached, printed, and circulated in simplified terms, and related to local conditions. The principles contained in them are universally acceptable, although the practice does not always conform to them. There are many social-study groups, and there are extension courses for labor

leaders in the University Colleges. Strangely enough, there are
as yet no extension courses for industrial or business leaders who
might also require some teaching in the matter of social responsibility. There is a multiplicity of societies studying and
dealing with social problems, and there is a good flow of literature and propaganda; but there is little cohesion between the
various groups, and too little constructive effort in their field.
Profit-sharing, admission of workers to a share in the control of
the enterprise in which they are employed, and a wider distribution of property are reforms extensively advocated but little
practiced. Organizations preaching rural revival and teaching
better agricultural methods, both technical and managerial, are
showing signs of vitality and beginning to achieve some results.

Here, as elsewhere, the term "social security" is acquiring an
almost hypnotic popular influence. Politicians raise the party
wind by wild promises of more and more security for more and
more classes in the community. Ireland has not developed the
extravagant social and medical services that the English are
providing for their people; but we tend to copy all the English
social experiments, and there is developing here a popular demand for similar social services which the politicians cannot
afford to ignore.

The entire Irish social set-up is unhealthy. The ever-falling
output per man and per hour, both in industry and agriculture,
is incompatible with an ever-increasing demand for more and
more expenditure on social services, and precludes any real
progress in social-economic reconstruction. Irish imports are
not balanced by exports, and the day of reckoning is bound to
come.

The political climate of Ireland is dominated by our external
relations and colored by our long history of centuries of subjection; but only the briefest reference to our history can be included, and this must be confined to very recent times.

Previous to 1921, as we have said, the whole island formed an
integral part of the United Kingdom of Great Britain and Ireland. It was heavily garrisoned by the British military and
policed by a large and well-armed police force. In 1921, after a

bitter struggle, the British Government made a treaty with the "underground" Irish Government, which was supported by a guerrilla army. Under the terms of this treaty, a limited amount of freedom was conceded to twenty-six of the thirty-two counties of Ireland; six were retained as part of the United Kingdom, and the treaty contained a proviso that the position of these six counties was to be revised at a later date.

Since 1921 the Government of the twenty-six counties gradually extended its powers in its own area, until in 1949 it declared Ireland a Sovereign Independent Republic. A written constitution enacted in 1937 claimed sovereignty and jurisdiction over the whole island. The problem of Irish partition has been so befogged by claim and counterclaim that it can only be made intelligible to foreigners by reducing it to the simplest possible terms. We, who constitute more than seventy-five per cent of the population of the island, assert that this country, and the whole of this country, is ours. The English Government, probably under pressure from its military general staff, appears to consider that a foothold in Ireland is essential to its strategic security; and England has the guns and the power and the planes to enforce this viewpoint. Twenty-five per cent of our people, mainly in the six Northeastern counties, support the English view; and while there is a puppet Government in that area with limited powers, the area is still represented in the English Parliament.

Customs barriers with all their wasteful and irritating obstruction separate the two parts of this small island and provide a perfect example of a failure in human relations and a fruitful source of internal and external tension. High-sounding principles of freedom, liberty, and self-determination, advocated for other people, sound a hollow mockery to us when we note the failure to apply them in our particular case. The situation here would seem almost Gilbertian were it not so serious and so provocative of tension between the parties concerned. It is an obvious application of the dictum that "might is right."

Our major external problem at the moment is to determine the position of Ireland in the new European set-up. Our Government is refusing to function as a European unit until its sovereignty over the whole island is re-established and recognized.

There is a written constitution; the President has powers similar to those of the Constitutional Monarch in England, there is a two-chambered legislature, the Dail—similar to the English House of Commons—and the Senate, with powers similar to those of the English House of Lords, but elected on a limited franchise. Election to the Dail is on the proportional representation system, with adult suffrage for both sexes. This system tends to return a large number of small parties and independents. It is difficult for any party to obtain an overall majority and give the "strong Government" which coalition and compromises find it hard to achieve.

The present Government of Ireland is a coalition of a large number of parties and independents, with the opposition being confined to one major party which has held office for sixteen years with an overall majority. The lines of demarcation between the policies of the major parties here are so thin as to be almost indiscernible to outsiders; but the atmosphere of controversy and conflict seems unnecessarily bitter. There is general agreement on external issues; on internal issues, disagreement is mainly on procedural methods and is aggravated by a "hangover" from the internal schism which provoked a civil war in 1922 after the Anglo-Irish treaty of 1921. There is no avowed Communist in the Dail, and whatever Communist activity there is in Ireland is necessarily underground. There are two Labor parties, labor being split on the issue of Irish workers remaining members of British trade unions.

The important internal political problems, at the moment, are to restore our shattered and weakened economy, raise our output in all fields, and secure a balance in our internal and external trade. The balance of political power is in the hands of the urban population, although the majority (53 per cent) of the people of Ireland still live on the land. Urban business and labor interests are better organized, and legislation always tends to favor the groups who are able to exert organized political pressure.

Party politicians, eager for power, promise political miracles; their magic touch will produce "rabbits out of the hat." No one will have to work harder or longer, but there will be increased production. Incomes will be maintained, but prices and the cost of living will fall. Taxation will be lower, but there will be more and better social services. The illusion is cultivated that there is an inexhaustible well of public finance, out of which funds without limit can be pumped for public services. The gap in the external balance of payments will be closed by some form of financial wizardry. Lincoln's dictum "you can't fool all of the people all the time" may be true, but it can be nationally disastrous if, in a demagogic democracy, designing politicians can fool a majority of the people most of the time. Lord Boyd-Orr, former director of the Food and Agriculture Organization, consistently and trenchantly points out that the struggle both of the individual and the nation is primarily for sustenance. If adequate sustenance for all could be assured and fairly distributed, a major step in the promotion of peace and relief of tension would have been taken.

Ninety-five per cent of the population in our sector and forty-five per cent in England's sector of this island are Catholics. And all of these are practicing Catholics whose lives are greatly influenced by the teachings of their Church. Our constitution is based on Catholic social doctrines and recognizes "the special position of the Catholic Church"; but all other denominations are recognized and freedom of conscience and free practice of religion is guaranteed. There are no state endowments for any religious group. The proportion of clergy to population is probably the highest in the world, and great numbers of volunteer clergy and nuns devote their lives to missionary work all over the world. In proportion to our population, Ireland is the greatest exporter of Christian missionaries in the world. This feature must be regarded as evidence of genuine religious fervor and Christian zeal, and not simply a part of our emigrant stream. The clergy at home and the foreign missions are all supported by voluntary contributions; there are no payments to either clergy or nuns from State funds, except salaries to those employed as

teachers in State-aided schools or as nurses in public hospitals.
Many of our voluntary hospitals and almost all our institutions
for deaf and dumb, blind, mentally defective, orphans and derelict children, homes for the aged, and rescue homes, are owned
by religious orders. Large numbers of nuns are employed as
nurses in our public hospitals.

There is free primary education for all and religion is taught
in the schools. The vast majority of teachers in primary schools
are lay, and the Manager of the Catholic School is in every case
the parish priest. Special schools are provided for the small number of non-Catholic children. Secondary education is subsidized
and is almost entirely in the hands of religious orders, male and
female, or secular clergy, and a great majority of the students
go to the professions, the civil service, and the Church. Post-
primary vocational schools, giving technical and business training, are slowly extending and are entirely under lay control
and financed entirely from public funds. University education
is also subsidized and is under lay control; but a large number of
Catholic clergy fill professorial posts in our University Colleges.
Ireland exports the majority of the graduates from her Universities; eighty per cent of medical graduates have to seek careers
abroad; and the proportion of engineering graduates who have
to emigrate is nearly as high.

The attempt to revive the national language by governmental
action is an interesting educational and psychological experiment. The Education Authority insists on teaching children in
the primary schools through the medium of Irish, although the
home language in ninety-five per cent of homes is English. This
procedure seems educationally and psychologically absurd, and
has had most disappointing results. The popular jibe is that "the
rising generation is illiterate in two languages."

Our psychological climate is largely conditioned by our history and the environmental and social factors accruing from it.
We were conquered, and occupied for centuries by a superior
military force; we had a chronic underground resistance with
frequent sporadic rebellions, invariably defeated; we suffered
famine and pestilence, gross exploitation, and religious and

political persecution. Our attitude tends to persist even now, when the authority in control is that of our own people.

It is doubtful if there is such an entity as a national consciousness or a national psychology. When we speak of such, I suggest that we are thinking of the average individual, or the national prototype, that has been moulded by the particular heredity, environment, tradition, religion, education and all the other factors which go to the shaping of personality in every country. The national character and temperament is just a good average of the characters and temperaments of the people of the country concerned. The typical Irishman is of the extrovert type, airy and gay, quick-witted and effervescent, often improvident and irresponsible, lacking in that stubborn stolid persistence which is such a feature of English character, and prone to periods of morbid despondency or excessive exuberance. Some of our expansive jingoes tend to exaggerate our good qualities; and we hear such extravagant claims as "We are the last outpost of Christian civilization in Europe." While a little national pride is excellent, it is wise to cultivate insight, and recognize that we cannot set ourselves up as paragons of all the virtues or as models that should be imitated. There is much speculation here as to what is the underlying psychological cause of our continued and persistently excessive emigration, when there are adequate possibilities and opportunities for all our people at home if we set ourselves seriously to the task of developing our own country.

There is a theory that the national panic engendered by the great social disaster of the famine years in the middle of the last century has not yet been allayed. In three disastrous years nearly a million of our people perished of hunger and disease, and in those and the following ten years another million fled in panic. The flight still continues at an excessive rate, and the urge seems to have become almost instinctive. Those of us who are old enough to have heard our grandparents describe the horrors of those times can understand how widespread was the feeling of insecurity here, and how urgent the desire to fly to some place that offered better prospects. Some ascribe our present social inertia to the ac-

cumulated effects of our past disasters and project all the
blame on to foreign misrule. The social atmosphere and mental
outlook of Ireland is changing rapidly. We are rapidly losing
all the characteristics of an isolated peasant people. Modern
science here as elsewhere is breaking down the barriers,
modern transport has put all our people in contact with the
towns and cities, the cinema and the radio are teaching them
the synthetic way of life, which is the way of the world today.

The traditional family bond is weakening in Ireland, but
it still remains a potent factor, particularly in the rural areas.
Excessive isolationism is not feasible today, neither is it desirable; but no nation will be able to contribute much of
cultural or social value to the world if it does not set its own
standards and foster them in its own social and political soil.
In spite of our religious teaching and traditions we, like too
many others, are looking too much to modern science to solve
for us problems which can only be solved by the strong discipline of a religious code which is lived and not merely pro-
fessed.

The English philosopher Bertrand Russell, dealing with the
English contemporary scene in his Reith Lectures 1949,
summed up England's social objectives as "Security, Justice
and Conservation." Ireland could accept these objectives, but
we would reverse their order and say that our social objectives
should be: to conserve all our resources, material and spiritual,
and use them to produce to the maximum our material and
other needs, to achieve justice in the distribution of the products and services; and then security would automatically
follow.

Ireland can make no worthwhile contribution to world rehabilitation until we have achieved our own social reconstruction by stemming emigration, restoring rural values and the
sense of community they give, maintaining a proper balance
between town and country, between industry and agriculture,
keeping industry decentralized, so that workers will not be
completely divorced from the soil, and basing industry mainly
on raw materials available at home. Rural stocks are the foundation stocks everywhere, and if they decay the nation decays.

The average survival time for a family in city conditions is
three generations. We will achieve internal order and stability
by pursuing these objectives; we will reduce internal tension
and thus be able to contribute something to the relief of international tension.

In the pursuit of justice we must recognize and act on an
accepted code (we say the divinely revealed Christian code)
in all our relations. Applied in small units such as the family
and spreading to larger units, this fundamental code should
permeate the whole body politic and replace the smash-and-
grab mentality so dominant in internal and external relations
today. There is an old Irish saying "As I am, so shall my family be. And as my family is, so shall my country be." Our internal
critics note an increasing absence of civic spirit, more vandalism
and destruction of public property, and a reluctance to give any
form of public service without pay. There is more profiteering,
black-marketing, smuggling and a general tendency to do as
little as one can for as much as one can get. There is an increase
in juvenile delinquency, a weakening of the family bond. We
seem to be developing a social apathy amounting almost to public negativism. Real patriotism is a Christian virtue, applicable
at all times, and not a pagan survival useful only in time of war.

If we accept the logic of our belief in the supreme value
of the individual, and his nature, destiny, rights and responsibilities, we must make this belief the base of our social pyramid
and work up through the family and the smaller groups to
the State. Only then can we look forward to a world which
will be a happy family of happy states.

There is no value in cultivating more antagonism and hostility to ideologies which we condemn and abhor; we must
accept and practice the positive alternative which we have
in the Christian code. To apply a medical term, which fits the
case, one can say that the world today is suffering from "Malignant Hypertension." Since the beginning of this century
there has been a rapid worsening in this field, until today we
see a state of international tension and friction which is the
worst in history.

Excessive nationalism is not real patriotism, and people

must learn that selfishness in this field has the same undesirable results as the selfishness of the individual in the smaller field. Excessive internationalism with the imposition of standardized conditions based on any authoritarian system is a more deadly evil. International morality is at a low ebb; it can only be raised to a higher level when higher standards prevail in the relations between individuals and groups in all countries. The best preventive of tension and friction between nations is to promote such internal conditions in all countries as will make for stability, social justice, and a way of life in conformity with the Christian Code. A people which has achieved such internal balance will not be aggressive in its relations with its neighbors. The World Federation of States, which is the ideal of so many visionaries, need not be so remote if we achieve stable internal federation of our own conflicting groups.

ISRAEL

Abraham A. Weinberg, M.D.

Psychotherapist, and President of the Jerusalem
Branch of the Society for Mental Hygiene in Israel.

FEW chapters in the history of mankind, from the
psychosociological and psychopathological point of view, can
teach us as much about the factors governing interpersonal
and intergroup relations as the history of the Jewish people.
These people are now rebuilding their national home in the
country from which they were expelled almost nineteen centuries ago. Also, few problems are so ubiquitous and nevertheless generally so badly understood as the Jewish problem,
the bearing of which on world tension has generally been
recognized. Yet it was the acuteness of this problem that was
the cause of the return of the Jewish people to its ancient
homeland and, ultimately, of the establishment of the State
of Israel. It would seem a rather hazardous—and perhaps impossible—undertaking to present the multiple and intricate
aspects of the origin and the first stage of development of the
State of Israel. It may, however, be useful to give a brief outline of a few features of the general Jewish problem and to
dwell in greater detail on some actual psychological and sociological questions.

With the abolition of the ghetto, the Jew who entered the
non-Jewish world found a society with a civilization different
from his own; arts, science, and technology were in the process
of rapid development. He who had so far devoted himself
mostly to the study of the Holy Scriptures suddenly discovered
new fields of science which stimulated his inquisitive and contemplative faculties. He sucked in, as it were, everything
which this new world offered him. But essentially he was dif-

ferent; he felt this himself and was made to feel it by others
as well; deeply imprinted in his soul was a fear and distrust
of his environment. In many cases physically less well developed, the Jew acquires in infancy a feeling of inferiority, for
which he is forced to overcompensate, if possible, by climbing
socially through the acquisition of knowledge, fame or possessions. He thus often loosens his connection with his original
environment, since, in striving to become a distinguished member of the new society, he must try to cast aside what differ-
entiates him from it. In this tendency towards mimicry he has
to repress his Jewishness. Except in unusual cases, however,
the Jew cannot belie his own nature. Consequently, his attitude
towards the non-Jew may become more or less distorted. His
apparent calm and self-discipline may at times be perturbed
by emotionalism, combined with expressional movements be-
traying his differentness. His attitude of self-confidence may
be disturbed by a self-consciousness of which he need not be
aware. It is thus possible that this neurotic behavior gives rise
to the tragic phenomenon that the Jew who tries to distinguish
himself from other Jews because he considers their Jewish
characteristics and conduct to be the cause of antisemitism
furthers, by his own disharmonious behavior, that same antisemitic discrimination and exclusion which he desperately
tries to avert.

Many assimilated Jews have never been completely admitted
to the non-Jewish world. Others have not even secured partial
admission; they are still so much tied to their old in-group
that they have been unable to go up in the non-Jewish group,
the out-group. But as they could not remain a nation within
a nation, they organized themselves as religious communities.
In this community very many found compensation for the discrimination, humiliation and even persecution in the outer
world. They found consolation in the Jewish traditional conception of life, in the thought of being God's Chosen People.
They derived a feeling of security in being rooted in the Jewish community, *i.e.*, their in-group. Though not so generally
as in the ghetto, many still preserved their mental equilibrium

by studying the Holy Scriptures and by the strict observance of the Law.

In several countries, the assimilatory tendency expressed itself in an effort to make Jewish religious practice as similar as possible to that of the non-Jewish environment. Another form of assimilation was to be seen among one group of the orthodox Jews, in that their conception of the mission of the Jewish people was no longer directed towards a return to the Promised Land, but towards the performing of a religious task in the diaspora (dispersion of the Jews). Yet, though at times repressed, the attachment to their people and homeland remained alive deep in the soul of the Jews. They continued for the most part to segregate themselves from the non-Jews; to cluster together in the cities and to follow those occupations which had become customary for Jews in an earlier period, those in which non-Jews were not interested, or those which became open to them as a result of recent developments in science and technology. Yet the process of penetrating non-Jewish society and gradually becoming admitted to it, went on; the Jew hoped that at long last he would be free from discrimination, seclusion and persecution.

But the disillusion was not long in coming. Shortly after the beginning of the emancipation, the Jewish world was startled by the pogroms in Damascus in 1840; the old blood libel of the non-Jewish child said to have been killed by Jews for their Passover had again found acceptance. And this was not to be the last time. The blood libel was only an expression of deeper-lying intergroup conflicts which earlier had led to persecutions and massacres in the name of the Christian faith because of fear of epidemics (which, incidentally, claimed fewer victims among the Jews, owing to the observance of their nutrition and cleanliness laws) and because of fear of other catastrophes of which the Jew was accused of being the cause. These expressions later assumed the form of false political accusations (1881 in Russia), high treason (the Dreyfus case in France in 1895), and theories of Jewish racial inferiority and bid for world domination (Hitler). It is useless to pass in review all these dark moments in the history of civilization. What interests us here is the psychosociology of these phenomena.

The Jew, who is unable to adjust himself completely to the non-Jewish majority group which he enters and who cannot entirely repress his specific characteristics, disturbs the homogeneity of the group. He is, and remains, an alien to the members of the group who, while failing to understand him fully, nevertheless try to assimilate him. When this attempt fails, the group tends to expel the stranger or even destroy him. For the group is dominated not so much by the rational and moral conceptions of the individual as by the drives and passions of the unconscious. The individual may satisfy, perhaps unconsciously, through the medium of the group those urges which his conscience prevents him from following. If the stranger, in our case the Jew, can at the same time serve as a scapegoat, a second purpose is achieved; the discontent and hatred of the people can be diverted from its government or from its leader(s) to the hated stranger. The Jews have been accused of every kind of evil in order to find a justification and a rationalization for the campaign of destruction. Psychoanalysts have pointed to the circumstance that Jewish people, from whom Jewish-Christian ethics are derived, symbolized the conscience of the Christian group; thus a repressed (because forbidden) resentment against God—the Father—may express itself in hatred of the Jew.

The wish-dream of those Jews who believed that assimilation was necessary to solve their problem was not fulfilled. The entrance of a great many Jews into the non-Jewish society intensified the defense mechanisms on the part of the latter group. Modern antisemitism became a general social neurosis; sometimes it approached a mass psychosis. Rising nationalism among the non-Jewish group led to better integration and thereby fostered the trend to exclude all alien elements. Among the Jews this caused a threefold reaction. Some individuals tried to secure their entry into the non-Jewish group by baptism and mixed marriage. Others, while recognizing their Jewishness, tried to acquiesce to the position of belonging to two different groups, the Jewish and the non-Jewish group. The mass of the people, however, could not follow their example. Their attachment to the Jewish people and the Jewish homeland, and their idea of a Jewish mission, were too strong, especially in Eastern Europe, for them to be prepared to end the Jewish neurosis as the victims of murder or through the national suicide of assimilation. The various antisemitic outbursts during the last hundred years have made it increasingly impossible for them to repress their Jewish ties. After every new outrage new groups of emigrants went to Palestine. The mass murder of six million Jews during the Second World War made the establishment of the Jewish State inevitable.

An examination of the main psychosociological problems confronting Israel must be based on an examination of the elements making up the present population of the Jewish State. In 1882, when the modern Jewish settlement of Palestine started, about 24,000 Jews were living in this country. Many of these families had been established here for centuries, as Palestine had never been entirely without Jews; others were Jews who had come to Palestine out of religious motives. This latter group, the so-called "Old Yishuv" (settlement), for a long time led a more or less separate existence. But it is now adjusting itself to the ways of life of the other Jews. The immigrants can be divided, according to the period during which they entered the country, into six "immigration waves."

The first wave of 20,000 to 30,000 persons who entered the country between 1882 and 1903 consisted of pioneers who had become conscious of the necessity to build a new national Jewish life in Palestine after the Russian pogroms. Though insufficiently trained for agriculture, they realized that for the building-up of Palestine, a Jewish return to the land was a prime necessity. They thus became free farmers, though still making use of hired labor, and laid the foundation for a number of settlements, some of which later acquired great importance. Their descendants form an industrious part of the new community.

The second immigration wave of 35,000 to 40,000 persons

who came to Palestine before the First World War consisted also of young and ardent Zionists from Russia who wanted to translate their ideals of Jewish and social freedom into deeds. They realized that the re-establishment of a free national existence depended on a return to agricultural labor with their own hands. Skilled manual labor should again be given pride of place. They became the founders of a new collective form of settlement.

The third immigration wave of 35,000 persons came from Eastern Europe after the First World War; it consisted largely of convinced young Zionists who had already been trained for agriculture. The second and third Aliyah (immigration) gave the main impulse for the upbuilding of the Jewish National Home. The idea of a mission of the Jewish people, which had always remained alive among the masses, took on new meaning: that of building a new form of society as an indispensable prerequisite for the establishment of the Jewish State. Many of the leading personalities of the State of Israel have come from their ranks.

The fourth immigration wave of 82,000 persons started in 1924; though this wave, too, consisted partly of trained pioneers, its main element was the middle-class Jew who contributed to the development of the towns. These Jews went to Palestine driven by the economic crisis caused by Polish discriminatory laws aimed against them. The composition of this group of immigrants was not quite satisfactory; and when an economic crisis arose in Palestine, many of the new immigrants left the country. This crisis and the fact that for some years no violent anti-Jewish disturbances occurred in the diaspora caused a short interruption in the flow of immigration. This situation led to the amalgamation and consolidation of those who had immigrated previously. The Hebrew language meanwhile became the vehicle of the social, economic, and cultural life of the Jewish community in Palestine.

The rise of Nazism and the accentuation of antisemitism in general, as well as the plight of the Jews in the Middle Eastern countries, again led to large-scale immigration from

1932 onward. This was the fifth immigration wave (1932–1945: 278,000 persons). The large majority of these immigrants hailed from Germany, Poland, and Central Europe. The German immigration introduced new types of immigrants into the country; their cultural background was different, and among them were many intellectuals and representatives of commerce and industry. A great number of them were devoted Zionists who had nevertheless adjusted themselves to Western civilization, and it took some time before these Central European immigrants adjusted themselves to the Jews who had already found their roots in Palestine.

The sixth and most recent immigration wave has been made up largely of two categories: the survivors of the persecutions in Europe and those emigrating from the Arab countries. This mass immigration constitutes an economic, a sociohygienic, and even a psychohygienic problem of the first order. The fact that these new immigrants are often people who have suffered psychologically and physically, and that many of them are Oriental Jews whose cultural level differs considerably from that of modern Israel, makes this problem even more difficult.

The bearing of this problem and of immigration in general on the development of the State of Israel becomes even clearer if we realize that the Jewish population in Palestine numbered only 24,000 in 1882, less than 84,000 in 1922, but reached 909,000 by the end of the nineteen-forties. There were 649,000 new immigrants during this twenty-eight-year period; there was also a natural increase of 176,000 due to births in immigrants' families. This large share of immigration in the growth of the Jewish community in Israel gives the immigration problem a central place in the political, economic, and social life of the country.

Systematic inquiries into the problems of adjustment of new immigrants to Israel are urgently needed. Plans for investigation in this field are being prepared; how far they will be carried out depends on the financial and administrative aid to be made available. A modest beginning on a limited scale has already been made. Its results, and the general experience in this country, permit us already to give a general outline of some important problems, though confirmation by extensive research is needed.

For the new immigrant to become successfully adjusted in Israel, he must be placed in an environment which is not completely strange to him, and one in which he can find other Jews originating from the same country as himself. The presence in Israel of intimate friends from the country of his origin also increases his chances of success. Sound information on conditions in Israel, too, is a contributing factor; a too-rosy picture leads to disappointment and lessens the chances of integration. The knowledge of Hebrew also promotes the sinking of roots. After about three years in Israel, most people seem to be fairly well adjusted. But it takes about ten years to become really rooted in the country.

The younger the immigrant, the easier the adjustment. The children of immigrants from Western and Central Europe adjust themselves more easily and more quickly to the new conditions than their parents. The conflicts thus arising between children and parents are conducive to neurotic and other disturbances. Fortunately, the youth movements and the communal settlements are important preventive agents. They serve as a kind of substitute for the deficient family life.

Children who have been rescued from the persecutions in Europe are objects of special care. Not only are these "displaced children" suffering from being cut off from their normal surroundings and missing parental love and security of family life, but in many cases they actually saw their parents, brothers, and sisters being tortured or murdered. These children are under the special care of the Department for Children and Youth Immigration of the Jewish Agency and that of the Ministry of Social Welfare. They are placed in children's homes where they live as members of a large family. Neurotic and psychopathic children are treated along modern principles of child guidance and psychotherapeutics. The facilities for suitable treatment, which until recently were very limited, are now being expanded. But the lack of trained psychiatrists and other personnel will be felt for some time to come.

There is also the problem of the adjustment of those immigrants who have been driven to Israel by the need of the times. While many members of the previous immigration waves had come to Palestine out of a Zionist conviction, and therefore realized their attachment to the Jewish people and to the Jewish homeland, there are many among the recent new immigrants who have come only out of necessity. Many of them, after arriving in Israel, become conscious of their attachment to the people and to the country. But with others this is not the case. The psychological problems of those who have come to Israel by force of circumstances beyond their will are particularly difficult. They run the risk that rebellion against their fate may unconsciously sabotage their possibilities for adjustment (by "inability" to learn Hebrew, by constant "bad luck" in looking for a suitable job, by acquiring nervous or psychosomatic diseases). Such persons are much less able to bear the disappointments that are often unavoidable in the process of mass immigration than those who recognize in advance the difficulties which may be awaiting them. Everyone who changes his country or place of living, who makes a transition from one sphere of culture to another or even from one climate to another, incurs a heavy tax on his personal adjustment.

The adjustment of new immigrants is not only influenced by individual factors; it also depends upon group factors. This holds good for every new immigrant, though the difficulties vary for different categories, and especially for those who have not yet overcome their Jewish exile-neurosis. The immigrant meets a different type of Jew in Israel, and a form of society other than that to which he was accustomed in his country of origin.

During World War II the integration of the various groups of Jews in Palestine made enormous strides. The group tensions which existed were discharged towards the common national enemy. External pressure, and in particular the hostile attitude shown by the Mandatory Government since 1939, promoted this integration in no small measure. It found expression in an ever increasing number of "mixed" marriages.

In general, the differences between Jews who had come from different countries begin to disappear during the second generation. Only the gap between European and American Jews on the one hand, and Oriental Jews on the other, cannot be so easily bridged; though here too there are signs of mutual adaptation.

I have avoided a discussion of the special psychology of the Jewish people for two reasons: first, such views are so easily influenced by a pro-Jewish or anti-Jewish attitude and, second, it is impossible to arrive at a correct definition of the Jewish personality. To do so, it would be necessary to eliminate the group tension caused by the special minority position of the Jews in the diaspora. Only the freedom guaranteed by a Jewish state will reveal the special character of the Jew or of the various Jewish groups. The influence of the greater measure of freedom which the Jews have enjoyed in Palestine can already be observed. This is most noticeable in the communal settlements.

The striving after the realization of Zionist socialist ideals, and even more the hard necessity of setting up agricultural enterprises under very difficult conditions, has led to the establishment of communal settlements. Since the foundation of the first settlement of this type, Daganish-A, in 1909, this form of society has secured for itself a decisive place in the life of the Jewish community in Palestine. In 1948, the number of communal settlements in Israel was 187, with a total of 52,000 inhabitants.

The communal group is built upon the principle that the farm property belongs to the group and not to the individual. Every member of the group gives his labor for the benefit of the whole group. He receives no material reward for his labor other than the satisfaction of his needs, and care in the case of illness and disability; nor has he to worry for his old age or for the future of his children. Within the democratic system of the communal settlement every member is eligible in principle for any function, for the management of the farm as well as for the various technical and cultural committees.

Children are educated in groups; they see their parents in the afternoon after the latter have finished their work. The fact that he is a member of a community of his own gives the child a certain measure of independence from his parents, who have fewer possibilities of dominating or spoiling him; there is, on the whole, less danger of undesirable conflict-ties, assuming that the nurses and teachers are well trained in the principles of modern child guidance.

The fact that the children grow simultaneously as members of a family and of a group enhances their inner security and their psychological equilibrium. It increases the chances that, when grown, they will be among the sound builders of a more peace-loving society.

The years have shown that life in a communal settlement also has its drawbacks. Not everybody is suited for it. Some people, while wanting to maintain cooperative buying and selling, do not wish to give up the individual responsibility for their farm or the full privacy of family life. People of this frame of mind have established smallholders' settlements which in 1948 numbered a total of 105 with 31,000 members. During the last few years a new type, intermediate between the smallholders' and the communal settlement, has developed. This is the cooperative settlement. Here the farm is run collectively, but each family takes care of its own meals and other personal requirements, buying its own supplies in the cooperative store. Some people advocate a reorganization of the communal settlement in the direction of the cooperative settlement. There is a danger, however, that when wages are paid, even to a limited extent, or when more facilities are given to private family life, the basic idea of the communal settlement will be lost. There is a widespread awareness of the problems of communal life, and a readiness to examine how improvements can be introduced into the system without impairing its specific and beneficial character.

It is generally admitted that the "kibbutz" (group) has rendered incomparable services to the regeneration of the Jewish people. This is best seen in the youth born in Israel. These

young people have a matter-of-fact approach to life; they are
no longer victims of the desperate striving after self-assertiveness which so often characterized the frightened Jew of the
diaspora. These young Jews are also different physically: a
new generation has grown up, tall, strong and broad-shoul-
dered. In the Jewish war of liberation, they demonstrated a
quiet courage and performed acts of heroism without falling
into masochistic pseudo-heroism.

It is difficult to estimate how widely the kibbutz movement
has influenced the spirit and the character of the Jewish community in Israel. That it has exerted an influence, and by no
means a negligible one, may be considered certain. In the
towns and the villages there are workers' cooperatives in industries in which, in other countries, capitalist enterprises
would usually be active. Large cooperatives, affiliated with
the General Federation of Labor, play an important part in
Israel's economy. The kibbutz has contributed to restoring the
dignity of manual labor among the Jewish people; the difference between the standard of living of the manual laborer and
members of other occupations is gradually being leveled. On
the other hand, the usual problems of the relationship between
employers and employees are also found in Israel. These problems are complicated by the rapid transition from a backward
country to a highly industrialized country, and by differences
in the behavior of people originating from all parts of the
world.

The adult Jew who has found his roots in Israel also experiences the beneficial influence of freedom within his own group.
He shares a common ideal; he is no longer the object of discrimination. He becomes more free, more self-confident. However, the tempo of life in Israel is quick, and people work hard
without paying due regard to the demands of the climate. The
struggle for life in the towns is not easy. It is complicated by
the existence of different cultural standards among the various
sectors of the community.

There are great differences in religious views and practice
in Israel. Some groups adhere strictly to the orthodox tradition

which, though basically identical throughout Jewry, has assumed certain minor variations in different countries of the diaspora. These variations persist in Israel. The stirrings of a religious revival are felt among large sections of the population. Even among the so-called freethinkers one often meets a more or less conscious religious approach.

The people of Israel are independent of mind; they show a keen interest in international as well as in national politics, and sharply criticize conditions and the views and actions of political groups differing from those of their own party. Yet Israel shows a highly-developed national discipline. This is partly due to the fact that our people are aware of the dangers which threaten our young state from the outside. Their differences in the religious, ethical, and political fields thus do not acquire the importance, at least for the time being, which they would probably have had otherwise. Meanwhile the process of mutual adaptation continues.

The new immigrant, especially the one who is not yet sufficiently free from his Jewish exile-neurosis, is often confronted with a type of Jew that is strange to him. While people are hospitable to a very high degree, everyone has his own worries; with all their helpfulness, the settled elements of the community do not have sufficient time for the new immigrant. The latter must frequently find his way with little or no knowledge of the Hebrew vernacular. Although he is very often assisted in a language which he understands, and can obtain advice from information services that are doing excellent work in spite of being overburdened, his problems are not always sufficiently taken care of. It is a prerequisite for the undisturbed development of the state that it aids its new citizens, who have often suffered so much, in the difficult process of adjustment. This is especially true when they are afflicted with the diaspora-neuroses.

The task is vast: not only will the problem of the adjustment of new immigrants have to be solved, but also the problem of the adjustment of the Oriental Jew to the modern Jewish State, and the problem of the adjustment of such non-Jewish minorities as the Arabs and the Druzes. The raising of the social and cultural standards of these minority groups, and their adjustment to a more Western form of society in Israel, requires an active policy in accordance with the concepts of modern mental hygiene. The Jewish community readily accepts this task. A primary condition is the non-existence of hatred of the Arabs among the Jews. The Jew's love for his state is so genuine, his work for the realization of his age-old ideals so intensive and varied, and his self-confidence and reliance on Providence so great, that there is no room for fear, aggression or hatred. In spite of all differences in cultural standards, the Arabs are considered as a related group. The possibility of identification, at least for the achievement of such aims as collective freedom, and equal political, social, and cultural development, is definitely present. The chances for good intergroup relations can, therefore, be considered favorable.

The Jewish State has existed since May 14, 1948. Many doubted whether it would be able to survive. Though attacked on all frontiers, it has survived. This is not surprising to those who understand the history and development of the Jewish problem. The Jewish people, facing the danger of destruction through persecution or assimilation, conscious of the need for a free national existence, have begun to rebuild their ancient homeland. Here they have acquired a feeling of inner security; their energy has been released for the building up of their own community. With great love they have put themselves to the task of developing a new society, politically, economically, and culturally.

The Jewish State will not be aggressive as long as its security is not seriously threatened from without. Such fears of aggression might be felt, especially by those who do not know the citizens of Israel and look upon them as they do upon the Jews of the diaspora, whom they have never understood, often distrusted, and many times feared. Such attitudes could not be changed suddenly at the moment the State of Israel came into being.

A full understanding of the changes in the Jewish people who have taken root in Israel will be helpful in dissipating suspicion and in remedying the fallacious idea that intimidation or threats are a successful political measure. For this people, as we have seen, is well on the way to recovering its health. A sound people, like a psychologically healthy individual, is aware of reality. Consequently, as much as the Jewish people need peace and want friendly relations with their neighbors, they will be prepared to meet menaces against their security. They will defend themselves with determination, from whatever side an attack should happen to come.

It is evident that very many Jews all over the world have recently gained more inner security and a freer attitude toward their non-Jewish co-citizens. There is now a fair chance for better intergroup relations between Jews and Gentiles in the diaspora. These relations have been favorably influenced by the fact that at last a state has arisen, a state ready to take up the cause of the suppressed Jew, a state ready to receive him whenever he wants to leave, or is forced to leave, his native land. The new state might also be influential in the alleviation—and possibly even the cure—of antisemitism, the social psychoneurosis of the non-Jewish world and the counterpart of the Jewish exile-neurosis. This would mean the dissolution of one of the most powerful pseudo-arguments for intergroup conflict.

ITALY

Nicola Perrotti, M.D.

Member of the Chamber of Deputies of the Italian
Parliament; President of the Italian Society of
Psychoanalysis; President of the University of
Rome School of Social Work; Editor of the review,
"Psiche."

TO speak of international tension today means to
speak of the tension between the Eastern world, led by Russia,
and the Western world, gravitating towards the United States
of America. This tension, which is excessively strong, seems to
be a foreboding of worse calamities for mankind. Quite aside
from the implications of a new fighting war, the situation is
already causing diffidence, uneasiness, and poverty among all
peoples. Such political tension concerns all men, because economic capabilities and incapabilities depend on it. Moreover,
these factors exert a function of primary importance on the
private life of all men, even those most removed from politics.
They influence their existence, their well-being and their tranquillity.

Hence the questions which scholars and thinkers seriously
concerned with the destiny of mankind put to science appear
fully justified. They deal with the meaning of international tension, with the forces causing it, and with the reason for its rapid
rise and immense spread in these postwar years. One may ask
whether psychology can offer mankind something to attenuate
the noxiousness of this tension, and to utilize the immense
quantity of wasted psychic energy in other less harmful activities
having higher human and social values.

Answering these questions is a hard and unpleasant task. We
must base our answers on facts which are complicated and which
invest the fundamental problems of life. But it is a duty the psy-

chologist of today must undertake with the greatest care: "intelligence oblige." At this present moment of our history there are millions and millions of people who have lost all faith, all idealism, all safety. They look to science and more particularly to psychology—ultima dea—with trust. They hope to find light for understanding and advice for acting. The fact that all turn their eyes to science is not without a deep meaning; it is a sign that, in contrast with the passiveness and suggestibility of the masses, a need for a scientific truth is felt. Psychologists, therefore, if they want to be faithful to themselves, must have the courage to fill the role of spiritual guides of mankind.

The first doubt, as far as international tension is concerned, arises from the very definition of the question. We speak of this tension as if it were the cause and messenger of all evil. But is it really true that it has an altogether negative and pejorative meaning? Is not life itself conditioned by incessantly renewed tension? Is not every progress, every enlargement of the vital powers, the result of tension, of very strong tension? And is not anxiety (that anxiety by which the whole of mankind seems to be tortured, and which is the ineluctable satellite of every strong psychic tension) actually the sign of strain, of an effort made by mankind to "relive" a new life whenever it perceives that its vital sources are dried up?

The study of the psychological condition of the Italian people in these postwar years should be extremely fruitful, because the bipolar tension existing in the world at large is reproduced in its essential traits inside Italy.

Among the Italian people there is too big a difference between those living in well-being, comfort and political power, and those living in squalid poverty, chronic unemployment, and perennial uncertainty of the future. Similarly, there is a serious inequality between the tone of life in North Italy and in South Italy.

If we also bear in mind that Italy, geographically speaking, lies at the very border of the Eastern and Western worlds, it is easy to understand how the Italian people are influenced from both directions.

In addition to the political struggles, which have been extremely lively, there is another obvious symptom of strong tension in the Italian people. It is a feeling of restlessness, uncertainty, and anxiety that is common to all Italians. This feeling reveals a deep psychic conflict. In order to understand the value of this strain, one must observe the psychological reaction of the Italian people to the events of war.

It should be borne in mind that the Italian people, because of the war, had to face the following dreadful conditions: 1) a state of constant danger, mostly due to air raids, but also to destruction and reprisals both by Germans and Fascists; 2) a want of food, which caused many to go hungry, but which also caused all to be afraid of death by starvation; 3) a large-scale destruction of dwellings, public buildings and all that was the patrimony of Italian social and civil life; 4) the dissolution of the entire state organization, especially with reference to public safety and the administration of justice.

The Italian people, then, no longer trusting their mother country and no longer sheltered by a paternal government, and faced by the dangers of war and by the even more painful fear of starvation, allowed all links of collective affection to break to pieces. The Italians had to face the essential problems of life without the aid of social force, faith, or ideals. Victorious over the German invaders but defeated on the military ground; rich in life force, but poor in raw materials; exceedingly individualistic and thirsting for social justice; fundamentally irreligious but superstitious and Catholic on the surface; active in work but passive in politics, the Italians found themselves in a state of deep and painful disagreement with themselves. They were the victims of an uneasiness and an anxiety that were only partly hidden by a superficial euphory.

The reaction of the Italian people to such a state of things was excessively active. There might have been a general depression and social disintegration. There was, instead, a widespread feeling of euphory and a restless activity towards reconstruction. The readiness with which the instinctive mechanisms of both collective and individual defense were put in motion made it possible for the Italian people to escape catastrophe and limited the moral and material damage.

However, social cohesion was saved from disintegration only at the expense of a remarkable psychological "regression." The ego-instincts and personal interests prevailed on the social and collective ones, and an almost absolute individualism was established.

Those most capable and unprejudiced took advantage of the danger and of the general economic uneasiness in order to reach a position of relative safety. It was an "insurance against the anxiety of the future." Those who could not, or did not know how to achieve security in some way, came to a state of open vindictiveness and fierce rebellion.

The Italians, therefore, divided into two different groups: on one side those who, after the terrible fear of being left helpless, now see in every and any innovation a menace to a position so painfully reached; on the other side are those who still are in a state of anxiety, and who are therefore inclined to change the social order. The tension between the "beati possidentes" on one side, and the "disinherited ones" on the other, threatens to grow even stronger.

Going deeper into the study of the social and political struggle, we perceive that it is not confined to a simple contrast of interests. It is upheld and fostered by a very deep psychological conflict of a more general nature. This conflict, in its turn, is fostered by individual conflict. The existence and importance of such personal conflicts may be traced in the psychology of all Italians. They appear more evident in politicians, for the reason that their public life renders their deep personality more transparent. These conflicts are most clearly revealed through the analysis of neurotics.

A renowned professional man, affected by a serious anxiety hysteria, developed a phobia of the *Communists* and *communism*; he was afraid that he was disliked, watched and spied upon by the Communists. He was also afraid that should they come to power, they would certainly persecute him.

The analysis showed that, though apparently mild and sentimental, he was unconsciously very aggressive. He was horrified at having to acknowledge being arrogant and tyrannical, he feared that the instincts of aggression might break into his inner self and that he might become as violent and as intolerant as a Communist (according, of course, to the opinion he held of them in his imagination). He perceived this internal danger and turned it into an external one through the psychological mechanism of projection. The patient rationalized his anxiety and built up a complete philosophical and social theory against communism.

This patient took part in political activity for the relief of his internal tension. His political activity allowed him to justify and use much of his aggressiveness in the anti-Communist struggle.

We have only to imagine one thousand or one hundred thousand people with the same psychic gears, to understand how a psychological conflict, shared by many individuals, can not only become the determinant cause of a political party, but can affect the destiny of an entire people.

A contrary case was that of a patient, a fervent Communist, who was affected by an obsessive neurosis. In the complex psychic unconscious motivation of his neurosis was a very strong inferiority complex and the usual duplication of the father's figure. Thus the patient felt an instinctive hatred of the Evil Father, forbidding and punishing (identified with the Premier, the Capitalists, etc.); he also felt a love and worship for the Good Father (identified with Stalin, the leaders of the Communist Party, etc.). The tension between his aggression and his passivity was extremely strong, and this patient had, with the aid of Marxism, wonderfully rationalized the situation.

A woman affected by agoraphobia fought hard against her temptations. She was an active and fervent Christian Democrat and was vexed by the idea that the Communists would kill her husband, a very modest industrialist, and would treat her as a bad woman. This was exactly what she unconsciously wished to be and consciously fought against. I might quote many other cases: a Socialist statesman, something of an exhibitionist, whose line of conduct in life was led by the need of showing off his "courage." He was consequently inclined to place himself and his political group in the position of being persecuted; this in order to show everybody that he was a man who stuck to his guns; another, again a Socialist, whose brother complex developed terrible violence against the hated Capitalists, but equally submitted to the senior brother, the Communist Party.

These particular cases have been mentioned to set in relief the fact that political men and political groups, showing orientations so different and in open contrast to one another, actually have a common psychological basis and a kindred mental form. In all cases, indeed, the conflict is stimulated and fostered by what we are now accustomed to call the "complex of oppression." The divergencies, characterized by the bipolar tension which has grown on such a basis, reveal the same forces at play in all cases.

All this is neither new nor surprising. It is known that both sadism and masochism, although they imply a different trend, still have the same meaning and the same value in relation to the personality. In fact, we speak of "sado-masochism" as a single problem.

All considered, the central problem with which we are dealing is the problem of aggression and the subsequent feeling of guilt. This problem is the fundamental social problem; the tension between the exigencies of the individual and those of the community may be traced back to it, as well as the tension between individual prepotency and social justice.

Tension takes on a different meaning and value according to its intensity and the psychological level on which it occurs; and certainly the conflicts which occupy us at present and which may be reduced to the tendency to oppress or to be oppressed (along with the feeling of guilt and the irritation this oppression implies) are among the most stubborn ones.

On this common ground, the reactionary-conservative feels, in the depths of his soul, that in spite of his denials he does not have a clean conscience. He actually believes he detains goods and power to the damage of others; but above all he feels he may become arrogant, brutal, and sadistic towards those who might menace his privileged position. He thus struggles against his own propensity to aggression and trembles in front of his feeling of guilt.

Every Communist, on the other hand, though he feels he has a right to hate and overthrow the symbols of wealth and the exploiters of his work, unconsciously envies the skill and rapacity of his adversaries. He feels he could become like his hated rivals; above all, he trembles before his own passivity and at the idea that he actually endures his own condition of inferiority and his state of traditional subordination.

The reactionary-conservative struggles against his own sadism, the Communist against his masochism. The former represents a mild, generous, comprehensive being; he speaks of freedom and of vast social reforms. In actual life, he behaves as an oppressor and a forestaller of riches and power. The Communist stands for violent and impulsive prepotency, defending what he holds to be his sacred right. Actually, he behaves in such a way as to be always overcome, as if he could reach his own balance only when being persecuted, when he can then react against his persecutors. The reactionary-conservative fears a personal revolution through the irruption of the instinctive "dregs"; he sees the Communists as an incarnation of these "dregs." The Communist looks forward to a personal revolution of his own, so that he may get rid of the internal insistence which keeps him in an everlasting state of inferiority. He recognizes in his adversary the incarnation of his own forbidding insistency.

Both political elements build up an adversary not as he actually is, but conforming to the negative part of their own personality. In such a condition, the possibility of mutual understanding is ignored; tension becomes critically heightened.

When many individuals are in conflicting positions, both analogous and opposed, all the conditions for the formation of two "clusters," or psychological groups which form the substrata of every social and political struggle, are realized. This situation now exists in Italy.

When two people have different and opposed psychological views, there arises a discussion which first becomes vivacious, then harsh; if not stopped *pro nono pacis,* it may soon become violent and offensive, and might even degenerate into physical violence. What is clear and evident to one of the contenders is constantly doubted by his opponent. One charges the other with stupidity; even worse, he charges him with being in bad faith, with obstinacy, and with refusing to admit what to the other appears as plain truth. In such a situation both antagonists appeal for help to other persons, possibly in authority, who can support their respective theses. All are inclined to identify themselves with those having the same psychological views and therefore the same opinions. In this way social conflict arises.

Similarly, national borders are crossed, and an Italian group with a conservative trend inclines to identify itself with the peoples gravitating around the United States of America; those with a tendency towards innovation identify themselves with Russia.

The same thing has happened among other nations, and the result has been the formation of two immense groups, the like of which has never before happened in the history of mankind. Yet there is a common basis for the two antagonistic groups. In spite of the fierce contrast between them and of their deep differences, we are struck, on less superficial examination, more by their concordances than by their discordances.

In the first place, they have in common those characteristics which belong to all collective formations: a striking uniformity in the way they understand life and react to its problems, an easy suggestibility, a decrease in the powers of understanding and criticism, and an extroversion of aggression towards the antagonistic group.

In the second place, the absorption of the individual by collectivity is evident both in Russia and in America. Everywhere the individual appears to be less and less important, while state and society become more powerful and more invading. The enormous concern for public opinion in America and class-consciousness in Russia show that conformism is the normal life-praxis. The individual is of very little concern.

This general levelling and unpersonalizing appears to be the most salient factor in both groups. There is also a certain dogmatism, a sort of Messianic spirit, an intolerance, which are the inevitable consequences of the psychic processes that are involved.

No wonder, then, that the American man in the street cannot even conceive the existence of people with an ideal of life different from his own, a life of welfare, ease, progress, and social life. Or that the Russian worker finds it unbelievable that so many workers allow themselves to be exploited by capitalists; workers who not only do not think of rebelling but, on the contrary, are easily satisfied with the dish of lentils their masters are pleased to leave them. No wonder either if the former holds the latter to be stupid, backward, and devoid of energy and dignity.

Finally, a general state of disquietude and a deep sense of uncertainty add to the diffuse feeling of guilt that unites Russians and Americans.

The American people, in fact, feel that their increasing activity and incessantly growing production are the consequence of an instinctive, inborn, and poorly-masked rapacity. They feel that they can never feel totally assured of the results achieved. They feel something is false in the race towards so-called progress, and they develop a feeling of guilt because this progress is not based on social justice. Perhaps they even feel, unconsciously, that their welfare and progress is conditioned by the necessity of exploiting other people who live in conditions of inferiority and dependence.

On the other side, the Russian people, having recently freed themselves from more than a secular condition of slavery, do not yet feel self-assured; they have passed brusquely from being the object to being the subject of their own history; they have a vague sense of being still an inferior people, unable to govern themselves. Therefore they despise and at the same time envy the Americans.

Having mentioned the concordances between the two blocs, let us examine their divergencies. These few and not easily ascertained differences have little importance, because it is only through the similarity of the conflict situation that two collective "minds" can be formed. In this way, the cohesion of the two blocs is assured and, through a reciprocal extroversion of the aggression, international tension is raised to a high potential.

Psychological tension, even if enormously strong, must not be considered *a priori* as endowed with a purely negative meaning. The same thing can be said about those psychic conflicts which are found at the basis of the neuroses. In fact the neuroses must be considered today not only as a compromise between instinctive contrasting tendencies, but also as an attempt at resolving a social problem. In one sense, it is an effort to overcome a collective psychological automatism. From this situation we derive the impression of great spiritual richness the neurotics often give us as compared to the flatness of the common man. But it is equally true that the neuroses may cause unheard-of suffering and may completely inhibit and stifle the human personality.

It has been commonly said that the whole of mankind suffers from an immense psychosis of self-destruction. Be this as it may, it is only too true that the external manifestations of the conflicting groups in the world today remind us strikingly of the psychology of the neurotic.

If we stressed the analogy between the psychology of conflicting world groups and the psychology of neurosis, we would certainly find a number of interesting points of similarity. The same psychic conflicts are at the bottom of neuroses and of collective psychology. A neurosis may evolve both towards an overcoming of internal conflict with a subsequent enlargement of the personality and towards annihilation. Mankind, too, faces two analogous perspectives. Mankind is now at a decisive turning point; the atomic bomb is materially and psychologically a revolutionary fact. The world has before it either the way toward self-destruction (which might lead to a most depressing psychological automatism, with a social organization of the "beehive" type, perfect in its way but incapable of evolution or renewal), or the way toward overcoming the present conflicts, with the prospect of a new era of greater spiritual richness. This problematic condition of human destiny makes the study of international tension a truly absorbing problem.

In a neurosis, recovery depends on such factors as the amount of choked-up energy, its tenacity, and the level on which the psychic conflict takes place.

In the case of a conflict of peoples, the level of the individual as well as of the collective conflict is very low. This situation is due to the fact that the conflicts concern the primeval problem of aggression: oppressing and being oppressed, dominating and being dominated (all of which are equivalent to the fierce law of nature—eating or being eaten). In addition, modern man presents, as a consequence of his aggression, a strong feeling of guilt. The psychic energy adhering to these conflicts seems rather mobile and unrestrained, having possibilities of being transposed to a higher level.

In spite of this, nothing seems to offer hope for a spontaneous and favorable evolution of tension. Experience teaches us that when a situation tends to get worse with nothing to shake the psychic crystallizations, there is no reason to believe that the polarization of minds and the homogenization of blocs will not continue, and that international tension will not increase.

Shall we then have war? No one can seriously expect to give an exact answer to this painful question. The art of prophesying is a very difficult one. But there is no need to be a prophet in order to assert that there will be war within the next few years. The final solution of such strong tension can only be a new war, unless psychological intervention can prevent a conflict.

It does not seem likely that the particular and contrasting interests of some elements of the bloc will end by undermining the internal cohesion of the two groups and giving birth to internal tensions so strong that new situations of compromise and balance will arise, as has happened before. Such a disintegration does not seem likely because the psychological bloc led by Russia is, and will remain, compact (except for marginal situations such as that of Yugoslavia). It is just such a compactness that will take the place of the unity of the Western groups.

While reason may show up the uselessness of the slaughter

and of the inevitable damage to both victors and vanquished, it will never be sufficiently strong to prevent an irrational eruption of the unchained instincts. Apart from any other technical consideration, both blocs will base the aggression on their idea of defense and not of offense. In the meantime, a political and diplomatic *détente* may be expected; but a change for the worse in the psychological situation and in the impermeability of the two groups seems to be destined. War seems inevitable because there is no strength capable of channeling aggressive energy away from the conflict.

Has psychology anything to offer which would actually attenuate this tension, or at least neutralize the most brutally destructive part of human aggression and thus prevent a new war? Here, too, the smallest dose of optimism seems more of an illusion than a conviction based on real experience.

In spite of this justified skepticism, we all feel, in the depth of our souls, that man is not really inevitably damned by his nature. We feel, on the contrary, that he has, psychologically, the capacity of preventing war and its useless destruction and atrocities.

Is not man the only being capable of saying *no* to his instinctive impulses? Why should he not be able to check within himself aggressive collective reactions in the same way that he forbids himself personal and individual ones? Should this be possible, the problem would still be difficult, since we would have to find the way of putting such a capacity into action.

The way to be followed is the one shown by the very evolution of man from an instinctive creature to a civilized person. Part of the aggressive energy must be employed to repress that part of the aggressive energy that would burst out impulsively. We must find the way of employing the aggression of man in order to fight that collective aggression which is war, just as we succeed in fighting the individual murderous instinct of aggression. We should seriously declare war on war, not by solemn pacifist assertions, but by vigorous combative activity.

When a society, because of its irresistible need to unchain aggressive instincts, wants to bring about a war, it does not speak of this need; it tries to attenuate the image of the horrors induced by war, and it calls attention to ideal problems, to courage, dignity, and faith.

Thus it is that the most atrocious cruelties were performed in the name of Christian love. Barbarity and cruelty were invoked in the name of the highest ideals. But those who want no war must behave in the opposite way. We must no longer divert our attention from the atrocities of war; the representation of the atrocities, destructions, and terrible suffering should constantly be made evident by all the means of a far-seeing propaganda. We should thus give birth to a true artificial anti-war psychosis; people should feel towards war the same horror and repulsion they feel towards bats or snakes or rats. We must improve such a collective psychology to the point that at the mere idea of war, all will cling to peace just as the shipwrecked grasp a lifebelt, caring little whether the helping hand be that of a friend or enemy.

Is all this, or something like it, attainable? Or are these ideas merely the expression of one of the many illusions of mankind? Psychology must overcome this doubt. Psychology at present can do something useful for the future of mankind, something which cannot possibly be achieved by politicians, moralists, and philosophers.

There is first the matter of the diagnosis of international tension; then there is the matter of prophylaxis and therapy. The influence which could be exerted by comprehensive psychological action justifies any sincere effort and any personal contribution on the part of psychologists and thinkers the world over.

JAPAN

Tsuneo Muramatsu, M.D.

Professor of Psychiatry, School of Medicine,
Nagoya National University, Nagoya.

IT is a difficult task to determine psychological
trends characteristic of an entire nation. Although Japan is
small in territory, her long history and her internal social differ-
entiation have created many group differences in tradition and
outlook. Ruth Benedict has suggested that Japanese culture may
be regarded as relatively homogeneous when compared with
the heterogeneous patterns of the Western nations. But to the
insider, especially the psychiatrist, homogeneous aspects are
less apparent and perhaps less important than the evident differences.

To understand the character traits of the contemporary Japanese, it may be useful to summarize the more conspicuous differences between developmental trends in Japanese and American social and family life.

While Western peoples were seeking for—and establishing—
national independence and individual freedom, and while
Protestant pioneers colonized and organized America, the
Japanese were still living in a mediaeval, feudal, hierarchal family system and society. This condition persisted until the Meiji
"revolution" of 80 years ago. During the Tokugawa Era, for
about two and a half centuries preceding the Meiji Restoration,
an extremely rigid, stratified type of society and family was
characteristic of Japan.

In this system, status in the family as well as in social life was
determined at birth. One was educated and trained from early
childhood to adjust to the prescribed and appropriate way of
life in an authoritarian atmosphere. To the extent that the in-

dividual was obedient and faithful to his allotted position, and was content with his lot in family and society, he could have personal security.

The standards of life were strictly stratified by class: the kind of clothes and their colors, the size and types of houses, the kind of language, when and how to bow, and in general, how to behave. All these were prescribed for the status in society, which was calculated on such criteria as the individual's position in the family, economic condition, occupation, age, sex, and marital status. Conventional morality and traditional restraints were so stringent that the violation of these unwritten laws subjected one to ridicule, or even to exile from the community or family.

The family or "house" was the most important symbol in life. Preservation of the family line and its dignity was regarded as the most important duty to the ancestors. Consequently, a wife who could not bear children was sometimes divorced and dishonored. Members who disgraced the family were often expelled. Loyalty to the house, and if necessary sacrifice in the interests of the family, were demanded as a matter of routine. The status of the family was determined by the community. Ordinarily, the first son of the head of the main family was the heir. In place of direct inheritance, the other sons were established as branch houses, with subordinate positions.

During this same period, Americans were emphasizing individuality, spontaneity, efficiency, progressivism, rationalism, and mutual cooperation in a *gesellschaftlich*, or "contractual," relationship between individuals. In contrast, the Japanese were still stressing the concept of society as a unity under the direction of a single authority, uniformity in each defined status, the insignificance of the individual, with conservatism, conventionalism, traditionalism, and loyalty in a *gemeinschaftlich*, or "family," relationship between individuals. Thus Japanese society as a whole took on the type of unity and solidarity characteristic of the kin group, plus a special Oriental stress on parental authority and filial duty.

This type of hierarchal structure demanded obedience to superiors and elders, uncomplaining acceptance of one's own

status, devotion to and self-sacrifice for authority, and acceptance of the priority of group or family interests over those of the
individual. Conservatism preserved traditions; an archaic spiritual perspective was encouraged.

This intense emphasis on in-group characteristics in feudal
Japan resulted in exclusiveness, cliquism, and hostility toward
outsiders. War lords were set against other war lords; villagers
against strangers; and family members against persons outside
of the family. Elaborate rules were set up to govern necessary
out-group relations. From these developed those elaborate patterns of etiquette which are often regarded as characteristically
Japanese. With respect to governmental administration, the
common people were kept in a state of ignorance and dependence.

The major religious strains that have influenced Japan have
tended to support the ethics of the in-group social structure.
Confucianism, which teaches benevolence, righteousness, propriety, wisdom, and sincerity, emphasized obedience to parents
and self-control. Ancestor worship was stressed by the indige-
nous *Shinto* (Way of the Gods). Buddhism, which has been very
influential, stressed the view that one cannot exist without the
good will or help of other people and of all things in nature.
Therefore, one must be appropriately grateful for the debt one
owes to everyone and everything. Further, according to Bud-
dhist teaching, one should not "sacrifice" any animal for eating
except fish. One must be satisfied with a modest and simple life,
and not aspire beyond that. These religious influences possibly
helped to confirm the Japanese people in their conservative and
static approach to life.

Neither Buddhism nor Shinto preached a doctrine of original
sin. Therefore, rather than sin, a sense of shame was aroused in
consequence of the violation of religious prohibitions, traditional morality, or the regulations of the group or family. The
consequences of shame were primarily the loss of "face" or de-
prival of group protection. In this fact lies the great importance
of "obligation" to the Japanese people. Failure to observe one's
obligation to family or society at large, as well as to individuals,

resulted in serious deprivations. Obligation, then, as a system of unwritten law, bound individual to individual and individual to group in a tight network, without regard for individual right or desire.

In such an atmosphere, it could be expected that suppressed energies would find an outlet in pursuits which anyone might take up, regardless of class position. For example, growing chrysanthemums or dwarf trees, arranging flowers or gardens, and similar rarefied pursuits were common. Standards of taste, color, and form were exquisitely refined and reduced to a deliberately underplayed simplicity.

After the Meiji Restoration, Japanese eyes were first opened to the outer world. They were enthusiastic in adopting new objects and ideas from Western nations, and discarded or modified many of their old customs. The individual was released from feudal restraint, but at the same time the necessity for interpersonal competition arose. Modernization and industrialization developed rapidly, and the growth of industrial monopolies was marked. The population increase that occurred was primarily an urban phenomenon; the rural population remained fairly static. Living became more expensive, its pace more rapid, economically more unstable, and emotionally more tense and insecure.

The Western political party system was formally adopted soon after the Restoration. Several political parties were organized, and the Diet and House of Peers were established as the legislative organ. However, the intellectual and cultural Renaissance, which required four centuries in Europe for final consumation, has had only three-quarters of a century to develop in Japan. A complete Western-style renaissance was out of the question. Thus the newly established constitution made the Emperor the all-powerful and sacred ruler, even though this was essentially in name only. Many basic feudal conventions have continued relatively intact in family, school, and office, and especially in rural areas.

Moreover, members of the conservative British aristocracy were brought in as advisors, and students eagerly studied German philosophy, law, and science. The authoritarian German military system was adopted as a model by the army.

Governmental administration and education were completely centralized. Respectful emphasis on the government and disrespect for the people continued to be very strong. The Government was and often is called *okami,* which means the top or the above. Young men of intelligence and ambition aspired to entrance into a governmental school, and many looked forward to becoming governmental officials.

Authoritarianism was most conspicuous in the army and in the governmental bureaucracy. It has been customary in Japan for lower-rank officials to conduct governmental business. Because of their general arrogance, as well as their inefficiency, they have been unpopular with the people. This arrogance may possibly have developed from the general tendency, noted by Erich Fromm, for people who are extremely submissive to superiors to enjoy the exercise of power over powerless inferiors. In spite of the hostility toward authority, there was little widespread protest or revolt; in general, people were passively resigned. This attitude has been expressed in a popular proverb which says: "Contending with authorities is like trying to quiet a crying baby." Most of the people felt that government was a matter for superiors, and consequently they had virtually no participation in administration, foreign affairs, or even in matters which affected them directly, like the expenditure of receipts from taxation.

In Japanese family life, the authority of the father, the parent-child relationship, relationships with grandchildren, and the relation between husband and wife tend to resemble those in the German family, as described in Bertram Schaffner's *Father Land, A Study of Authoritarianism in the German Family*. An old Japanese proverb states that: "Fearful things in the world are four: earthquake, thunder, fire, and father." However, in this generation, authoritarianism and child discipline have not been as rigid as those of the German family.

From the end of the Tokugawa Era until the present day, there have been only four generations. Our grandparental gen-

eration was trained to the way of life of the strict feudal family.
After the writer's grandfather lost his position as a warrior because of the reform, he became a government official. When
he retired, in the middle of the Meiji Era, he continued to read
books about Confucianism, old Japanese and Chinese literature,
and refused to acquaint himself with Western ideas. He la-
mented the neglect of the traditional culture, and the eager
imitation of Western fashions. He governed his behavior in accordance with the old *samurai* code. When he visited the grave
of his war lord, he made obeisance as of old. Nevertheless, he
did not interfere with his children's desire to become Western-
ized; he even mocked his own stubbornness.

Our father's generation became remarkably liberal and individualistic, and seemed to be much more ambitious and competitive in respect to fame and wealth than either the
grandparental generation or our own. Our own generation seems
to be more liberal and also more skeptical.

Again, our children's generation seems to be considerably
different from our own. This is especially true for young men
and women between twenty and twenty-five, who were educated under the strong pressure of militaristic and nationalistic
concepts. They were forced to make an adjustment to war, and
to imperialistic and ultra-nationalistic ideology. All of this pressure is now gone.

The development of industrialization has led to a gradual decline in the extended and patriarchal large-family system. The
number of smaller families has increased. The rate of divorce
has decreased, and the standard and level of living have been
raised to some extent. Three conditions—family size, economic
circumstances, and size of dwelling—affect the relations between
the members. The larger the family, the more difficult is the economic situation; the smaller the dwelling, the more complicated
become the social and emotional relationships between the
members. Moreover, most Japanese houses are constructed
with much less individual privacy than the Western type.
The rooms are separated from each other by no more than paper
screens or thin walls of wood and mud plaster. The whole family

lives face-to-face almost all day long, and in many small houses they all sleep in one or two rooms. Often the father and mother bathe together with the younger children.

In order to keep interpersonal relationships in such a family at least superficially peaceful and smooth, the concept of "reserve" is invoked. This implies obedience to superiors and elders, with a minimum of complaints and no backtalk. Strong emotional tension, frustration, and hostility in some individuals frequently result from the consequent repression. More specifically, this reserve means the restraint of free expression of one's own wish or opinion, in consideration of the feelings, dignity, or face of others; and at the same time, the protection of one's own status or face in social or family life. Such reserve in practice often brings about a hesitation to express oneself frankly, to behave freely, or to assume initiative. This behavior, with its silence and its smile, may cause misunderstandings even among the Japanese, not to mention the difficulties that arise between Japanese and Westerners.

Another related mechanism, which serves to prevent the emotional complication of interpersonal relationships, is the go-between—a method which is used not only in arranging marriages, but also in transacting business.

Reserve is not only a mode of behavior toward superiors; superiors themselves are expected to behave with some degree of reserve toward inferiors. They must not be too frank, they must avoid hurting feelings, they must not demand too much, and they are also expected to be sensitive enough to penetrate the reserve of their inferiors and ascertain their real desires and opinions. Otherwise, the inferiors might accumulate hostilities toward them and develop disobedient or even aggressive and explosive behavior. In this system, since a frank argument with superiors is generally viewed as disobedience, a repressed disagreement may often be expressed by "yes" in words and "no" in act.

Generally speaking, because the Japanese are not accustomed to discuss things frankly, they are not trained to form definite opinions about a subject, to express them clearly, to listen to the ideas of others calmly, or to argue critically. The Japanese are often very timid in frank expressions of their own ideas, very sensitive to criticism, and very apt to become excited by objections to their views when discussion does occur.

Reserve-behavior is not only characteristic of interpersonal relations, but also of the relations of an individual to a group. Group solidarity, which emphasizes reserve-behavior and obedience to the person in authority (who guarantees the security of all members), forms the basis for the establishment of the so-called "boss" system in Japanese social life. Such boss systems appear everywhere in all kinds of groups and organizations—local, professional, school, office, governmental, and criminal. This tendency provided a foundation for the authoritarian and disciplined organization of totalitarian, ultra-nationalist, and Fascist groups.

The parent-child prototype relations, which carry over into the boss system, are also carried over into ordinary work relations of office and factory. Workers often transfer this attitude toward parents to their boss or employer. Workers often look upon their work in terms of a personal emotional relationship with the boss rather than in terms of simple employee-employer relations. The most striking example of this is found in the so-called craftsman spirit. Again, it is often found that workers will put forward their best efforts, even when they are not paid, for a boss who shows appreciation of their skill, or inspires them with spirit, or to whom they are under obligation. But for an employer whom they do not like, for whom they do not have this personal feeling of obligation and relation, they will often fail to work hard, no matter how high their wages. While these tendencies are diminishing with the gradual spread of modern capitalistic technology and industrial organization, the general attitudes underlying them are still widespread in all levels of the population.

Hostility toward the father, and sometimes ambivalence toward the mother, commonly develops in many young people as a result of the oppressive psychological atmosphere of family and social life. The first age of rebellion is usually at four to five years; the second from thirteen to eighteen years. Individual expression of hostility differs—some suppress it, some develop guilt reactions, while others express their hostility openly.

As an adjustment to the oppression of convention and to real poverty, the Japanese tend to be industrious but inhibited, dependent, more or less pessimistic, and rather masochistic. Commonly, human existence is considered as full of unhappiness, sorrow, and pain. For many Japanese, happiness is merely a dream or an illusion, and the individual is insignificant and powerless. A movie or drama with a happy ending appears unreal to Japanese audiences, especially those above middle age.

For a majority of the Japanese, life is a hard struggle for existence; they are unable to think of it as enjoyable. Before and during the war, militarists constantly stressed the harsh pressure on Japan for bare existence. They pointed out that little Japan, with her large and still increasing population, could not exist without emigration or expansion. Their purpose, of course, was to justify the claim that urgently necessary emigration and expansion were being blocked by larger and richer countries that were forcing Japan to starve or to fight for her very existence. The authoritarian nationalists added that Japan, as the leader of Asia, had to liberate the peoples of the Far East from the present situation and at the same time defend them against Communism.

Critics were overwhelmed by the traditional prestige and power of this group. The people followed an old proverb: "Be wrapped by a long thing," which means: "Do not struggle in vain when you are completely enveloped." But even during the war, the professional military and higher bureaucracy seemed to be unpopular among a majority of the common people. It was commonly said, "This is a good time only for the Star (symbol of the Army), the Anchor (symbol of the Navy), and the Face (people with prestige)." Because of the lack of war material, "spiritual" force or power was emphasized very often by the leaders, who were accordingly criticized by the people as dominated by divine obsession or possession. The uprightness and justice of the Japanese Army and Navy and the contrasting cruelty of the enemy were reiterated so strongly that the people were made to think in terms of either victory or death, with no other alternative.

The feudal spirit was strongly emphasized along with patriotism and Shintoism. Young boys were trained, almost hypnotized, to deem it a great honor to die for the Emperor or for the country of their ancestors.

The lack of fanatic and last-ditch resistance to the entry of the Occupation Forces in 1945 was a great surprise to many Japanese. While the command of the Emperor was effective in ending resistance, the people had already come to the realization that they were losing the war.

To be resolute is considered a virtue among the Japanese. They have been trained by repeated earthquakes, typhoons, floods, conflagrations, and numerous other natural disasters not to complain too much or too long about past misfortunes. Not to be a good loser is considered cowardly. But a loser sometimes easily becomes an obedient and at the same time very dependent follower of the victor. Thus a victor may sometimes be considered as a new boss who has a real obligation to look after the weaker followers.

Generally speaking, the Japanese often feel inferior in the face of modern Western civilization. Since the beginning of the Meiji Era, the Japanese have felt that they lagged behind Western science, thought, and industry. Imported objects and ideas are commonly considered better and more reliable than the corresponding Japanese products. Japanese self-confidence often seems to be weak. This attitude was exceptionally apparent with the end of the war.

After surrender and occupation, most people appeared to be in a stupor. They did not know what to do; they did not know what would happen to them next. While they were frightened by the Occupation, they were very much impressed by the humanity and generosity of the Occupation Forces.

With the promulgation of the new Constitution, there has been extensive formal reorganization along democratic lines. The widespread changes in attitude and in receptivity toward democratic ideas which have taken place are truly notable. But it would be a mistake to assume that the democratic renovation of Japanese thinking is complete. It is obvious that complete psychological reorganization will take much more time, because democracy, in its fullest sense, requires independence and maturity of the individual.

The postwar food, clothing, and housing shortages, combined with a sharply rising inflation, have driven most people to devote all their time and thought to such immediate concerns as preserving a minimal level of existence. The total caloric count of the daily food ration in the city of Tokyo during the last four months of 1945 was around 1,200—far less than the bare minimum requirements. People became physically exhausted, uneasy, and demoralized. Criminality—mainly larceny—increased rapidly, especially among young people and children.

Many parents and school teachers, under the stimulus of new ideas, have become skeptical of the old authoritarian principles of training and education, since authoritarianism has been formally abolished and democracy put in its place. But democracy is a new concept; it is surrounded by uncertainty. Consequently, there are wide differences in the interpretation of democratic behavior.

Among many young people there is strong feeling of having been deceived by their leaders, teachers, and even by their parents. This is particularly true for the twenty- to twenty-five-year age group, which was oriented toward an authoritarian, imperialist, ultra-nationalist ideology before and during the war. They were, so to speak, poured into a warlike mental mold from their primary and secondary school days. Told how to think, feel, and behave, how to live and how to die, they were not trained to think critically or to behave independently. They were given much less of a general cultural education than older people. With the Occupation, this convenient and rigid frame for their life vanished. They were consequently disoriented and confused. Conventional morality lost much of its authority and, along with Confucianism, Shinto, and Buddhism, it seems to have little to offer confused young people. The number of Christians is still

small, although conversions appear to be increasing in very recent months.

Consequently, many young people seem to have lost their
conventional hopes and ideas and have not formulated new ones
to replace them. Some give the impression that they will never
trust authority again, and will strongly resist any attempt to
make them do so. Others are pessimistic or even nihilistic. Some
young people seem to be simply hunting for pleasure and enjoyment, and relations between the sexes is considerably freer
in many areas. Others are extremely egotistic and do not seem
to care about their family, their society, or even their nation.
Some are seeking new philosophies, ideologies, or religions;
and Communists seems to be increasing among college and uni-
some have become fanatics. Thus, the number of both Christians
versity students. There has been a rash of new "religions," the
foundors of oomo of which are apparently paranoid.

Such characteristic Japanese traits as neatness, cleanliness,
and politeness have been less apparent in urban areas since the
air raids. People were in no position to observe these virtues, and
carelessness and impoliteness have tended to become habitual,
concurrently with weariness and poverty. An increase in teen-
age amateur prostitution—the *pan-pan* girls—is one of the striking postwar social phenomena. The *pan-pan* give a striking impression of real enthusiasm and enjoyment—perhaps from a
feeling of emancipation and release from traditional restraints
surrounding the role of women in Japanese society. Many of
them, of course, come from war-broken and impoverished families, but some are of middle-class origin. Many of these girls are
mentally subnormal and have unstable personalities.

The economic situation in Japan has improved steadily. Production of all kinds of goods, as well as foreign trade, has effected
a not inconsiderable recovery. The general interest in public
health and welfare, in social work, and in prevention and rehabilitation of delinquency has risen considerably in the last
two years.

It can be said that the Japanese have been diligent students of democracy. They have learned much, and have done their best under very difficult circumstances. New leadership has emerged, especially from the ranks of farmers and workers.

The development of the labor movement has been remarkable. After the right of labor to organize was given by the Occupation, the idea of union organization was accepted with enthusiasm. Unions appeared everywhere, even in the hospitals. Hospital unions usually took on a closed shop vertical form and included all physicians and nurses except the director, the assistant director, and the chief clerk. These latter were regarded as the "management" class according to the new union ideology. Moreover, "Patients' Unions" were organized in many hospitals for the purpose of inspecting the entire hospital administration, including the distribution of rations. Such examples illustrate typical postwar insecurity, hostility, suspicion, and defensiveness. Many such unions remain. However, after the first enthusiastic phase, many have disappeared or have been modified.

Superficial verbalistic imitations of democracy, as well as imitations of American fashions and mass-cultural elements, are to be found everywhere. These phenomena are in part due to the loss of self-confidence and to the vacuum created by the disappearance of the simple submissiveness to those in power. On the other hand, many old organizations remain prominent. Even a street girl cannot pursue her trade unless she gets permission from the boss of one of these guildlike groups.

In families, traditions like "obligation" and "face," or appearance before the world, remain very important. Such deeply-rooted ways of thinking cannot be expected to vanish overnight.

The physical and mental exhaustion of a majority of the Japanese since the war has not yet been entirely alleviated. Economic difficulties, spiritual confusion, and political insecurity, national as well as international, do not admit of immediate solution. Overcrowding is severe, so that many repatriates and the jobless have difficulty in finding refuge even in their home districts. These conditions easily make a majority of the people emotionally insecure, tired, anxious, pessimistic, tense, and irritable, whether they are aware of these reactions or not. In general, however, people are willing to work hard with at least overt good humor.

Young people in the age group from twenty to twenty-five are now playing the most aggressive roles in the "activist" radical sections of the labor union movement in Japan. Needless to say, people of this age group are generally the most active ones everywhere in all social movements. But in addition, this is the generation in Japan which was the most severely victimized by the war.

These young people, having lost the ideological and submissive-aggressive orientation given them by militarist-dominated education, have shown a variety of responses. They may react with helplessness and immaturity, seeking something to depend upon for authoritative guidance and direction. Often this particular group is prone to accept any authoritarian ideology which, like communism, presents itself as attractive and as offering solution to daily problems. Others seem indifferent to any ideas or to any group; they are concerned only about their existence; they often revert to the traditional attitudes and values. Criticism of social change is prominent in this group, though rarely audible publicly.

Often the response of helpless and immature people to an insecure world takes the form of membership in a rebellious or power-seeking group dominated by a boss. A new generation of young gangsters and black-marketeers has appeared. Finally, the resurgence of labor unionism, under strong though often uncertain leadership, has provided another vehicle for the hopes and the needs for dependency and security so apparent in the younger groups. There are dangers, of course, in the seizure of these democratic unions by unscrupulous bosses and political leaders.

Whether the response is aggressive and rebellious or submissive and retiring, a basic authoritarian attitude seems to be present. Certainly those who join revolutionary ideological groups and criminal gangs are merely transferring their former loyalties to Emperor and the military to the new groups. The submissive response, on the other hand, seeks the lost authoritarianism in traditional verities. Aggressiveness and withdrawal-behavior may both be expressions of basic insecurity, particularly when the people concerned have a background of repressive training. Such persons require someone to give them orders because they cannot face responsibility. Correlatively, they need someone to blame for their unhappiness or insecurity, and will join movements which provide targets and a sense of accomplishment. The dynamics are the same; the responses differ.

Many of the intellectuals who were not strong enough to stop or prevent the war, and who instead criticized the militarists with hopeless cynicism, at present continue weak and inactive. Generally, they show eagerness in developing democracy in Japan, criticizing both the extreme political left and right. However, their attitude seems to be defensive, rather than one of trying to convince people of their point of view.

In the final analysis, the majority of the Japanese are probably too busy with immediate problems of daily life to participate in ideological discussions. But they seem to show a general dislike and distrust of the aggressive policies of the extreme left. Being primarily concerned with security and peace, their fundamental attitude probably remains very conservative. Thus there is danger of a resurgence of authoritarianism. As an example, some PTA's are already criticized as "BTA's," or Boss-Teacher Associations.

This general passive tendency of the Japanese is historically conditioned. This fact must never be forgotten in any program of social change. It is not difficult to imitate the formal aspects of democracy, and it is not difficult to amend regulations and pass new laws. But it is very difficult to change the forms of interpersonal relations, custom, and emotion in such a way as to conform to the psychological prerequisites of democracy. It may therefore take generations for genuine democracy to appear in Japan.

There is, and there will continue to be, a danger that aggressive minorities will seize dominant power, and that a majority of the people without open protest will again revert to the psychology of "being wrapped by a long thing." Social protest appears when one can think independently and critically, when one realizes the power of his own opinions. The Japanese must learn that democracy is more than a word, it is a complex way of life. And while one must not expect a Japan remade entirely in the Western democratic pattern, certain basic reforms in this direction are necessary and desirable. Many of the basic and preliminary steps have already been taken; only the future will tell if the full stride can be made.

LUXEMBOURG

Ernest Stumper, M.D.

Medical Director of the Psychiatric Hospital of the
Grand Duchy of Luxembourg.

THE distinguished psychologist William McDougall
described a number of activities which contribute to conflict
among individuals and peoples. Among these activities were
the "tendencies of fear, of anger, of curiosity; the tendency to
seek and consume food; the tendencies to assert ourselves
amongst our fellows, and to find satisfaction in their yielding
to us their submission, deference to those who are powerful."

Faced with the problem of the psycopathology of international relations, several preliminary matters need to be explored.
The essential points seem to be an effort to unravel what is morbid in the behavior of individuals who dominate other people,
and what is morbid in the structure of these dominated peoples
themselves; and to consider the problem of the regression or reversion to a primitive stage in the complex manifestations of
present-day behavior. It might very well be that, without vio-
lating the limits established by Anglo-Saxon psychology, these
manifestations no longer correspond to what we assume to be a
high level of modern civilization.

It is evident that this last-mentioned point is most important.
For if, as some authors believe, evolution has been the fatal consequence of an irremediable deviation of instinctive life, all hope
would be vain, even if economic and social (in the strictly proper
sense of the word) problems were susceptible of a satisfactory
solution.

Since the dawn of history there have been several principal
causes of conflict among peoples. Vivid and lasting memories
of these conflicts remain fixed, like psychological barbs, in the

hearts of people. Although the Hundred Years' War was originally a war of dynasties, the antagonism between the English and the French has never completely disappeared since the time when an English king claimed to impose his rule upon the French. And just as the historical rivalry in colonial affairs between France and England still troubles some Frenchmen, the ghost of Bonaparte continues to haunt certain British minds.

Luxembourg is such a tiny country that the value of its testimony might be questioned. But this small country, an innocent victim of many international conflicts, has learned much in the course of the centuries. War-ridden, devastated, and plundered numberless times, it has not had the courage to develop a national ideal. Nor has it had the time. The country has been transferred, exchanged, sold, conquered, and reconquered too often. Remaining forcibly attached to ancient agricultural and religious traditions, its inhabitants have acquired a well-marked skepticism for nationalist phraseology. Cruelly tried by every European war, they have learned to consider the future without optimism.

For a hundred years Luxembourg has been, in spite of the smallness of its territory, the object of certain neighbors' covetousness. The attitude of the Germans in particular has never inspired confidence. German annexation aims, hidden at first and openly revealed in 1914, resulted in a *de facto* annexation of Luxembourg in 1940. May the tenth, 1940, was not a surprise to the people of Luxembourg, even though the French, speaking of a "drôle de guerre," were inclined to underestimate the real danger of the European situation. In the early morning of the tenth of May, the disbelieving French alarm posts had to be warned by Belgian and Luxembourg inhabitants in their flight from the German army. At the risk of appearing paradoxical, one might say that while there is often international tension without a war, at that moment there was a war without tension, at least as far as the French were concerned.

It was in a way the sleep of the just, unjustified though it was. None of the wars of the past can be compared, in terms of the number of violent deaths, to the most recent one. All that is related about Germany in these pages is but to serve as a lesson and a warning for the future. For can one deny that this country produced Goethe? Must one abandon hope that the nation of Kant will one day evolve in a human way? The German spirit, so dissociated and ambiguous, is the eternal incarnation of the Faustian problem. A spirit that is pliable and rigid in turn, sometimes formed by an iron fist, and sometimes given up to the most exalted mysticism. What a riddle! What a mystery for the future! Peaceful nations fear above all that the germ of evil-mindedness, once spread, might develop elsewhere. Sir James Jeans has pointed out that the human mind, the real creator of the universe, appears in certain people as if it were incapable of reconciling reason and instinct.

The misfortune Luxembourg suffered brought in its wake both an opportunity and a lesson. The country could admire the common sense and balance of the Americans no less than that empiricism which, of course, is not without theoretical difficulties.

Once possessed of democratic traditions, which suited her well, Luxembourg remained skeptical of ideological myth, whatever its origins. She did not allow herself to be invaded by a primitive spirit, nor did she assume a passive attitude. She refused to accept irrational, antilogical, or antibiological dogmas.

To the east of our national boundary, people think differently. In 1913 a German student told me: "It is only force that counts. The strongest people, being the best, will obtain supremacy over other nations and will dominate them forever. And it is good that it should be so." It was a time when the romanticism of force was cultivated in military and university circles. Today the cult of force remains fundamental—and not only in Germany!

Three stages in the history of international antagonism can be distinguished. The archaic stage is characterized by vital necessity. It involves the ideal of adventure and the problems of dynasties and successions. This archaic period was followed by a more recent one of colonial and economic rivalry. This period, in turn, was succeeded by the contemporary period, characterized by oligarchies grouped around violent and cunning personalties devoid of scruples. Such leaders play upon their people as upon an instrument specially made for them. The present period embodies an aggressive and expansive ideology.

Following the Second World War, we learned that a number of Germans belonging to the elite had conspired against the regime. But only the German mass could decide the fate of its idol. And it was this German mass which threw itself upon the funeral pyre containing the moral corpse of its Führer. Such behavior brings to mind the Hindu widow who follows her husband to death in the flames. Once seduced by the voice of the "well-beloved" chief, people lose their sane judgment and their old way of looking at things. Society loses its regulating and moderating power, and we come to a state analogous to the one William McDougall discusses in his book, *Energies of Men.* There he evokes the hypothesis of a mankind in which society has no influence on the shaping of character. In such a world, human beings would be cruel and without charity. They would be as egotistic and as little accessible to moral considerations as the lower animals.

Such a state was indeed attained by a people whose leader succeeded in substituting an ideal of mere force, and the myth of the fair-and-fiery-haired superman, for traditional Christian morality. This myth assumes various aspects. It is not necessary to emphasize the Marxist-Leninist economic dogma and the manner in which it differs from fascism and national socialism. It is only the resemblance which is interesting. They are brought closer together by the myth, by the ideology in the form of an intangible dogma, by the dictatorial domination of a people by an authoritarian oligarchy. No one knows whether the rule of the Marxist-Leninist oligarchy will lead to a war. No one knows, indeed, whether they desire a war in a way the national socialist oligarchy desired war. They try to clear themselves of this suspicion. But do they make efforts to ease international tension?

Whether the danger is imaginary or not, the fact remains that nations who have had a taste of revolution are less inclined to renew the experience than those who lived under a feudal form of government up to a recent age. In Luxembourg, social conditions never brought about a real revolution. Our economic evolution was, in spite of some uneveness, smooth and peaceful. Owing to our prudent farmer- and small bourgeois-mentality, violently extreme solutions have always frightened our people. They dread uncertain developments.

Even at a period when this country lived miserably, social problems did not breed serious trouble and revolution. The so-called revolutions of 1789, 1830, and 1848 were limited to transformations and adaptations of the aristocratic and bourgeois world. The misery and destruction, slavery and deportations, and manslaughter and political murders endured from 1940 to 1945 gave bolshevism no appreciable number of adherents. This in spite of the admiration our people felt for the heroic conduct of the Russian people. Consequently, at the moment, international tension is being interpreted here in the same way as in other Western nations. While not everyone is well-to-do in the country of Luxembourg, instinctively or deliberately we tread in the footsteps of such peaceful nations as France, Great Britain, and the United States of America.

The Second World War did not shake our conviction that the Hitler and Mussolini dictatorships had brought about the catastrophe. Everyone agrees that riches and material comfort are not everywhere equally distributed. But the course of every past revolution teaches us that, although each is considered as final, it is in fact limited to a changing of oligarchies, the last one of them being charged with all the crimes. Must we not after all be grateful to the Germans? They put us through a hard but useful school. They taught us by example that the "other" animals, of which McDougall speaks, are not the most wicked, that we do not live in the best of all possible worlds, and finally that we must distrust those who try to sweep away the past. It is deplorable to imagine a future in which a world cataclysm, started once again by a gang of adventurers, might arise.

Every dictatorship must falsify history wherever it conflicts with its outlook; it draws a *cordon sanitaire* around its terrorized people, isolating them from the civilized world and preparing them for a new war of conquest.

He who believes that the people themselves start wars must be of a naïve mind. Wars are due partly to the wild desires of rulers and oligarchies, partly to the passive and sometimes enthusiastic submission of the masses. The dictator must make the minds of his people uniform. Only the absolutely safe conformists are tolerated. Outside this dogmatic circle live only the decadent, the uprooted, the rotten, the cosmopolites, the stateless, those who sold themselves, and the pseudo-scientists, pseudo-writers, and pseudo-artists. Blind passive obedience in all things! Submissive "people's tribunals" sentence to death the opponents of the regime. In the eyes of the world, people paralyzed by fear appear as the accomplices of the dictator. By the heinousness of his crimes, he destroys his bridges behind him and renders future relations between his people and other nations exceedingly difficult. Every attempt at a revolt is at once smothered in blood. A strange sight it is to see the rebel at the bar of the people's tribunal confessing his "crimes." If these confessions sometimes are the result of torture, one must admit that they often come out of a state of mind similar to that of Dostoevski, who left his Siberian prison with the words: "My punishment has been just, because I carried within my heart bad intentions against my government. But it is a pity that I should be made to suffer now for theories and for a cause which are no longer mine."

What a striking resemblance between this great writer's state of mind and the spineless submission of entire nations. Such an unexpected resignation, which no longer has anything rational in it, is the expression of an instinctive factor, of an overwhelming masochistic passivity. Masochism explains the sudden collective passivity, the silence of scholars, and the enigmatic cowardice of economically—and even politically—strong persons and groups. Such a total eclipse makes one believe in the existence of a tendency to enjoy a passive state in which one feels safe. People who lived for years under Nazi domination, saw the cowardice of reasonable, cultivated, and human Germans who, while despising national socialism, trembled before their barbaric and amoral masters. Moreover, these "enlightened" Germans passively and even voluptuously obeyed the most absurd and cruel orders of the regime.

The extreme readiness with which the Germans accepted the militarist virus was increased by the existence in Europe of clearly-marked nationalisms. Even the Soviets, advocates of a world brotherhood, are now withdrawing more and more into a narrow-minded nationalism which might well be nothing more than a masked pan-Slavism.

Nietzsche once said: "As a people of the most stupendous mixture and concoction of races . . . the Germans are more elusive, contradictory, unintelligible, incalculable, surprising, and even terrifying than other peoples are to themselves." This monstrous originality makes many things clear. First, it explains why the Nazi ideology gathered such a small number of adherents in occupied territories. In Luxembourg, after the occupation, only a few hundred persons threw in their lot with Hitler. The increase in swastika flags allured some thousand more—all of them opportunists and scoundrels. Only a few dozen of real volunteers joined the German army, while more than 12,000 Luxemburgers had to be enlisted by force. What a shameful failure of the "race-instinct" hypothesis in a supposedly German country and by supposedly German blood! What a riddle for the German and his *Widerspruchnatur!*

We experienced—may we never have to again—the fulfilment of Nietzsche's words: "Nearly all that we call 'higher culture' rests on the exaltation of cruelty into a spiritual ideal." Equipped with similar aphorisms, the Germans set to work. And who would assert that they did not succeed? The French, thoroughly tired of martial games since the time of Napoleon, saw themselves dragged into three wars; Great Britain and the United States were involved against their will in the last two.

Why did Germany not become wiser after 1918? In order to answer this question, we must turn to the unconscious, to that instinctive and emotional sphere which is the source of mental disorder. Professor W. H. R. Rivers has said that "during a period of stress, recent tendencies weaken, ancient levels rise, revealing themselves in symbolic form . . . They are manifestations of early forms of thought, through which repressed tendencies find expression when the control of higher society levels is removed." This dynamic process is as true of the mass as it is of the individual.

The primitive mentality, "mystical rather than logical," re-

sembles the regressive symptoms of a mental disease. According
to the level of their civilization, people come under the influence
of the myth, which is the expression of the primitive soul, of the
return to the past, of the impulse of the human beast, of the invasion of magic memories and a romanticism drunk with instinctive force. The compensatory imagination of propagandists
creates a fascination capable of overriding even religious values.
Rosenberg's assertion that "the Nordic blood represents that
mystery which supplants the old sacraments" seems stupendous.
But it shows clearly what an unbalanced people wants. The
faithful swallowed these wild fancies which, according to them,
the simple-minded mortals making up the rest of the world
would not even understand.

We know too well how much this enslaving of a people's soul
can influence its neighbors. Dictatorship spreads like wildfire
among the swarming mass of adventurers in neighboring countries. The fear which a violently aggressive people inspires can
rally hesitating sympathizers as well as cowards. It stirs all those
who believe that by acquiescing they can indefinitely keep their
customary way of life.

Hitler's antibolshevist policy early in the 1930's was a balm
for the well-to-do in Europe. Many approved his anti-Jewish
crusade. They did not understand that this maniac, like all diseased people, charged others with the very crimes he proposed
to commit. As William Brown said: "Hitler and the German
people imputed to their enemies their own bad intentions and
bad faith." Today, millions of people are convinced that a non-
committal or even benevolent attitude in the face of a newly
rising myth will guarantee future peace.

One cannot escape the question of how it became possible for
dictatorship to strike a decisive blow upon a people as educated
and as industrious as the Germans. True, there had been Frederick II, Herder, Fichte, and Nietzsche, as well as those who
never gave up their desire to revenge past defeats. But even the
swastika, that symbol of a myth so flattering to so many troubled
feelings, would not have sufficed had it not been extolled by de-
moniac oratory, by an apocalyptic legend, and by the gloomy

Nordic romanticism of the twilight of the gods. It was what C. G. Jung would call the archetype for a *Zeitenwende,* for the making of a new age.

Never in the past had so many Germans believed that the hour of the German mission in the world had come. The few friends of peace who dared lift their voices were quickly brought to silence by sarcasm and threats. A series of fallacious dogmas, called the program of the national socialist party, directed the dynamisms of an entire people towards catastrophe.

It was Hitler who created and promoted the movement. But once more the German people made things easy. What providential and unique gifts they attributed to this Führer! To these vile flatteries he modestly answered on February 24, 1940: "I am nothing but a magnet constantly passing over the German nation and drawing the steel out of this people."

Is it astonishing then that such a dictator should feel a revelation stirring within him? He is the man of destiny, elect, unique! To believe himself the rival of Jesus, Mahomet, or Napoleon is but a step. He sincerely hopes to surpass them all in space as well as in time. The important point is that the Führer communicated this belief to his people. As a consequence, the German mind ceased altogether to function in a normal manner.

It is quite certain that the man whom Hindenburg called the Bohemian Sergeant was a psychopath. Eloquent though he was, he united in his person a number of morbid traits. He showed an innate aggressiveness, with a tendency toward depressive states. He hatched sly plots and revealed furious paroxysms and emotional explosions. He was filled with cruel intentions, which he hid under an inoffensive exterior. He pretended, after the manner of Nero, to be an artist, a painter, and an architect. His exhibitionism, his theatrical bearing, his total absence of scruples and humanitarian sentiments (except when they were useful for misleading his adversaries), and his hysterical reactions (shown as early as 1918) mark him as a political criminal. He was animated by the mystic conviction that he was intended to play a providential part made possible by the prophetic and strategic gifts he attributed to himself. Herald of a millennial empire, this

psychopath with a mystic faith in his own destiny was above all
an unconscious mystifier who cheated his people and himself
up to his last days in the shelter of the Chancellery.

This failure of common sense takes us back to the fundamental problem of the mass and the elite. Dictatorship establishes itself as a result of an unwholesome competition between
these two groups. The failure and decline of the two governing
classes occurs when a succession of great men comes to an end
or when the leaders leave the right road for the purpose of flattering the instincts of the mass. The latter, abandoned and left
to itself, is capable only of vague and emotional feelings which
are formless and abrupt, though sometimes mixed with explosions of collective generosity. "Crowds," Gustave Le Bon writes,
"sometimes make a show of heroism, of blind faith in certain
causes, but never of judgment."

Naïveté, emotionalism, and credulity are the character traits
of the crowd, making the crowd the predestined victim of adventurers and psychopaths. However, a reasonably high standard of living can keep a people from contamination by a totalitarian economic myth. Also, historical experience can help
distinguish the light from the dark and thus promote international friendship.

In countries such as Belgium and Luxembourg, people prefer
the security of an honest living, a flourishing trade, and a well-
paid job to the "myth." To equalitarian objections they answer
with the question: Is it at present easier to succeed by work in
a true democracy or in a totalitarian state? It is true that a number of age-old values were on the point of being carried away by
the war. And this situation has left individual malice to feed
international tension. There is the hatred of the guilty towards
those who were honest during the occupation; and there is the
resentment of those deported and later rescued from concentration camps, who see justice overlooking the scoundrels who had
"collaborated."

The fate of Luxembourg has been the same as that of other
countries exasperated by the shameful contrast of real misery
with the unpunished luxury of schemers. These persons, by

dubious dealings, procured for themselves the riches which allowed them to avoid just sanctions. Here as well as elsewhere, each of the various political parties, none of which came out of the storm spotless, claims the crown of resistance. The silent sacred union of the Nazi period has vanished. Those who escaped in 1940, and who later were saluted as liberators, are now blamed for having taken shelter; those who suffered the moral agony of Nazi slavery are treated as collaborators. Everyone has a grudge against everybody else. Malice and desire for revenge abound. If there were not a new threat in the air, serious internal struggle might arise. Such a situation, however, would be as nothing compared to that which might come out of the present world anxiety: a real Nothingness, the genuine "retreat of the existent" as expressed by Heidegger.

Whatever be the attitude of the disinherited of this world (and they certainly deserve the aid of society), the dictatorial solution is but a short-lived remedy. Parasitic leaders take the place of the decadent elite. They swallow the worker who formerly was sweated by capitalist societies. Moral slavery is added to material serfdom. Far-sighted oligarchs and their faithful followers shirk active service in time of war. Instead, they keep watch on people's minds.

As to a war to liberate mankind, has it ever been proved that good can come out of evil? What is the value of the dream of a perfect society if it is to be paid for with the lives of millions of men who ask nothing but to live?

But there is little use for rational arguments against a dictator who breeds within his people a psychosis of distrust and who poisons the world by arousing fear. A dumb anxiety is created. Everyone simulates death. This is the "feigning-death" reflex of the animals. It is the fascination the wild beast exercises over its fear-ridden prey. It is the re-awakening of prehistoric ages, the crumbling of the brittle layers of the last civilization.

Pessimists believe that since there is always a war in the long run, the same causes must always lie behind it. Whether economic competition, an ideology or a dictatorship are at work, the factors engendering tensions and wars are nothing more than the "tendencies" described by McDougall: fear, food, domination, submission, deference, etc. Only the mechanisms take on new exterior forms and hide reality. War in the last analysis tends only towards rapine and booty.

If this distressing hypothesis is adopted, it is quite useless to suppose that the mass has surrendered to primitive instincts. The aggressive tendency latent in the group would need only to be focused by determined individuals who are gifted with violent prestige and strong powers of suggestion, individuals who by their very existence form the spark which produces the explosion.

The psychological background of world tension is a result of instinctive and emotional "clouds" raised by the combination of the dictator and the crowd. The basic problem of the present and of the future is that of leadership.

Bertrand Russell recently said, "For a society to progress, it must possess exceptional individuals whose activity, useful though it may be is not of a kind which can be exercised by a majority. Far advanced societies always have the tendency of excessively checking the activity of these individuals. But if, on the other hand, society exercises no control whatever, the same sort of individual initiative which might lead to useful innovations is liable to give rise to crime." These words contain a formidable truth. They also constitute a program that clearly states the problem remaining to be solved.

THE NETHERLANDS

F. W. Zeylmans van Emmichoven, M.D.

Director of the Institute of Psychology of Peoples
and Nations, The Hague.

THE human species displays a great variety of types
according to race, nationality, and region. The two World Wars
which the first half of the present century brought with it have
made it clear that we can entertain no illusions about peaceful
cooperation between these various types.

Deeply rooted in racial difference lie differences of philosophical outlook and physical constitution which seem practically unbridgeable. Conflicts arise whose roots are not to be
sought in the economic and political field alone, but which can
be shown to be due to differences in psychological disposition.
Tense relations can also exist between inhabitants of different
districts within the borders of one country.

In the various districts in Holland contrasts are marked. The
Dutchman in the south is an entirely different being from his
fellow-countryman in the North. South of the Moerdijk a more
free and easy atmosphere begins to predominate. Life is characterized by a certain joviality, cafes become more numerous,
people like living out of doors more, and despite that earnestness
which is generally typical of all Dutchmen, people in the south
cannot bring themselves to view life's various problems with
that tragic seriousness of mind so beloved by the northerner.

The Frisians in the North feel themselves a people apart.
Strict and rather severe in their Protestant conviction, they have
little in common with their Catholic compatriots in the South;
the rest of the Netherlands is another world for them. Whenever
they leave their own province they say they are going "to Holland"—meaning anywhere else in the country outside Friesland.

There are innumerable differences of this kind which could be mentioned. But despite this, all the different parts of Holland have one thing in common: they are all inhabited by "Dutchmen." True Dutchmen who, in spite of all the contrasts of character, feel themselves to be one people. The last war afforded yet another convincing demonstration of this fact.

It is beyond doubt that, however great the differences between its various component groups, a people really does form one psychological whole. This psychological whole which we know as the Netherlands and which, during the course of centuries, has developed a character of its own, stands in a definite relationship to each of the nations which surround it. It is the purpose of this chapter to describe the nature of these relationships and to seek certain principles governing their origin.

Originating sometime in the last two thousand years as a delta, partly marsh, partly forest, between the branches of the Rhine and the Maas rivers, the Netherlands is, more than any other country in Europe, a "self-made country." The provinces of North Holland, South Holland, of Zealand in the West, and Groningen and Friesland in the North, together with parts of other provinces, are what they are today thanks to a hard struggle with the sea and inland waters. A French novelist says jokingly that all countries were made by God—except Holland, which was made by the Dutch. What he says is true, at least as regards the latter half of his pronouncement. In the last four centuries, large tracts of the country have been reclaimed from the water and turned into fertile fields and meadows. The struggle with the water, which is still proceeding (witness the draining of the Zuider Zee), has left its mark on a large section of the population. It stands to reason that this struggle strengthens the people's love of freedom and independence. Deep in his heart, the Dutchman loves this land which he has won with such heavy labor.

During the period of the last four centuries this love of freedom found added expression in the struggle which had to be fought against the Hapsburgs in the Eighty Years' War (1568–1648) in order to secure that freedom of conscience and religious toleration which the Dutch regard as essential. During this long war, the Empire of Charles V, "on which the sun never set," was forced to see this small people win its freedom under the able leadership of that noble man, William the Silent. It also saw it grow in the latter stage of the war until it became one of the most powerful countries in Europe.

Side by side with the struggle *against* the water, expansion *across* the water began more and more to influence the character of the people. The East India Company, a commercial venture led by the powerful merchants of Amsterdam and other commercial towns, penetrated further and further into the Southeast Asian Archipelago and made Holland one of the great colonial powers. On a smaller scale, the West Indian Company succeeded in establishing a connection with a few South American islands. In those days the merchant fleet sailed on every ocean in the world, while the Navy seemed invincible. After four wars with England, however, this supremacy had to be surrendered to that country, whose power exceeded Holland's; all the same, Holland has succeeded in maintaining her position as a colonial power of great significance up to the present time.

A curious antithesis which still persists in the Dutch soul owes its origin, in part, to the two factors mentioned. J. Huizinga, a great historian, describes the Dutch people as "bourgeois," though not in any derogatory sense of the word. "The bourgeois conception of life has communicated itself to every group and class in our people, both rural and urban, propertied and propertyless. Our entire history reflects these bourgeois aspirations. Our forefathers kept up their resistance to the Spanish for the sake of the freedom of the bourgeois citizen. The political characteristics of the Republic were rooted in middle-class morals. . . . Our unmilitary, predominantly commercial spirit originated out of this middle-class 'bourgeois' environment."

While this "bourgeois" character is typified by life in an atmosphere of intimacy and homeliness on a small scale (which is also witnessed by the old towns with their high, narrow facades ranged along the quiet canals), there is at the same time a certain breadth of horizon, a tendency to live as one with the rest of the world. In the West and the interior of the country the old towns lie for the most part in wide-open polderland, protected from the sea and the rivers by dykes. One can imagine how safe and protected one feels living in one's own intimate little world in small towns like these. But at the same time the thoughts of the people range over the entire globe, following the ships as they sail in the oceans of the East, the West, and the South, to fill their merchant houses with goods from all over the world. And thus, in the seventeenth century in particular, there existed in the Dutchman's soul that remarkable antithesis between bourgeois "intimacy," which led, more often than not, to an intrinsic narrowness of mind, and a feeling that he was a world citizen in the widest sense of the word. Just as the seafarers ranged over the oceans of the world, men of learning and artists visited the European cultural centers of the time. Painters, sculptors and musicians not only found new inspiration in the cultural centers of Germany, Italy and France, but they also introduced into those countries much which young and vigorous Holland had itself brought forth.

However great the change may have been in Holland's relationship to Europe, Asia, and America, these intrinsic traits of character in the Dutch people still persist. The Dutchman can still be characterized as a man who feels an intimate, personal bond between himself and his home, his family and his circle of friends. At the same time, he absorbs with the greatest interest—indeed, it may well be with rather too much interest—everything which comes his way from other lands and continents.

The European peoples bordering directly on Holland are the Belgians in the South, the Germans in the East, and the English to the West across the Channel. Although economic and cultural ties exist between the Dutch and the Scandinavian countries to the North, the relationship with them is of less significance than that with Holland's three immediate neighbors.

For centuries a strong tie has existed between Holland and Belgium. The North and South Netherlands fought together for some of the time against the Spanish in the Eighty Years' War. After the fall of Napoleon there was even a brief period during which an attempt was made to unite the two countries in one kingdom. After 1830 the two kingdoms existed side by side, the relations between them being now friendly, now strained. Antwerp and Rotterdam were great trade rivals, and a number of problems arose. The question of Belgium's having direct contact with the Rhine was one such problem.

The difference between the national character of the two peoples creates both mutual attraction and mutual repulsion. The Dutchman likes going to Belgium, where he meets with a still greater degree of that freer, rather more easy-going and heartier manner which is to be found in the Southern provinces of his own country. Life in the large towns of Brussels and Antwerp has a certain southern allure for him. A quiet beauty reigns in the smaller towns of Ghent and Bruges with a touch of mysticism which provides a contrast to the intimate bourgeois character of similar small towns in Holland. Conversely, the Belgian enjoys coming to Holland and feels respect for the spiritual and intellectual capacities of the Dutch cultural leaders and admiration for the Dutch feeling for organization, order, and tidiness.

There are however, certain negative reactions which rise up in the deeper levels of consciousness. The Dutchman often regards the Belgian as nonchalant, disorderly, untidy, and as a gadabout. What he in one way finds attractive in Belgium he sees from another viewpoint as a mark of inferiority. The Belgian, on the other hand, regards the Dutchman as sober, cold, intellectual and haughty. Difficulties arise, particularly in economic matters, because the hearty, jovial manner in which the Belgian likes to do business comes up against the cold, calculating tendencies of the Dutch businessman who is out for his own advantage.

Thus in the relationship between these two closely connected countries, one sees emerge one of the central problems of the psychology of peoples—the fact that every trait of national character has both a positive and a negative side. The positive side is consciously recognized by the intellect, but the negative side finds its expression in the form of tension in the subconscious mind. At times this tension can develop into hate. Thrift and economy have as their negative aspects greed and avarice. Orderliness entails a certain pedantry. Exaggerated propriety and neatness banish goodheartedness. On the other hand, warmhearted, human joviality is in danger of driving out a deeply earnest attitude to life. An openhanded, generous character can lead to extravagance, while clinging to a comfortable material existence easily brings a kind of superficiality with it.

Thus Holland and Belgium stand in the relationship of two peoples destined to live together side by side like brothers. While they doubtless desire to do so, they are at the same time insufficiently permeated by an understanding of their differences. Holland's relationship with the Flemish-speaking part of Belgium is naturally stronger than her relationship with the other part. The French-speaking part is, by nature, more closely connected with France than with Holland.

Although France does not border directly on the Netherlands, French culture has nevertheless had a great influence on the development of the Dutch. Towards the end of the nineteenth century and in the beginning of the present century, Dutch literature bore witness to this. If one reads the "Hague" novels of Louis Couperus, one becomes aware of the fluency and the delight with which French was spoken in certain circles at the time.

It appears to have been France's especial task in recent centuries to exert a cultural influence over great areas of Europe. And, after all, what language lends itself to such a task better than French, with its subtle feeling for form, rhythm, and harmony? England has undergone the same influence since William the Conqueror crossed over from Normandy. In Germany, it was chiefly Frederick the Great who was strongly influenced by the enlightened thought of French philosophers, and who invited Voltaire to his court. In Russia, as the novels of Leo Tolstoy show, it was customary to use French in aristocratic circles.

And thus in Holland, too, and from the nature of things to an even greater extent in Belgium, French influence was very considerable.

In the course of the centuries, the relationship with England went through various different phases. After the four wars with England already mentioned, wars by which the struggle for world power was decided in England's favor, Holland was driven back to occupy a more modest place in the world of the eighteenth century. In the beginning of the nineteenth century, after the fall of Napoleon, Dutch colonies were even under British control for some years. After the middle of the nineteenth century there was a definite recovery in Holland, which, as often appears to be the case, showed itself in the fields of economics and culture simultaneously. The Boer War, however, engendered a very definite dislike of British politics among the Dutch people. Small in number but stubborn in their resistance, the Transvaal Boers of Dutch origin succeeded in holding out for a long time before they eventually got the worst of it. The rich mineral deposits of the Transvaal seemed to possess a great attraction for England, which was already powerful and still expanding. In those years, the Dutch people, unable themselves to give large-scale aid to their South African brothers, lived in hatred of "perfidious Albion."

Even in the First World War, the sympathy of a very large proportion of Dutchmen was with Germany; this was especially so in Rotterdam, which maintained continuous contact with that country via the Waal and the Rhine. Afterwards, however, an even stronger bond developed with England. The close relationship between the two countries became clearly apparent. By nature both are democratic and parliamentary, and despite all party differences they both have a strong streak of liberalism. A certain soberness of mind causes them to dislike extremes, while a certain practical-mindedness prevents them from losing themselves in political illusions.

Although economic competition exists, many products are exchanged; and by the gradual improvement in communications, the two countries were able to come into ever closer contact with one another.

Thus the English language became better known in Holland and gradually drove French into second place. Indeed, in some circles people preferred to use English expressions, and "sorry" took the place of "pardon." Sports like football and tennis made the English more and more popular. The diffusion of English literature also increased, with innumerable detective stories and subtle novels of psychological importance.

Like France, England also exerted a cultural influence on Holland. The inner discipline and self-control which are more or less natural to the Englishman, as well as his dislike of rowdiness, did not fail to have a civilizing influence on the Dutch. Not, however, without evoking a certain irritation at deeper levels. Phlegm plays a fundamental role in the unconscious life of both peoples. But the Dutchman's phlegmatic nature is clearly colored by a sanguine streak. Just as the weather is constantly changing in coastal areas with wind, thunderstorms, and rain occurring suddenly, and with the air in constant movement, so the Dutch mind has its sudden changes. The Dutchman is more emotional, more active, and more restless than the Englishman, whose placidity often irritates him. He is less of an onlooker regarding what is happening in the world. He feels that the Englishman takes rather too long to abandon his role of an observer and to take action.

Germany, bordering on Holland's eastern frontier, represented an important hinterland for trade and industry. This being so, a very strong bond has existed between the two countries for centuries. For Hollanders of smaller means, Germany was also favored as a tourists' country. Here and there, just beyond the Dutch border, begin the splendid forests with which Germany is so richly endowed, while the Rhine Valley, with its mountains and its old romantic air, had a great attraction. If one also takes into consideration the fact that up to the First World War living in Germany was very cheap and that everything breathed an air of neatness and goodhearted hospitality, one can easily understand why every year thousands of Dutch holidaymakers found enjoyment there.

In many faculties in the Dutch universities, the German element predominated. German textbooks were used for the study of philosophy and psychology and in several fields connected with medical science. They were thorough, systematic and exhaustive, and were much sought after for study, despite the compression of the style and their piling up of facts, which made their reading an almost impossible task. They could always be consulted on any subject as a kind of encyclopaedia. One could always turn with pleasure to a witty French book or a practical English one for further guidance.

Practically every Dutchman felt a strong dislike for the Prussian element which always made itself felt in Germany. In this respect, the Dutchman's love of freedom and independence, the product of centuries of development, came into conflict with the German tendency to get involved in a system and to subjugate oneself readily to its compulsions. His soberness of mind and his realism were always put off by the atmosphere of illusion in which those who believe in systems, and think they can find an expression for spiritual ideals in them, live.

The Dutchman has little sympathy for militarism. Indeed, one can say that everything to do with the military system and with "drill" is anathema to him. But this does not mean that he will not make great sacrifices for the defense of his country and even risk his life for its sake. This was sufficiently demonstrated during the German occupation in the Second World War. But he wants to be free to fight for his liberty himself, on his own responsibility, and in his own way. At the same time he is guided in this respect by a great love for traditions which in his own country are as good as holy: the traditions of freedom of speech, freedom of the press, freedom of philosophical belief, freedom of association with those he regards as his spiritual brothers, and freedom to harbor all those in need. Thus it was that centuries ago the Portuguese Jews found hospitality in Holland; later the Huguenots found similar hospitality; and more recently, the great number of those who fled from the national socialist regime in Germany found refuge in Holland. Books prohibited in other countries were already being published in Amsterdam in the seventeenth century. After the First World War, countless German, Austrian, and Hungarian children were cared for by Dutch families.

From the psychological viewpoint, it was the greatest of the national socialist regime's blunders to trample on this tradition the way it did. The notices "No Jews Allowed," which were put up during the occupation in all the public parks were sufficient in themselves to cause the Dutch to rise up in rebellion, even though there was no especial sympathy for the Jews in Holland.

Huizinga points out that the Dutch people has, in the course of the centuries, made itself familiar with the spirit of the French, British, and German peoples. "If there is one respect," he said, "in which the Dutch might well be proud, it lies in the fact that no other people has shown itself capable of assimilating, so evenly, three different cultural influences and of understanding so precisely the spirit of each of the three." And he very rightly draws attention to the fact that the possibility of assimilating these foreign cultures so evenly depends on our possessing a language of our own, by means of which we are able to preserve a certain impartiality and to provide ourselves with our own mirror in which to catch the reflection of what is foreign.

One does not on the whole observe any impulse in the Dutch to exaggerate their own nationality; indeed, in certain circles just the opposite tendency is remarked. The Dutch are, by nature and inclination, born world citizens, though in their hearts their relationship to the world may find its expression in a "bourgeois" form. In the South Netherlands and particularly in Flanders, where a similar inclination towards world citizenship is present, the development of this sense of world citizenship is to a certain extent hampered by the conflict of tongues.

Is it possible to discover a psychological basis for the differences between the various peoples of the world? Whether it is or not, it is necessary to make the attempt. Attention has been paid in this chapter to a limited group of European relationships —and to the Dutch point of view in particular. There are, however, many other countries in Europe whose culture has not been without its influence on Holland. Italy and Spain, the Balkans, Russia, Poland, and the countries of Scandinavia have lent Holland something of their spirit, their literature, their art, and their economy. Europe presents a picture of a collection of peoples of great number and variety which have emerged from a process of development which has been going on for two thousand years. One can find Dutch towns which were originally built as forts by the Roman conquerors at the beginning of our era. Eight centuries later, Charlemagne built a castle in Nijmegen. Its Carolingian chapel still exists. This process of historical development often began much earlier in other countries.

An endless complexity of alternate growth, decay, and revival of individual peoples and of their relationship with other peoples needs to be analyzed. Yet political history—the history of the formation of national states and of wars—tells us but little. Cultural history and the history of art provide the necessary addition, but even when all this material has been collected, one cannot help feeling that many of the developmental processes to be studied in connection with the various peoples still slumber in the secret recesses of the mind.

One can well understand why Americans find it difficult to grasp the complexity that is Europe, and why they often ask why the smaller and larger states which comprise Europe cannot join together in one united whole. A study of the psychology of peoples which takes all the factors into account makes it clear that a union of the nations of Europe is not only a far more complicated question than that of the United States of America, but is also a problem of an entirely different nature, of a different spiritual order.

However, a start has been made with Benelux, a union of the three small countries of Belgium, Holland and Luxembourg. From the economic and political point of view, this union is a matter of necessity. But many are possessed of the will to go beyond mere necessity and to work freely to forge a spiritual bond of such strength that one day one will be able to speak of a true community of peoples.

Although Luxembourg is small, it has a by no means unimportant metal industry. It is also a very pleasant and much-visited tourist country. Many Dutch people spend their holidays there. Culturally it has still to develop a marked character of its own. Its men of learning usually study at colleges in Germany, France,

or Belgium. Yet it seems that this modest attempt at cooperation between three countries could serve as an example for many
others.

It is of the greatest importance that the psychology of peoples
be applied in practice. Only when this is done can we expect that
the international tension which still exists in the world will be
replaced by mutual understanding. Then, instead of causing catastrophes time and time again, these tensions will lead to the
enrichment and the strengthening of the mutual ties between
countries.

Much would have been gained if political leaders would let
themselves be advised by a board of experts on the psychology
of peoples. Such a board would consist exclusively of people capable of judging the problems that arise from the point of view
of psychology and common humanity. They would need to be
completely disinterested.

From the beginning of this century we have been "one world."
It is our task to make this "one world" a place where individuals,
nations, and races can achieve full inner and outer development.

The difficulties involved may seem to many to be great, perhaps insuperable. There is certainly no room for illusion. Yet by
the international cooperation of many experts in the fields of
science, art, sociology, economics, and politics, it will be possible to break new ground.

And thus one may ask: is any other choice possible? Are we
not faced in this "one world" of ours with the alternative of either
having to die together or live together? And does not to live together mean to work together to create that "one humanity"
which all of us, from the depths of our being, desire? Is it not a
sacred ideal which has been proclaimed for us by all the truly
great minds that have ever existed?

SOUTH AFRICA

Bernard Notcutt, Ph.D.

Professor of Psychology at The University of Natal,
Durban.

PLATO, in his *Republic,* developed a parallel between the organization of the individual and of the state. He
sought an understanding of justice in the individual by studying justice in the state. This was the first attempt in European
thought to build a parallel between psychology and politics.
Since then the theme has been worked over many times. A great
variety of fruitful analogies has been developed.

The title of our book implies that war is something like the aggressive acts of an individual. Hence we are discounting purely
sociological descriptions, which tell us that wars arise from
population pressure, or are the inevitable results of technical
change, or of ideological differences ("communism and capitalism cannot live side by side"), or result from the malignant activities of armament manufacturers, international bankers, anarchists or propagandists. No one would deny that any of these
may be important elements in an international situation, but insofar as we are trying to use psychology for understanding war,
we must bring the problem back to the motives of individual
human beings. It is not our business to give a complete account
of the causes of war, but merely to show how psychology is relevant to the solution of these problems.

The second implication of the title is that international tension is pathological, a disease, something that ought not to occur.
The suggestion is not merely that war is evil, but that it is in some
degree unnatural and exceptional, that the ordinary and proper
state of nations is one of peace. This seems obvious, a truism, to
most of modern Western society. But it would not have been

taken for granted in other times and places. It is a characteristic belief or postulate of a business man's society that every man really wants his own good, understood in terms of life, wealth, happiness, and other utilitarian values. There is the assumption that no sane or decent person wants or could want war; that conflict is not inevitable, but deeply based on a natural human aggressiveness. It hints at a rejection of the "struggle for survival" school, who suppose that war is a continuation of the general biological process of natural selection, and also a rejection of the "you-can't-change-human-nature" school, the "underneath-a-thin-veneer" critics.

The title of our book is one that fits well with the American dream, the belief in a plastic human nature, to which any extreme of good or evil is possible in the right or wrong setting. This is a modern and slightly toughened-up form of the old belief (so widely prevalent in the eighteenth century when the Republic was founded, and so deeply woven into its Constitution) in the natural goodness of man, and the natural harmony of interests, when these are not perverted by the machination of priests and kings. Such a faith would not go unquestioned in South Africa, where a belief in original sin is strongly held in influential Calvinist circles.

The third implication is contained in the appeal to the scientist, rather than to the saint, statesman, or philosopher, for salvation. This is partly a tribute to the immense prestige of the American scientist, and is partly due to dissatisfaction with the customary discussion of international affairs in terms of morality. In many ways moral argument on such questions appears inadequate and unconvincing, especially in a relatively free country, where you can hear several sides to a question. Our systems of moral thinking are not so objective as to elicit the same answer from every observer, however he is situated. Moral judgments, whether founded on religion or on some irreligious philosophy, have too much local coloring, are too dependent on geography, to be altogether reliable. Most moral systems are expressed in universal terms as systems of obligation that are impartial and independent of time or place. But in their application they take on a national or sectarian coloring and are easily subject to rationalizing and other manipulation ("I am determined, you are obstinate, he is a pig-headed fool").

Emery Reves, in his book *The Anatomy of Peace*, brought this out in an impressive way. He gave an account of political history between the world wars from the points of view of five great powers in turn. He showed that, without any gross distortion of facts, each of the five could make a case to show that it alone had consistently followed a path of virtue and justice, while every other nation varied between weakness and malevolence. It is plain that moral ideas are too slippery and ambiguous in their application to be of much use for solving international disputes. To believe that we are right and they are wrong is no doubt necessary once the shooting has started, but the wise man delays this moment as long as possible.

Political philosophers like James Burnham and E. H. Carr have made this point of view familiar to a wide public in recent years. Many people, despairing of moral argument, have hoped to find stability in the objective approach of the scientist. Traditionally, science stands apart from morality, yet in the social sciences there is a borderland in which scientific results appear to have a direct significance for morality. When a doctor gives a patient advice, he does so because he can assume that the patient's aim is health. The health of the body is an idea that most of us understand fairly well in a general way. But the health of the mind is a much less definite concept. Except in extreme cases, there would be little agreement about its application. It is possible for a psychiatrist, under the guise of giving a patient advice about how to preserve health, to smuggle in a lot of his own moral opinions. There is, of course, no reason why a psychiatrist should not have opinions on morality. But it is undesirable that they should masquerade as scientific knowledge, and borrow the prestige of his medical skill. Particularly this applies to the present project, the analysis of the causes of war. If the psychopathologist can apply his knowledge to a better understanding of war, he will be doing a service to humanity. But he must beware of putting up a prophet's signboard, and announcing that if only people will follow his advice, everything will be all right. In their present need, people will turn anywhere for help, and we must be careful not to borrow the prestige of Science (with a capital S) to put across our own opinions. We must avoid, too, those forceful tones that worried people so often assume in times of crisis, that insistent rap on the table, and the strident voice crying "Listen to me, or else!"

We must remember, too, that there is an important difference between the study of the individual and of society as a whole. In studying the neurotic individual, the psychopathologist takes as his norm the society in which he and his patient live; he can ask whether his patient is adjusted to society, whether he fulfills its demands, is accepted, finds a place in it, can be happy and effective there. In studying international relations, there are no such criteria of "normality." What usually happens in practice is that each observer takes as his norm the standards of his own society, or such of them as he approves of, and praises or condemns the rest of the world according as it fits these standards. As Emery Reves puts it, this results in a Ptolemaic description of a world that needs to be Copernican. (In Ptolemy's account of astronomy, our earth was the center, just as for amateur political philosophers, their own country is usually the center).

The psychologist who hopes to contribute something to the preservation of peace must be prepared to stand outside his most cherished beliefs. He must not approach the problem with the assumption that peace is possible only under communism, socialism, capitalism, Catholicism, democracy, or some other arrangement. To say that there will never be peace until everyone is like yourself is the mark of Ptolemaic man.

Let us now look more closely at this body of knowledge that we call psychopathology and see what it contains that will help our task of understanding war. The relevant parts of the subject are concerned with disorders of motivation, and the wide range of human misfortunes that they can induce. There are certain common features in the background of all such misfortunes. There is an illogic of the emotions, different from, and often contradictory to, the logic of reason; the art of psychopathology consists in learning how to understand this illogic. Its significance for political affairs lies in the fact that the same kinds of illogical thinking are found in the privacy of the neuroses and in the public arena of politics. Plato's parallel still holds good.

Disturbances of motivation consist sometimes in wanting things that the outer world denies us, and sometimes in wanting simultaneously things that cannot go together. One of the commonest backgrounds of neurotic disturbance is some form of mental conflict, usually the fear of one's own impulses; the recognition that some desires are so intensely felt that they would, if carried into action, bring one to destruction. The wishes that are most likely (in the Western world) to get us into trouble are of three kinds: (1) the need to excel, to be "first horse," to be on top. If we invest our emotions too heavily in success, we become vulnerable; (2) sexual desires, which are often insistent and unmannerly, and cut across the established rules of society. They offend those by whom we wish to be loved; and (3) aggressive impulses, desires to hurt, to kill and to destroy.

Although conflicts over these desires are usually at the root of the trouble, they are not often conscious to the person who suffers from them. The possibility of self-deception has long been understood, both in the self-analysis of religious meditation, as in the *Confessions* of St. Augustine, and in the cynical observations of social critics like Voltaire and Thackeray; but it is only since Freud that we have come to realize the full scope of this process.

The reasons for our failure to understand our own motives are chiefly two: one is that the knowledge is painful or humiliating, so that we find one device or another for avoiding or neglecting it; the other is that many of our attitudes are residues of experiences that we had in early childhood, when we were too young to understand or remember them properly, and when our circumstances were so different that it is hard to see the connection with the present. Although these experiences of early childhood naturally vary from one person to another, they contain certain common features, or familiar patterns: experiences relating to choices of protection and freedom; those relating to receiving and getting food and drink; attitudes to authority and discipline; early experiences of sexuality, and the mode of its suppression; experiences of hate, jealousy and aggression, and the means of controlling them. Early experiences, partly forgotten and partly repressed, established basic attitudes which are likely to last throughout life.

Some psychologists would add a third reason why our acts may be unintelligible to ourselves. Our acts, they hold, are not merely ours. They also repeat experiences of our remote ancestors, whose goals and thoughts we have in some mysterious way inherited. In the English-speaking world, however, this kind of explanation is usually considered unnecessary. The problem is handled in a different way, by means of culture and personality studies. Here social psychologists working among primitive tribes have been able to show the adult personality typical of a particular tribe is in large measure a reflection of the methods of child-rearing that are customary there. Just as Freud was able to show many subtle relations between a child's early experiences and his adult personality, so by an extension of his ideas it became possible to do the same for a cultural pattern.

National characters perpetuate themselves not merely by imitation, but as a direct response to customs of child training. We can expect that those who are reared under the traditional stern dominating father and tender submissive mother of the classical Oedipus complex will develop an authoritarian character, with admiration for power and contempt for weakness; that an American child brought up in an aseptic regime, bottle-fed on a formula at regular hours, and prematurely toilet-trained, will grow up with unsatisfied mouth cravings (shown by a continual need for candy, cigars and sweatergirls), a habit of referring to his wrist-watch, and a compulsion to do things in a hurry; that a Zulu baby whose mother has enormous breasts and feeds him generously on demand until he is eighteen months old will grow up with a cheerful disposition and small inclination for insurance policies or thought for the morrow. Had we but world enough and time, we might be able to map out a program for baby-rearing that would reduce aggressiveness in every country, and prevent war in this way. But we need to act quickly. It will be a couple of generations before Dr. Gesell's "new" method of feeding babies will have decisively altered the American character. And world peace will not wait for that.

The technique of national character analysis is very new. It may be expected to have a considerable effect on world affairs when its methods are improved, as they undoubtedly can be. It involves far more than a study of infantile feeding habits, though these are convenient for illustrating the method. In every culture there is a set of what Shils calls "implicit hypotheses" about the nature of man and the meaning of history, which are acquired early, and hardly ever formulated for discussion. These implicit hypotheses belonging to the cultural tradition correspond to the unconscious memories of the individual. Just as the residue of early experience molds one's individual character and opinions in ways that one does not ordinarily suspect, so the cultural tradition in which we grow up is taken for granted as a background for thinking. A good example is to be seen in the English and Afrikaner communities in South Africa. Most members of the Afrikaner community have ancestors who took part in the Kaffir wars of the nineteenth century, and who shared in the eventual conquest and pacification of the natives. These achievements, typified by the Battle of Blood River, which is celebrated annually at the religious ceremonies of Dingaan's Day, form the center of a group or national tradition, which is constantly reinforced in home, school and church.

In contrast, most English South Africans have no ancestors who fought in the Kaffir wars. If they have, the memory of them usually has no great emotional importance. The British soldiers who fought the Kaffir wars usually did so as a professional duty, without considering themselves the founders of a nation or the saviors of a creed. There are no committees, churches or celebrations to recall their achievements today. The liberal and humanitarian thought of eighteenth- and nineteenth-century Europe, which formed so important a part of the English settler's heritage, did not directly reach the ancestors of the Afrikaner; when it did reach them, it was rejected as unsuitable to the needs of frontiersmen. The Voortrekkers trekked partly as a protest against the enforced liberation of their slaves.

This contrast in backgrounds makes a difference in the "implicit hypotheses" of the two groups, most markedly in their attitudes to the natives living in the country now. To the typical Afrikaner, any weakening of caste domination is at once a danger signal. It is an act of treachery to the Founding Fathers, to whom he owes everything. He recognizes a duty to be just in personal dealings with the natives, and to teach him Christianity, but never a duty to recognize him as an equal or to share citizen's rights with him. To the typical English South African, the caste system is a convenience, and indeed a present necessity if his civilized standards of life are to be maintained. But to him the system has no inherent validity; indeed, he is often uneasy about it, and expects the present inequality to diminish gradually with the spread of education and other civilized practices. It is not surprising that each group finds the other's concepts of native policy not merely irritating and peculiar, but a threat to justice and future security. Psychologists may be able to render important services to humanity by making nations more intelligible to one another.

The unconscious memories based on individual experience are not entirely separate from the implicit hypotheses derived from cultural history. We can see the unity of the two by the study of group identifications. A growing boy is said to identify himself with his father when he aims at growing up to be like father, to take father's place in the world, to marry some one like mother, to inherit father's property. Identifying with a person in this sense does not mean suffering from any delusion that one is really some one else; it simply means imitating the other person or feeling his interest to be one's own. As people grow up, they can go on to many other group-identifications, often derived from the original father-identifications. Many types of institution—a political party, church, regiment, business, may become a parent symbol, or be regarded as an extension of himself. It is principally through this mechanism that man's primary selfishness is overcome, and effective organized activity is made possible. Most significantly for our purpose, a man may turn his country into a father- or mother-symbol (fatherland, mother country, *la patrie, vaderland*).

These identifications may shift about in a surprising way without disturbing one's private illogic. When a South African team beat a New Zealand team at rugby football, the weediest officeboy in Cape Town threw out his chest and felt that he had done something pretty good. Here the rugby team, and South Africa in general, had become himself. At other times, one's country becomes a powerful protecting father, stern but just, who metes out punishment; a kindly smiling mother who nurses one's baby self, or an unhappy female ravished by an insolent invader. These images are constantly employed by writers and cartoonists, and find a ready response in the unconscious memories of readers. It is through this identification of the state with the parents that the operation of conscience may be extended from the family to society in general, so that a sense of duty comes to operate to some extent in public affairs. We develop a "cultural superego." This includes the duty to serve the state, to obey the law, and to respect authority.

Of course people do not always love and obey their parents; but the identification of the parent with the state can work equally well for those who do not. Many revolutionaries, especially of the middle-class radical type, have begun by hating their own parents, and have later transferred their dislike of authority to other forms of government. The poet Shelley is a famous example of this logic. Many criminals appear to reason in the same way; William Healy found that many young delinquents had been rejected by their parents in childhood; so that aggression against society meant (among other things) a revenge on their parents.

The identification of the state with the parents, however, is not automatic and inevitable. When the parents themselves are strongly against the government, or when the state in some way rejects the love of parent or child, then there may be discord between attitude to parents and attitude to the state. Particularly this problem arises in a caste society like South Africa, where there are large sections of the community who occupy an inferior status. If this is an established arrangement, people may acquiesce and live comfortably within their status; but if their status is made insecure, or depressed still further, it might become impossible to identify the state with the father. In such cases we might find a strongly developed sense of obligation within the family, which does not effectively extend outside. One has the impression that this often happens with native criminals in South Africa, though not much good evidence exists. If the state does not succeed in becoming a father symbol, then its authority depends merely on its success in punishing criminals.

When such an identification of state with parent is made, the powerful ambivalent feelings belonging to early family situations get mixed up with public affairs—the politics of the nursery confuses the politics of the world. The complications introduced by these emotional forces make international disputes so difficult to settle, particularly when they are conducted in public. Diplomats in private can afford to adopt a sensible utilitarian attitude to give here and take there. But in public everything is a matter of honor; we live in a world of symbols. The very mechanism by which man is able to overcome his selfishness and take a public-spirited part in great affairs is also the greatest obstacle to peace between nations. The unit with which one identifies may vary greatly in size, from an individual to a huge state or area like the U.S.A. or U.S.S.R.; and there is no tendency for identification to weaken as size increases. One individual may, of course, make a whole hierarchy of identifications—with the city of Durban, of which he is proud to be a citizen, with the province of Natal, with the Union as a whole, with the British Commonwealth. This has led many people to wonder whether this allegiance could not be given, at any rate in some degree, to some universal symbol which would transcend national loyalties. To some extent this has happened, as when Basuto tribesmen revered the Great White Queen Victoria, whom they had never seen; as the Delphic Oracle was a common court of appeal for all Greece; or as the Pope was in some degree during certain periods of the Middle Ages.

Could the United Nations come to serve as a "good father"? Indeed, there is no theoretical reason why this should not happen. But we cannot expect it to happen easily or automatically. One requirement appears to be the presence of some contrasting image, just as one cannot see a figure except against a contrasting background. Some cynics have even supposed that the United Nations will never unite except to repel an invasion from Mars. In any event, the father-image will grow only with actual evidence of its power to command, punish, and protect, and as its symbols become part of daily experience and common reverence. We need to know much more than we do about group identification. We have general ideas about it, and can usually recognize its occurrence, but cannot predict at all accurately how an instance will work out. We need to study the phenomenon by methods that are more scientific and less dependent on intuition than is customary in this type of work.

A large field of psychopathology consists of a study of the devices by which we avoid direct recognition of a painful and devastating reality. These protective devices (repression, isolation, projection, reaction formation and so forth) successively deceive the person who adopts them and sometimes deceive other people as well. But they often fail to solve his problem; they fail to create the happiness and security that he desires. Sometimes they may create a kind of security, but at the cost of happiness, as with an obsessional, who, by restricting his activities to a limited sequence of rituals, may remain relatively free from anxiety. But more often we find that the very device that is used to escape from one anxiety helps to create another.

This situation may occur in various ways, but one way is particularly relevant to understanding international tensions. I am afraid of a neighbor because he has power over me, and I feel hostile to him because of some supposed threat; to justify my own hostility, I assume that he feels hostile to me; this is *projection,* a defense mechanism so universal and automatic that it often seems like genuine logic. As the situation develops, every hostile act on either side produces more fear, more hostility, and more projection, so that a vicious circle is set up. Any severe and prolonged neurosis is based on such a vicious circle. People are unkind to me, so I cannot trust them; but when I do not trust them, they withdraw their love, and so I hate them all the more. Thus a device originally adopted to protect one from anxiety really serves only to intensify it.

It is obvious that this vicious circle of fear, hostility, projection, and fear, plays a great part in international tension. Fears which perhaps begin as an illusion gradually create their own reality. Neighbors become dangerous because they are feared. My neighbors are dangerous, and I must arm. They are afraid because I am arming. To suggest at this stage that if one disarmed, it would lessen fear, and also lessen hostility, conjures up images of being delivered helpless to a powerful and ruthless antagonist who would instantly take advantage of one's simplicity. And indeed the outcome is unpredictable. Switzerland gained, Holland lost; Sweden gained, Norway lost. Either horse is a gamble. In the individual neurosis, as in international tension, we get the dreadful feeling that everything we do to avert the crisis only serves to bring it nearer.

How can such situations ever be resolved? It is hard to sum up compactly, and in many cases we are much surer about the fact of the cure than about its cause; but so far as the individual neurosis is concerned, there are two main ways: one is by a radical change in external circumstance—someone dies, loses his job, leaves home, inherits money, breaks his leg; the whole web of personal relations has to be rebuilt, and with it the symptoms may disappear. The other way is through psychotherapy, and though we cannot enter here into the dynamics of this disputed process, we can say that one important element is gaining universal logic on the problem.

So far as we in South Africa are concerned, the immediate fear of powerful and threatening neighbors has not seriously affected our country during the last forty years. Though we have participated actively in both World Wars and our men have served on many battlefields, the quarrel has been for us not a strictly personal one, and we have been able to adopt, until recently, a high-minded and disinterested attitude toward world affairs. This was one factor that enabled General Smuts to make so great a contribution to the founding of the League of Nations and of the United Nations. Our direct acquaintance is not with the enemy across the border, but with the schism in the soul. The Union was founded on a series of uneasy compromises, typified by its two capitals, two flags, two official languages (apart from half a dozen unofficial ones spoken by the majority), two national anthems (or possibly three), and four categories of citizen status. No wonder that Smuts wrote a philosophy of holism!

While these complex arrangements indicate a spirit of tolerance and mutual adaptability, they also indicate the presence of strains and anxieties. The different races and cultural groups within the community show little tendency to coalesce. We are not a melting-pot. And in the attempt to find a workable adjustment, our statesmen meet all the problems that are seen on the larger scale of world affairs. International politics, like charity, can begin at home. The problems are as urgent to us as are the larger problems nearer to the world's storm centers. And the need for wisdom is as great.

SPAIN

A. Vallejo Nágera, M.D.

Professor of Psychiatry, University of Madrid, President of the Spanish Neuropsychiatric Association.

WORLD tension presents particular characteristics which cannot be interpreted without a previous knowledge of the background of the present psychological situation. Spaniards have been living in constant torment since the revolution of 1931, which marked a change of political regime that brought personal persecutions, confiscation of properties, burning of convents and churches, and open assassinations. The suffering built up during the first five years exploded in a frightful Civil War (1936–1939) which caused a million casualties on the battlefields and 300,000 officially verified assassinations of citizens who were guilty of no other crime than that of holding anti-communist ideas.

After the Civil War, Spain was forced to remain neutral in World War II, threatened by a powerful enemy on the Pyrenees frontier, which kept her from enjoying her well-earned peace. This delicate position continued when the victory of the Allies permitted Russia her imperialist expansion for vengeance against the people who had declared themselves against communism and had defeated it on the battlefields. The situation prolonged the agony of a Spanish nation longing for quiet.

The warlike climate that has been reigning in Spain for twenty years is reflected in the people, who oscillate between more or less intense emotional reactions and deep psychological disturbances. Spanish psychiatrists have been well able to note these psychological reactions, as the practice of their medical specialty brings them into daily contact with persons whose nervous systems have become unbalanced.

The peak of Spanish anxiety came during the Civil War, in which every person took part; whether he wished to or not, every Spaniard participated in the revolution and the counterrevolution. Some were at the battlefront and some in the ranks of the political parties. But no one could remain outside the struggle. Whether on the National or the Communist side, Spaniards knew that it was a war without quarter, for victory or death, with their own destiny and that of their children at stake. Loss of their dear ones and destruction of their properties had as much effect on Spaniards as the roar of battle or the bombardment of cities. The spirit of twenty million people was submitted to intense anguish.

The victory of the Franco party in 1939 brought tranquillity and peace to the great majority of Spanish homes, since hardly a tenth of those who were responsible for the horrible criminality of the war had to suffer the consequences of their defeat. The mildness of the punishments and the later amnesties relieved the people, and the lack of political parties augured an era of peace and work, unfortunately interrupted by the outbreak of the Second World War. The geographical position of Spain made her a prize coveted by both belligerent groups, and it was difficult for her to preserve neutrality, even though the desire to stay out of war predominated among the Spaniards. Today Spain is in exactly the same position, but now the nation understands that it will be forced to participate in a future war, and this realization accounts for the special psychological condition of the national state of mind. The population fears the end of the peace that it bought with its own blood.

This chapter is being written without any political purpose; dictated according to orthodox scientific criteria, and is intended as an impartial report on the pathological mental conditions created by the anxiety that grew out of the Spanish Civil War.

Laymen and far too many specialists in the field have conjectured a great deal on the so-called war psychoses or mental disorders. Impartial observers of former wars, such as the Franco-Prussian war of 1870–1871, realized even then that many people remained psychologically unchanged by going through the un-

interrupted ordeals of war. In the same way it was observed that
while some citizens, comfortably situated in the rear areas far
from the battlelines and their danger, would undergo serious
mental disturbances, the great majority of combat soldiers maintained perfect mental health.

Actually, the emotions and dangers of war are no longer limited to the battle areas nor to the civilian population close to
them. War has ceased being a chivalrous and more or less honor-
able pastime for those who are willing to take part in it for reasons of position or patriotic duty. In our day, military service is
obligatory, and when war arrives the civilian population is mili-
tarized and forced to abandon family, home, work, social life,
and all comforts. Apart from those few who benefit from the
war—like farmers and shopkeepers—the immense majority suffer
damage to their interests, and all risk their lives. A single bomb
can destroy a community, and the planes carrying them over
enormous distances at inconveivable speeds drop them almost
at random.

The population participating in a war is thus submitted to a
most intense emotional tension. But if the psychological reactions caused by this tension are briefer and less intense at the
battlefront than in the rear areas, this is because at the front the
reactions are inhibited or compensated for by the state of concentrated anger directed against the enemy and the desire to
satisfy personally one's thirst for vengeance. In the rear areas,
the pathological reactions of the mind are the results of prolonged mental states which sensitize the personality and prepare
it so that the most insignificant and unexpected stimulus can destroy mental equilibrium. The mental changes that appear spontaneous really come from long before, as a result of an unconscious elaboration on the war experiences and of the constant
though unconscious rumination and mulling over the disagree-
able incidents of the war and the personal dangers involved.

World tension originates in fear and the uncertainty of the
future. This pathological mental reaction to war should be studied more from the point of view of mental hygiene than from
that of psychiatry. Actually, there are no such things as war psy-

choses, since the mental disorders observed in wartime are no different from those noted in peacetime. The specific psychoses observed are an index of the reactivity of the people to the fear of war.

It is curious that the forms of mental reaction to war should be so very limited, and that they should restrict themselves to a few types, always the same for the millions of beings all over our globe. This limitation of the qualitative psychic reactions is due to the biopsychical structure of the human being which is controlled in its formation and development by predetermined laws and which consists of inherited bodily and psychological mechanisms which assure its survival. These somatic (form of body) and psychic (temperament) structures offer a limited number of variations, so few that biotypology—the study of biological types—is concerned with but three or four.

The forms of mass pathological reaction are still more limited than those of the individual. For when the individual psychological processes are interfered with (especially the higher-level functions of the mind), the masses are animated more by feelings than by ideas; they lack the control to hold back the free manifestation of their instinctive tendencies, and it is the latter which come into play. The masses wander in indecision, orienting the collective psychological reaction to the effective environmental values.

The abnormal states of mind of the mob have more influence on the production of induced mass psychoses than on the origination of individual reactions. It may be inferred that the present world tension caused by the imminence of war causes definite pathological conditions, more of the mob than of the individual. On the other hand, when emotional factors pile up on the particular individual, or when he finds himself in exceptional emotional situations (loss of family or property), individual war psychoses sometimes result from the morbid intensity of the state of mind. In other cases he subconsciously takes refuge in mental disorder, raising a protective barrier against his environment. He ignores the war with its dangers and incidents.

In the production of pathological psychic reactions, which we generally call war psychoses, both psychological and physical factors take part. The world anxiety of the moment does not exclusively bring about the fear of death, but a rather varied series of conditions. The nature and importance of these differ somewhat with each nation, but they are approximately the same in all countries. In Spain some of them acquire special characteristics due to political and economic circumstances and to the perils the country has gone through.

The anxiety of people in our time can be explained if we take into account the fact that the state of mind brought about by a psychic incident lasts longer in the conscious and subconscious than does the mental picture corresponding to the particular emotion. Conduct is thus controlled for a certain length of time even though the original event may seem forgotten. Ordinarily there are four psychic incidents which maintain the emotional state of the masses and which give rise to the pathological reactions we term war psychoses: *anguish*, a severe mental or bodily pain when facing a decision or fear; *anger*, caused by injustices experienced; *terror*, in the face of tragedy; and *despair*, caused by irreparable losses.

The courageous or timid conduct of the soldier at a given moment is more the result of his emotional reaction than of any reflective thought he may have had. The rear-area citizen has much more time to think about things, and for that reason he is much more fearful than the man fighting at the front. Certain definite environmental factors have a decided influence on courage and fear, and can push the masses towards heroism or shameful flight. We have been able to observe in all wars, national and foreign, that the emotional tensions of the armed forces and of the rear-area citizens go through great oscillations according to the course of events; and that the enthusiasm of the first few months of war usually changes to confident optimism for the victors and to progressive defeatism for those losing the battles.

For many, the war destroyed the economic present and future, and they are now going through austerity and poverty which are all the more difficult because these people previously were sufficiently well off to satisfy their needs and even their whims. Also suffering from the war are persons of a more modest social class who, through work and economy, saved up enough to assure them a comfortable old age. Other persons were beginning brilliant careers which were interrupted by the war, and it has been hard for them to overcome the obstacles in their paths. While there may be a few who have profited from the war, the great majority of the world population are anxious about the future that awaits them. A new war would increase their misery to an almost intolerable degree.

This anxiety about the future particularly affects our financiers and capitalists, the principal victims of our civil war. On the other hand, it does not concern the Spanish working class, for they alone have received advantages from the present political regime, not only by the institution of social security, higher salaries, and shorter working hours, but also by being freed from political struggles, forced strikes, and syndical quotas. They are able to work freely and without drains on their earnings. The mass of Spanish office workers, however, worry over the necessity of earning a livelihood, since their economic situation is not as balanced as that of the laborer.

First our Civil War and then World War II produced fat benefits for unscrupulous speculators. They led a life of luxury and squandering. The example of these profiteers caused envy among the masses and also disproportionate ambitions and desires to equal them. The popular idea is now to get money at any risk. The result has been a new form of immorality.

This kind of behavior, along with fraud and bribery, flourishes principally among businessmen and officials, since the pay of the latter scarcely provides enough for personal and family needs. On the other hand, no one thinks of saving, for it is feared that the successive inflation will depreciate the currency, and people therefore dissipate everything they get. They live only for the present, in the best manner possible and without scruples or conscience.

When the Civil War ended, the victorious side found that in the Communist zone, which was really the richest and most productive, the economic disorder and the laziness of the laborers had brought famine on the people. Vitamin deficiency was widespread and the lack of food was general. As the National troops retook the country the food situation improved accordingly, but what was available had to be divided up among a greater number of consumers. It consequently became necessary to set up a rationing system.

Even though agriculture and cattle-raising were reorganized, the Spanish people still remained hungry from 1940 to 1943 because harvests were light and many necessary foods had to be exported to obtain other necessities. The food situation has improved steadily to date without yet being completely balanced, in spite of the traditional frugality of the Spanish. We no longer see the terrible cases of avitaminosis, particularly among the children, that were seen in the first years following our war; but still a part of the Spanish people does not receive the quantity of food that it needs. This insufficient diet causes a mild collective psychological excitation which could increase, if circumstances permitted, to a social disturbance.

The nervous exhaustion which contributes to world tension is the product of the present conditions in the struggle for a livelihood, of the dissipation of energies in pleasures and entertainment, and of insufficient rest and sleep. In reality, it is more a question of mental fatigue than of nervous exhaustion; the organism can protect itself against it by sleep; but, like food, there is not enough of it for the majority of the population.

Many Spaniards of the middle class now work in wearying conditions. The difficult livelihood, together with the so-called "new necessities" like bars, movies, and other amusements, require an increased income gained through supplementary work, which takes still more hours from relaxation and sleep. Nervous exhaustion then results, because in the individual's balance of energy there is more going out than coming in; it is in this way that continual anxiety is ruining the Spaniard of our time.

Spain has always consumed large quantities of its rich wines without what one could call alcoholism, especially that condition that enervates the masses and contributes to universal anxiety. Unfortunately the consumption of spirits of poor quality and high alcoholic content has been introduced among us. These spirits, in conjunction with other kinds of daily and voluntary poisons like sedatives, hypnotics, antineuralgics, and opium, morphine, and cocaine, have harmed the mental health of the Spanish people.

We have already declared that there are no specific war psychoses, since in both war and peace we note the identical forms of pathological reactions. However, during war these reactions grow in intensity, due to the multiplicity of external factors which cause mental disturbances. In fact, war operates like a fine sensitizer of the special psychism of psychopathic personalities, of the mentally deficient, and of those hereditarily disposed to mental illness. But it is certain that people considered sane and healthy do not escape either, as it is rare for them to preserve their perfect mental equilibrium in the course of a long war.

The experience of war, especially of the terrible modern wars, has a profound and direct effect even on the most robust personalities. The normality or abnormality of a person is shown by the faculty, differing with each person, of recovering the mental balance disturbed by war emotions.

Many people believe that mental disorder is contagious. In one sense this is true. Psychological symptoms can be spread to great multitudes, and then a psychic epidemic, or a kind of mob psychosis, is produced.

In psychic contagion there are three elementary forces: suggestibility, imitation, and obedience. To these forces may be united other psychological factors, among which are the suggestions which the masses exert on each other, emotional resonance, and the versatility of the crowd. The individual submerged in the mob is incapable of maintaining a critical attitude toward what is going on; he allows himself to be invaded by emotion; he automatically transmits his feelings to the people about him. When we share the feelings suggested by the crowd, the emotional excitement we feel is re-transmitted even more strongly, and the emotional burden of the individuals making up the crowd is thereby intensified.

Psychic contagion is an effect of mass suggestion, and is facili-

tated by the psychological primitivism of the crowd; this is the
true key to the disorders and movements of people—political
and social, revolutionary and anti-revolutionary. The masses are
incapable of reflective thought, and the factors we have outlined
as causes and stimuli of psychic contagion favor the propagation
of certain religious or political doctrines, and of movements for
or against war. The contagion acquired by ideas and sentiments
that have been absorbed by the masses imposes a specific
orientation on individual acts, insofar as the subject sacrifices
his own interest to that of the mass.

While advantage can be taken of mental contagion to transform the masses into an enthusiastic and disciplined group, psychic infection usually has catastrophic repercussions on humanity because of the tendency of the mob to destruction and
perversity. Psychic contagion affects people in every epoch, and
when they are influenced by ambitious or malicious politicians,
they can readily be sent to war as cannon-fodder.

The type of national tension or anxiety arising at a specific
moment in the history of each people depends on the type of
mass social reaction then existing. This reaction, in turn, is governed by the level of civilization the nation has reached, the
ideas and sentiments it values, and also the interests of the moment. In times of war, revolution, and famine, the type of mass
social reaction is determined by feelings, inasmuch as ideas have
but little influence on the masses. This psychological factor must
be taken into account by political leaders, because it can happen
that the public may easily swing to the pole of self-denial, al-
truism, and patriotism. Propaganda for or against a war is made
by provoking a definite type of mass social reaction, such as
stimulating the imperialistic ambitions of one population, or the
desire for moral and material vengeance of another.

At the cry of "War!" the people rush out of their offices, work-
shops, factories, orchards, farms, and homes to take up arms and
fight the enemy until he is destroyed. In the popular masses of
every country there is awakened a great enthusiasm for their
respective causes. Without going into an analysis of the psychological motivation of the people's enthusiasm, nor into the ethi-

cal and spiritual quality of the sentiments stimulating this enthusiasm on both sides, it is well known that both sides offer their lives in the holocaust of their ideals.

This collective enthusiasm shown by the masses in the early days of a war is simply an effect of psychic contagion; it never results from a formation of doctrine pushing them to war to defend their specific ideals. The fervor and enthusiasm of the masses in wartime arises from the exaltation of the so-called patriotic sentiments, and also from the mass emotional complexes of rancor, resentment, envious rivalry, and ambitious drive. Mass enthusiasm can be fatal when it inhibits thought and when individuals, submerged in the mob, act impulsively on the sentiments current in their environment.

Wars, particularly those for religious or political reasons, keep up the emotional tension of the people during the development of the conflict by setting up reactions of passion connected in one way or another with the outcome of the war. It is during these periods that the public believes the most absurd news and people perform the most insensate acts.

The disorders of war exalt the paranoid facets of the gregarious personality; vanity, mistrust, false judgment, and selfish conduct. The nation is vain about military triumphs during a war, about the part it is playing in the victory, and about its discipline and obedience. During a war the public is distrustful, suspicious of hidden enemies and of espionage by traitors. The people defend their errors in the complete conviction that they and they alone are in possession of the absolute truth. During a war people kill, steal, rape, and commit every sort of attack against social order. In so doing they believe they are assisting toward a final triumph of the armed forces. Those people who do not act in a paranoid fashion during a war may take refuge in simulated mental or physical illness, defeatism, and ultimate surrender.

In war both sides commit massacres, pillage, arson, and destruction in the name of heroism and patriotism. Under the influence of the brutal passions which are released during a war, men can be brought down to the level of the beast, uniting the

instincts of destructive animals, associating the ferocity of the
tiger with the excesses of the monkey and the cunning of the
fox. However, criminality in war is more external than internal:
that is, it does not arise so much from innate individual tendencies as from environmental influences.

War constitutes an exceptional period in the lives of nations,
one in which the law is neither respected nor enforced. It is
therefore during wartime more than under other politico-social
circumstances that criminality increases. The declaration of war
liberates psychological tendencies of the utmost bestiality. Free
rein is given to the most abominable instincts of cruelty, criminality, and excess. The public knows no limits, and satisfies its
passions no matter what the cost.

A psychological study of world tension would have no purpose
if we did not deduce the means to counteract it from its causes.
The problem is one for those psychologists who specialize in
mob psychology and for the psychiatrists who have observed
the effects of war on the public.

In spite of the very high level of culture a people may reach,
they will always be excitable, impulsive, versatile, impassioned,
irrational, undecided, and liable to act in the most varying and
contradictory ways. They are highly susceptible to suggestion,
violent passions, and elementary feelings called up by demagogues. They are superficial in their reasoning, stubborn in their
decisions, and able to assimilate only the simplest arguments
and conclusions. It is only natural then, in view of these psychological conditions, that the masses can be made sacrificial victims by clever propaganda. They allow themselves to be dragged
unknowingly towards the most absurd beliefs and the most
senseless revolutions because they act by impulse and not by
logical reasoning. As examples of the simplicity of mob psychology, witness the triumph of the Labor Party in Britain and
the wave of communism in Europe and North America at the
end of World War II.

Considered psychologically, what we call world tension is
reduced to a state of mass anxiety of various degrees and shad-
ings. It is a product of mob suggestibility, which has deprived

the popular masses of their capacity to reason. Today the world fears war. To be exact, it fears a war unchained by a communistic Russia with huge masses of soldiers in its country and political supporters all over the world. The Russians had absolutely no military prestige until they won in this last war in collaboration with the Allies, even though separated from them by political ideology. Now that Russia has gained military importance, those nations becoming its satellites and supporting communism unconditionally find themselves threatened at the same time by war from within as well as from without. Here indeed is a cause of world anxiety.

Having examined world tension psychologically—at least in Spain—we come to the conclusion that it results from the following factors: (1) The existence of a state of mass emotionality, resulting from knowing what the results of the last war were for both victors and vanquished; and how the victors have seen their political regime changed forcibly and their economic situation paralyzed by a disguised Marxist revolution. (2) The diminishing realization of the individual's responsibility, because he is being swallowed up by the mass of political parties, allowing himself to be swayed by contradictory propaganda and guided by instinctive and subconscious tendencies rather than by reason. (3) The tendency of the masses to suffer group psychoses, by which a guess or a hint becomes immediately converted by the crowd into absolute truth, thus giving rise to clashing political movements and mass emotional effects. (4) The public's abandon to all sensual desires, which creates new economic obligations followed by the lack of balance between earnings and expenses. Thus the individuals of the world are being brought to social ruin.

SWITZERLAND

Oscar L. Forel, M.D.

Privat-Docent in Psychiatry, St. Prex; Former President of the Swiss Psychiatric Society; Former Medical Director of "Les Rives de Prangins," Institute for Medical Psychotherapy; President of S.E.P.E.G. (International Study Weeks for Child Victims of the War).

THE political neutrality of Switzerland does not prevent its citizens from taking part in international political problems, expressing convictions, and experiencing tension. But as a nation, the people have only recently permitted themselves to take an active part in their neighbors' disputes.

During the war, Switzerland granted temporary or permanent asylum to hundreds of thousands of exiled and persecuted political refugees. There can hardly be a country whose population has had closer contact with a relatively greater number of foreigners representing every political shade. Moreover, the Swiss people are well-informed, thanks to a press issued daily in German, French, and Italian.

Till now the Swiss political structure has resisted every storm. This explains why many people consider Switzerland to be a pattern of world communality. But that which suits a community of four millions is not necessarily desirable or applicable on a world-wide scale.

Foreigners visiting Switzerland are struck by the political and social mosaic, by the persistency of local customs, and by the number of societies, clubs, and newspapers. Whether this situation is caused by the many valleys separated from one another by the high mountains, or whether it is the effect of a compulsory introversion seeking an outlet in these little groups, the fact remains that there is a persistent diversity of character in the various regions of the country.

The Swiss is courted on all sides; everyone endeavors to enlist his support for the current ideology. Moreover, the Swiss is stubborn with regard to certain principles. He believes in evolution, politics, tolerance, mutual concession, and the need for compromise. He knows how to preserve the fruits of his political evolution and of his experiences, and how to maintain individualism and regional idiosyncrasies. Mistrusting revolutionary doctrines, he avoids any form of anthropolatry. The Swiss knows how many generations had to suffer in order to establish the present constitution of his country; he knows how many centuries of struggle went to evolve a regional autonomy subservient to the national superior interests, and to protect federalism from the centralized excesses of modern economics. These are some of the reasons that make the Swiss a defender of the established order. The Fascist, National Socialist, and Marxist revolutions barely touched him. Dictatorship, with its political principles of "might is right" and "the end justifies the means," excited a kind of national indignation.

Certainly there are tensions which Swiss statesmen have not been able to elude entirely. For example, there are the differences between Catholics and Protestants, even in the Federal Councils. But these differences are to maintain equilibrium, to insure that one function does not impose upon the other. When there is a question of filling an important post, the candidate's religion or political views are of less consideration than his personal value. The exception, of course, is when the country is in danger.

Every day the Swiss contact people with different ideologies and interests—civilization bearing another stamp. In a way this should be an enrichment, an incitement toward suppressing tensions. But at the same time everyone is tempted to stress his loyalty to his native canton, whether in self-assertion or self-defense, whether German, Romance, or Italian, Catholic or Protestant. This situation, in extension, implies a cultural allegiance despite any powerful neighbors. The population of Ticino proved themselves to be more anti-Fascist than the Romance, and the German-Swiss more anti-Nazi than the French-Swiss. On the other hand, the latter would express views on

France analogous to those heard in Germany, while the Romance-Swiss discussed German affairs with a French bias that was probably more accentuated than the views of the Bretons and Basques. In 1917 we heard our German-Swiss confederates coining the following incisive jest: "France would like to make peace with Germany but French Switzerland won't allow it!"

Not being in the possession of colonies, nor of influential zones, the Swiss are exempt from the most dangerous causes of international tension. Like all nations which have no colonies, have lost their colonies, or have known subjection, the Swiss dread imperialism and dictatorship in any form. They fear any expansion, save for changes due to culture or economy. There is an animus against all colonialism.

Thus far we have studied the past as a basis for the examination of problems relating to the future. Let us first consider a cause of international tension which has in all times played a preponderating and nefarious role. This factor is resentment in politics.

In the origin of many individual conflicts, resentment is often found to follow failure or wounded honor. This feeling determines the thoughts and conduct of the individual, causing him to appraise everything as through a distorting prism. One may even trace historical resentments (defeats, vassalage, colonies, colored races, etc.) which may form the unconscious and collective mortgage of a whole nation.

When envy, jealousy, and other analogous sentiments burst forth in consequence of certain events and remain attached to those persons who started them, a group of feelings emerges which from the first excites collective reactions. A panic can break out in the twinkling of an eye among a hitherto peaceful crowd; a lynching may develop like a blaze started by a spark. The tendency to react by aggressiveness or fear pre-exists in every normal individual. These are quasi-reflex reactions, unreasoned reactions that form part of the defense mechanism of all animals. Once the danger is past, the reaction ceases unless it has wakened a latent condition which awaited an opportunity to install itself permanently.

The success of a demagogue depends on the presence or absence of the latent feelings he attempts to excite. The demagogue then becomes the loudspeaker of the collective unconscious, of what everyone feels but is unable to express. Such a leader will be immediately followed, because the crowd was already in a state of incubation before his speech. The repercussions of resentment among crowds are more profound and more deleterious than the unchaining of "normal" passions. Resentment methodically gnaws and destroys the individual and his victims.

The appearance of a resentment depends on four premises: (1) *a real or an imaginary prejudice,* in which the individual places himself in among the frustrated victims of a system which he repudiates; (2) *feelings of personal powerlessness,* from which proselytism leads to a hope for revenge, and recourse is taken to demagogy; (3) *personal revaluation,* which ensues from the refusal to admit the fact of inferiority: the individual considers himself to be superior to those who humiliated him and those he holds responsible for his failures; (4) *tension and dynamism of the "resentful,"* which issues from those who dare not revenge themselves, but are obsessed by the desire of revenge. This state of mind can last for years. It may even become lifelong and entirely dominate thought and action.

Resentment is an accumulation of impotent yet active hate. It animates those who are frustrated in life, those eternal rebels who are ready to revenge themselves on destiny and on its presumed iniquities. Yet the motives for their failures are found in their special psychology, along with other initial errors, youthful "complexes," rebuffs, vexations, and desire for vengeance. Resentment is so diffused and well-camouflaged that insufficient attention is paid to it. Yet it can transform characters, create furies and misanthropes, and fan the hate and tensions of mankind. And with a ready receptivity, prepared conditions, and proper atmosphere, individual resentment can permeate an entire group.

The "Resentful Man," at once impotent and dynamic, avenges his own humiliations by humiliating others; he recruits his followers among the envious. The resentful constitute a deleterious element in the centers of all mankind.

Quarrels, duels, feudal dissensions, and above all, political strife and wars have at all times served as outlets for passions and, in consequence, have reduced the number of resentments. Today the increasing concentration of the means of production and of power in the hands of the Moloch States tends to augment the crowding together of humanity, to reduce individual responsibility, and to increase the opportunities for demagogues and dictators.

Retrospectively, it seems that the majority of Swiss people, especially those living in the country or the mountains, early perceived the Hitler phenomenon for what it really was—a collective psychosis. This psychosis was caused by the suffering of a Germany under postwar humiliations and resentment induced by a never-admitted defeat, shaken by treachery, haunted by the specters of unemployment and the rising tide of communism, fearing civil war, pinning faith to its military virtues and, above all, impregnated since Bismarck's days with ideas of expansion, of greatness, and even of "racial superiority."

The tendency towards limitless expansion is a characteristic of the hysterical and paranoic psychosis; it is found in fanatics (schizoids) and in some epileptics. This mental phenomenon explains why Hitler forged fresh and vaster plans of conquest after every success and at the same time discarded his collaborators and advisers, whom he later executed. More and more he withdrew from reality, saw himself surrounded by enemies and traitors, misjudged facts and possibilities. At first he misunderstood foreign conditions, later he misunderstood the situation in Germany itself; finally he listened to no one. Reduced to practically complete moral isolation, he committed suicide in a fit of impotent fury because he had not succeeded in destroying the object of his resentment—the whole world. In a supreme burst of hatred, he cursed his own people, who had afforded him every assistance in satiating his own resentments.

If we have devoted so much space to the phenomenon of Hitler, it is because he demonstrated so clearly what has long separated the Swiss from the Germans. Before Bismarck, the German was sentimental, poetic, philosophic, and musical. Later he became an involuntary soldier, "eternally misunderstood" and ever surprised to find that reason can be stronger than force. The Swiss introvert gravitates around his Alps; his aggressiveness spends itself at home, where his life is hard. Each day he plays his national card game "Jass," while the German plays cards with the world. The Swiss belongs to shooting clubs, to a chorus, and to a gymnasium; the German constructs Zeppelins, Krupp guns, a merchant fleet and a Navy in preparation for his attempts to organize, reform and embrace the whole world. He conducts himself in such a way that the world applies to him the régime he invented himself. Such has been the opinion of many Swiss from Bismarck to the catastrophe of 1945. They have since watched the evolution of public opinion and of politics; from the first they have helped their northern neighbors like the others. But one feels a reserve, a hesitation, a doubt in the face of recent signs of reawakening national aggressiveness.

There is the added fear of seeing some twelve million refugees, the victims of a policy that seems to be unable to assimilate them; these refugees may become a center of revolution and a spark of military recrudescence both for the Allies and for the Russians. All this, added to the increasing rearmaments, reinforces the reserve of the Swiss population.

The importance and diversity of the manifestations of aggressiveness prompt us to look closer at this element of individual, collective, national, and international tension.

Is there an instinct of aggression and even of destruction, as there is an instinct of self-preservation and an instinct of procreation of the species? I believe not. And this for two reasons: the one is in keeping with the definition of instinct, which implies an obligatory character. Instinct is a kind of unconscious intelligence, adaptable and plastic, dowered with "the memory of the species." It is a medley of desires, trends, and tendencies, conforming to momentary exterior circumstances, but of hereditary origin and due to the general constitution of the individual. Aggression, on the contrary, is a momentary and non-specific reaction, liable to appear in any circumstances. Visible or camouflaged, aggression pierces through our passions. It is the function of the momentary reactions that determine our attitudes and our conduct, insuring that instinctive tendencies follow an almost obligatory and pre-established course.

If, as we think, aggression is only an occasional manifestation, it would seem wrong to label the desire for domination, possession, conquest, and destruction as "instinctive," to imagine an instinct of death (sic), or to attribute an involuntary and innate existence to aggressiveness. One can be aggressive as one can be gay, sad or angry. For example, a game can suddenly be transformed into a fight, and love or hate can change to aggression. The source of instincts are inexhaustible, and instinctive impulses spring out of the depths of the subject, ever seeking satisfaction.

The fear of a menace is enough to release the reflex of aggression. This accounts for the entry into political life of an important source of international tension. Certain groups sometimes appeal to latent or rebuffed individual and collective aspirations in order to develop their own power or possessions, to obtain the vote for huge military budgets, or to maintain a state of alarm and a war psychosis. Talk of "vital space," after evoking the specter of famine, automatically releases the powerful instinct of nutrition; talk of possible, probable, or certain attack will prepare the mentality for a preventive war. When war is once unleashed, the human animal, roused and surrounded, only obeys the instinctive panic-fear. It is mechanism of protection, a warning to flee from a danger and, in defiance of a danger, there ensues attack with the courage of "fear in advance." The impresarios of war know the successive stages to be mounted in order to create a general war psychosis.

It is evident that the modern tendency towards the greater centralization of military, economic, and political power must culminate in the present situation, which divides humanity into two opposing parties within which aggressive propaganda rages. It maneuvers crowds, utilizes suggestibility, indifference, prejudices, fear, avidity, and resentment. But it also utilizes nobler inclinations: proselytism, the Messianic and reforming and even revolutionary spirit, the idea of bestowing the benefits of civilization upon presumed heretics, a social order deemed superior, a doctrine of guarantee for the future, and the happiness of the people.

Those who desire war have a choice of arguments; and no nation resists a well-planned propaganda. The keynote of this propaganda is based chiefly on fear.

A special propensity towards aggression, similar to that observed in various human types and temperaments, may be attributed to certain nations. It appears to be a quasi-innate need for conquest and domination. Every nation has passed through periods in its history when this propensity has led it to the battlefield. At other times it has been limited to economic competition and to the domination of money, even as it has taken the form of a political Messiahship enforced by armed might.

The carnage and fury let loose at the frontiers of Switzerland during the two World Wars served to strengthen the faith of the Swiss in their own political and social institutions. They remain convinced that their conception of democracy has helped to preserve them from civil wars and to keep them apart from the dissensions of their powerful neighbors. They have been able to develop their own humanitarian organizations, with the conception of neutrality implying solidarity. They have raised the Red Cross, national and international, almost to the rank of a State institution. Switzerland has created Swiss Relief and Swiss Aid to Europe; it has organized cultural and technical exchanges, sent a great number of social workers to war-damaged countries, instituted training courses of medico-pedagogic character destined to help victims of the war, and above all it has organized a large number of relief actions to collaborate with home efforts in the most devasted regions. This task was incumbent on the country, in view of its geographical, linguistic, and political situation. During the war, Switzerland undertook to represent the interests of the majority of the belligerents. She offered hospitality to a considerable number of wounded, sick, and refugees.

The fact that the concentration of world powers constitutes two great groups disputing world hegemony has restrained the majority of the Swiss from favoring any policy other than their own past. Moreover, should the Swiss abandon this standard of conduct, the country would doubtless again experience internal divisions and dissensions in comparison with which present tensions would seem but feeble family quarrels. Only ignorance of the political structure of Switzerland can explain the periodic attacks on the country's policy of neutrality. The policy has even been interpreted as the expression of an egoism equal to that of the Monroe Doctrine.

Certainly there are patriots who believe that the time for neutrality is past, that modern armament will exclude the survival of these little islands of refuge in a continental war. But the majority of the Swiss reason differently: as long as United Nations are divided and even in opposition, the only chance of not being drawn into a new war consists in stressing our attitude, while taking an active part in everything that consolidates peace for a world community. As soon as essential conditions are fulfilled, Switzerland will hasten to join a universal confederation, for it believes that it has solved on a small scale some of the problems which, on a world scale, have barely been touched upon. The Swiss will hasten to join not only because of their numerical weakness or the geographical position of their country, but also because the idea of universality, of solidarity, and of the federation of nations and international law constitutes their ideal in the matter of foreign policy.

All competition implies individual tension. And it is but one step from competition to rivalry: the next step leads to strife. Individual tension forms a part of normal life. Collective tension, on the other hand, is not indispensable. And it rarely appears spontaneously. The hate and fanaticism of the masses is usually actuated by joint political action or aroused by a demagogue. Moreover, suggestion or a forcible idea must awaken a response in the masses. It can be effective only when the inflammable material lies ready in the spirit of the listeners. The power of politicians, writers, the press, and the radio depends upon their ability to excite, appease, or inflame collective passions.

In support of this thesis, let us recall certain recent events. Few people had ever heard of "Fashoda." Neither the English nor the French had the least interest in disputing a territory of

no value in the Sudan. But Fashoda served as a pretext for a trial
of force to decide which of two colonial empires was to possess it.
It proved an awakening of latent tension. A Franco-Britannic
war was barely avoided at the end of the nineteenth century.

Similarly, Italy has demanded the return of the great Austro-
Hungarian port of Trieste because it is inhabited by a majority
of Italians. Yet Italy knows that this incorporation would reduce
Trieste to a third-rate area.

There is a policy that consists in exciting and exploiting collective tension, national resentment, and the spirit of revenge.
Everywhere those concerned desire peace; if they can work, they
forget past quarrels surprisingly soon. But with the appearance
of the demagogue, the old wounds reopen; he stirs up grudges,
refreshes memories, flatters vanity, and rouses cupidity. He plays
on the keys of prestige and the chords of passion vibrate. With
press and radio setting the pace, nations follow. Experience
shows that it is easier to lead the masses to destroy than to construct. Hate, defiance, or envy grow quicker than love and the
appeal to solidarity and constructive peace.

The principal sources of international tension seem to be fear,
defiance, prejudice, resentment, hate, and the spirit of domination. But these sentiments fade in the presence of opposing interests. They become camouflaged; there is talk of rights, justice,
progress, and ideals. As long as we are not directly threatened,
our political ideas determine our sympathies and decide our
partisanship. At the end of the last century, the Boers were heroes to the Swiss, victims of British imperialism. Yet England's
prestige steadily increased during the two World Wars, and
Winston Churchill was accorded one of the most enthusiastic
and unanimous receptions it has been our lot to see in Switzerland. During the Russo-Japanese war of 1903, the majority of
the Swiss hoped for a Japanese victory. But after Pearl Harbor,
the cause of President Franklin D. Roosevelt and the United
States was supported almost unanimously. At the time of the attack on Finland, anti-Russian tension was at its height. Inversely,
when Hitler attacked Russia, almost all Switzerland passionately hoped for a Soviet victory.

The impartial observer will note that foreign tension depends in a large measure on the equilibrium of the opposing forces; and many Swiss instinctively take the part of the weaker side. One puts oneself in the place of the weaker because one feels weak or threatened oneself. It is a dread of the man in power at the time. It is the eternal sympathy for David fighting Goliath.

In spite of our aversion to generalizations and the impossibility of our being able to sound public opinion in this matter, it will seem that tension has very greatly diminished since the war. The firm opposition of the Swiss nation to Nazi Germany has been succeeded by a feeling of duty to help our northern neighbor regain its place in the concert of nations. But experiences dating back to Bismarck's time (the Wohlgemuth affair) have rendered the Swiss mistrustful. They note every indication of German nationlist recrudescence. In their eyes, a two-powerful Germany means a risk of war. The German-Swiss particularly suffered too great a disappointment to again show confidence. To understand this reserve, it must be remembered that the Germany of "thinkers and poets" had profoundly influenced the culture of our confederates; and that the rise to power of Bismarck, of William II, and then of Hitler had progressively lowered the credit of the Germany of the wars of liberation, of Schiller and Goethe, and of the great musicians. The disillusion was in proportion to the former affection, and the wound is too deep to heal quickly. The German-Swiss had been poisoned by a campaign of infamous and insulting accusations launched by the Nazi press, a campaign which aimed at intimidating the so-called "racial brothers."

For many Swiss, the treaties signed after the two World Wars signified the political downfall of our epoch. For them, Woodrow Wilson was an idealist ignorant of European questions; the League of Nations was a fiction. The policy of reparations and humiliation nurtured Hitlerism; the amputation of the Austro-Hungarian empire delivered it over to ruin and incited it to ally itself with Russia, that other great power in the balance of Europe. The "Little Entente," the "cordon sanitaire," the entire anti-Russian policy led from Rapallo to the Molotov-Ribbentrop pact.

What is now left of Austria and Germany hardly fills a place in the European family. Though these populations could contribute to reconstruction, despair hinders them in view of the twelve million refugees without shelter. These refugees, abandoned to resentment, constitute an incandescent spark in the heart of the great hearth that is Europe. Assimilate Germany and Austria in Europe and then integrate Europe into a world community, or prepare for the worst; these are the alternatives in the eyes of many Swiss. They ask nothing more than to assist in a cause which touches them so closely. The language of the country and cultural affinities, no less than the best political and economic traditions, equip them for the task.

Still to be mentioned are those international tensions that affect the Swiss as well as every other nation. This tension is caused by the two opposing groups of great powers and their two fundamental ideologies. One imposes a Messianic character, inspired by a politico-social, economic and philosophical creed; the other organizes the defense of the established order, developed and adapted as much as possible to postwar conditions, according to the rules observed by Western capitalist democracies. Psychologically speaking, Switzerland made her choice, one might say unconsciously, simply because the Western doctrine agreed with her own tradition and mentality. It appeared to confirm her own principles. Yet a position so well adjusted to the West does not in the least imply the abandonment of solidarity and a neutral policy. It merely excludes the fact that a minority should impose itself within the country by means other than conforming to the rules of her political institutions. It also excludes the possibility of one of the power groups imposing itself by means other than abandoning part of its sovereignty in favor of a universal advantage.

The conception of neutrality rallies almost all the Swiss. They wish to develop an international organization, and they willingly assume the task falling to them. They know from experience that an organization of nations on a world plan implies initially a partial and generously conceded abandonment of national sovereignty and a submission to an efficient international code of rights.

Has the desire for peace so penetrated the minds of men that efficacious and lasting organization can be established? Will a world government shortly arise to fulfill a popular desire that has become almost universal? And if this hope still seems distant, what must be done to influence favorably the weighty and innumerable factors which are creating a change of ideas and bringing us to new political conceptions? Are we endeavoring to influence the deep trends which represent the shifting of the ideas of an epoch? What can we do to prepare the soil of public opinion, to create increasing links of solidarity, to facilitate osmosis among nations and to render economic and cultural interpenetration indissoluble? A beginning has been made. But if international organizations such as UNESCO and the World Health Organization prepare the way, the same is not true of "Atlantic" or "Pacific" agreements and pacts which are viewed as aggressive by those who are excluded and those who abstain for reasons of sovereignty.

There would seem to be no universally-accepted means to prevent a new war. Such is the belief of those who call themselves "realists." They cling to fatalism; they are often skeptical, if not cynical. The only lesson they draw from history is that war is the function of the varying equilibrium of forces, and that these variations are inevitable. They further say that should individual egoism be successfully repressed, this power would be delegated to the State. According to Schlosser and to Jacob Burckhardt, power is evil whoever exerts it; it is voracious and insatiable. Unhappy in itself, it is condemned to bring unhappiness to everyone else. These variations on the anarchists' motto *power leads to tyranny* impress themselves on our minds at a time when totalitarian regimes specialize in the art of molding opinion with the aid of press and radio. People are eminently open to suggestion. They can be incited to wars as well as to peace. Yet there is an essential difference; war satisfied our desire for conquest, risk, domination and exploitation—in short, it flattered all our egoistic tendencies. These desires can be moderated or repressed only by those which collectively constitute civilization. The fight for peace can succeed only in times of peace, because war propaganda is active at all times. Civilization, unlike war, is not "natural." It has been the greatest conquest of man.

What can education offer to alleviate international tension? If the history of human culture, rather than the history of wars, were taught, perhaps it would contribute to discarding the prejudice that politics is merely a game of force between nations. Youth should be for world communality; they should be immunized against the "virus bellicosus."

And what of the press? If it is inspired by a desire for peace, it is a precious instrument—especially if it unmasks that which instigates factions, encourages defiance and urges armaments.

But the press reflects public opinion more than it forms it. The public determines the market of demand and supply. It is the public that gloats over sensational news, is for or against Moscow, Rome, or Washington. This intolerance will sooner or later be exploited by fanatics. More moderate opinions, such as opposition to dictators and communist police but approval of certain of their activities, affect the masses no more than any other subtle distinction, such as to favor democratic liberty, but oppose the sins of capitalism. The people, like many of their present leaders, are at the stage of "black or white," "everything or nothing." It is an intransigent and critical stage of youth, for all that is moderate or seeks compromise is a feature of maturity and the prime condition of civilization.

As life becomes more civilized, human relations become more complicated. There is a greater need for effort and, above all, concessions from everyone. These mutual concessions bring about more individual liberty for everyone. A true solidarity is created, which makes possible an unmerciful fight against the egoism of individuals, groups and nations. This evolution is in its infancy. We are in an epoch of crisis in which everything is questioned, not only because of the effects of war, but because of dislocations due to technical discoveries. It is an epoch of transition, reconstruction and adjustment, lending itself to the most daring initiative. It is still a favorable epoch because multi-professional teamwork has tended to reduce, to an extent, individual error and ambition.

Four different reasons for world tension have been recognized: (1) *The absurd.* The origin of these tensions are found in pride, prestige, resentment, desire of conquest, and glory. Such tensions are puerile and immature. (2) *The artificial.* These tensions grow out of a pretended *Reason of State.* Under such guise whole populations have been displaced and a "Concentrated Universe" has been created. (3) *The traditional.* Such tensions result from incompatible ideologies, from doctrinal fanaticism, religion, and family or racial vendettas. (4) *The inevitable.* It is often said that the geographical situation of a country determines its relations and tensions with close and distant neighbors. Fortunately, civilized man is recognized by a standard of culture and morale where such "reasons" have no hold on him.

Everything that helps to dissolve our tensions, every institution that permits the individual to express his emotions contributes towards the prevention of the formation of resentments. Whether it is a free press, democratic institutions, a judicial system open to all, or quarrels and fights among children and discussions, polemics, and fisticuffs among adults, all are outlets that serve as safeguards. On the contrary, dictatorship and the domination of inquisition, terror, and oppression fosters resentment. This is especially true when such tactics are used for the profit of a minority, a class, or a caste.

Through education we seek to accustom our children to "good habits"; we develop in them a conscience which tells them at all times what is right and wrong; we praise civil virtue and we attempt to control egoism. Experience teaches us that aggressiveness engenders aggressiveness, and that the best protection against it in others is its moderation in ourselves. Two world wars have demonstrated the weakness of these educational efforts and indeed of the forces of civilization. The visible preparations for a new trial of force cause more and more people to ask whether there is not a more effective means of counteracting such a menace.

A new factor *has* appeared which may alter national relationships in a profound fashion. This factor is the knowledge, vague as yet, but increasing rapidly, of the increasing power of the means of destruction. It is bringing into focus the vision of apocalyptic horror which might be expected from now on. The solemn warnings of those who are alarmed by the consequence of their own discoveries in the realm of nuclear energy and "biological war," the feeling that the history of humanity has ceased to be prodigious and has become Dantesque since Hiroshima, Nagasaki, and Bikini, and the threat of total war are penetrating the minds of people all over the world.

This evolution will culminate on the day the news of the latest discoveries in biology and toxicology will be given to the world. It will be found that a very small quantity of toxin will suffice to kill every living thing within a considerable space. Moreover, a day later oxidation will cause the lethal effect to cease and will permit an army to penetrate safely into a region which twenty-four hours before was an inhabited country. This discovery will put to an end the monopolies of the great powers which alone possess the considerable means to manufacture atomic bombs. In the future, small countries, groups, and individuals may become more dangerous than Hitler. Man's sole recourse is to adapt himself as quickly as possible and to dominate his discoveries. Otherwise, he may disappear from the face of the earth.

Our minds are daily more oppressed by the dilemma: "To be or not to be." We know that if he had the means—and they were only barely lacking—Hitler would have precipitated his own people and indeed all humanity into the catastrophe that put an end to his own life. To declare that Hitler was mad, hysterical, and paranoic is no consolation. It merely illustrates to a disquieting degree that under certain conditions the pathologic dominates health. The patient does not ask the doctor to diagnose cancer, he demands deliverance from it! Humanity has reached this point. It is conscious of the cancer which is threatening it, and it is seeking a surgeon.

The initiated must assume the responsibilities incumbent upon them. Every problem must be considered on a world-wide scale. The menace to all, to the entire planet and the cosmos, forges universal links that are not as yet visible. For the present, it creates an atmosphere of perplexity. Man is seeking to recover his dimensions, his supports and the gravitation of which science has recently deprived him. In a panic, the sorcerer's apprentice retreats before his Mephistophelian creation.

It is no matter of chance that psychology is the vogue at present. It is being asked to explain that which escapes logic, to solve the mystery of our epoch, to unveil the unknown future. This is asking too much of it. Neither science nor law nor the state can protect us against mental epidemics. The true causes of dissatisfaction, suffering, revolt, physiological misery, and flagrant inequity must be discarded. Health organizations have placed the mental and physical well-being of the people on an equal footing. For the first time in history, mental epidemics are being combated in the same way as microbic epidemics. At a future stage in the development of man, who is now retreating in fear before his material discoveries, he will reconsider the problems which form the essence and the sense of his existence, his reason to be, and his hope.

The solemn appeals of the greatest chemists and physicists of our time should be issued throughout the whole world. The press and the radio in every country should undertake to inform their readers and listeners regularly and completely of the "progress" made in the means of destruction. A Nobel prize should be awarded yearly for the best popular work on scientific discoveries that can be used for destructive ends. Subjects reserved till now for the initiated should be made available to the unenlightened. The new generation should be methodically instructed as to the "volcanic" nature of our planet. They should learn that the earth is to be a field of strategy which may be reduced to a desert when destruction on a continental scale begins. It is important to diffuse the knowledge of these prospects of annihilation, for only a small proportion of the world's inhabitants are now aware of them. Only then could statesmen act on a universal plan. The preliminary conditions would then have been fulfilled. There would be a psychological atmosphere favorable to a world community which would be the natural sequence of the political orientation of an age and the spirit of a century.

At first sight it may appear shocking to evoke terrifying visions and to appeal to fear in the fight against international tension, especially since this method is contrary to the processes applied in individual psychotherapy. But the prophylaxis of war is a universal problem, the solution of which surpasses every other consideration.

It may be objected that fear creates a state of permanent alarm in which people tend to seek escape at any price, even at the risk of a catastrophe. It will be remembered that the Nazis called up the spectre of encirclement for the purpose of conquest, that the USSR ceaselessly denounces the "great conspiracy" against Russia, and that all great national propaganda asserts aggressiveness in order to justify rearmament. To the occult power of the partisans of force, those who speculate on "fear in advance," can we afford an education of youth based on fear as the sole permanently effective remedy? The contradiction is only too apparent. While "fear in advance" culminates in war, the fear of universal destruction might, on the contrary, form the beginning of a universal wisdom.

Surely education as an antidote to war merits all our efforts. It could contribute to the fight against passions, lies, and idolatry. For we all bear within us idols which, when defined, are taboo. These idols may be ideas or ideologies which merit examination and critical study. For example, young people learn to distinguish between patriotism, love of country, and aggressive chauvinism. They learn that certain idols have human shapes, and that we are naturally inclined to sublimate our parents, friends, great men, and conquerors. School and the press, books, the cinema, and all education should serve to "humanize" the idols, to show that they are endowed with the weaknesses inherent in human nature. Romain Rolland did not disparage Michelangelo by describing him as weak, undecided, vain, and full of the prejudices of his time and his caste. On the contrary, Michelangelo seems all the more sublime to have created masterpieces in spite of his weaknesses. Certainly nothing must be neglected to increase the effectiveness of education in preparing youth for its awaiting tasks: the preservation of future society from the threatening dissolution, and the creation of a civilization capable of resisting destructive agencies.

If we have dwelt upon the role of fear, it is because this powerful lever has until now been too often presented only in its negative aspect. If a "salutary fear" has the power to awaken the instinct of self-preservation to the detriment of destructive aggression, the ferocity of which we have already seen, then any hesitation would seem academic. Furthermore, there is no need to overexcite this salutary fear; it is latent in every normal man. Such fear exists in many varied and disguised forms. It explains the surrender of personal duties to an anonymous state; interest in the conquests of science and materialism to the detriment of humanism; flight into political phraseology, into grandiose but hollow phrases, and into stillborn programs; it accounts for the various "charters" and "declarations of the rights of man," even when it is known that they are hypocritical and inoperable; it explains the flight into a cinema-like unreality, an artificial paradise; into abuse of drugs, of alcohol, of narcotics and sedatives, lotteries and games of chance; it is also at the bottom of the flight into professional and intellectual irresponsibility, into safety-worship, and into an ostrich-like policy regarding dangers that no one desires, no one dares to deny, and few dare to meet with adequate defensive means.

This surrender is not surprising. The individual is losing one position after another. Nothing is left but companies, syndicates, trusts and holdings, and the Moloch state which dominates. For it is this evolution, this depersonalization of economic and political life, which threatens to characterize our modern human society. For some the development of this disquieting and drone-like character is normal and inevitable. For others it means regression to a previous phase of human development. They rank it among such other signs of discordance and disintegration as atonal music, dadaesque painting, surrealism, cubism, and similar trends. This cultural schizophrenia of the twentieth century is one of the manifestations of the cold panic and progressive disorder so widely denounced by those who judge our epoch.

Politics have become too serious a matter to be entrusted any longer only to politicians. Fortunately, they are shifting slowly but surely from the national to the universal plan. The maintenance of peace or the breaking-out of a war surpassing any imagination depends on our aptitude to solve the economic, political, and social problems on a world-wide basis.

The principal tension at the present time not only opposes two giant coalitions, it opposes two conceptions full of consequences: the one which irreconcilably proclaims the doctrines of the East as opposed to those of the West favors an immediate clash. It advocates a "preventive war" before the adversary shall have acquired the means of defense and counterattack. Partisans of a preventive war count on the latent "fear in advance" as being sufficient to create the favorable atmosphere for an outbreak of hostilities. The "cold war" and "war of nerves" make use of multiple tensions as pawns on the psychological chessboard of international relations.

The alternative conception, to which we subscribe, may be stated as follows: If we can succeed in maintaining peace in the immediate future, especially if we can counteract war propaganda by spreading the knowledge of the unlimited power of the new tools of destruction, it is possible that new formulae of reconciliation can be developed within the political coalitions now presumed to be incompatible. In the final analysis, the human, psychological, and economic conditions are the common factors of an epoch. And they are far more powerful than the formulae of our respective doctrines.

THE UNITED NATIONS

Otto Klineberg, M.D., Ph.D.

Professor of Psychology at Columbia University;
Former Director of the UNESCO Project on Ten-
sions Affecting International Understanding; Past
President of the Society for the Psychological
Study of Social Issues.

I T is not an easy matter to describe in brief compass
the role played by the United Nations in the solution of international tensions. In a very real sense nothing that the United Nations does is irrelevant in this context. Tensions, and the solution of tensions, are its business, its reason for existence. Directly
or indirectly, that is the meaning and purpose of all the activities
of the United Nations, as well as of the specialized agencies such
as UNESCO (the United Nations Educational, Scientific and
Cultural Organization) and W.H.O. (the World Health Organization). There are differences in method and to a certain extent in
underlying philosophy, but the final goal is one and the same.

It has become fashionable in recent months to ridicule the
United Nations; to dismiss it as a debating society or as a forum
for propaganda; to predict for it an early burial alongside the
League of Nations. It is true that there has been understandable
disillusionment among those who viewed it as a promise of permanent peace, and acute disappointment at its failure to prevent the present crisis. Especially at this particular moment of
history, reaffirmation of one's faith in the United Nations must
impress many as the blindest optimism. It should not be forgotten, however, that the United Nations has a number of important
successes to its credit, and that the world situation would be
considerably worse than it is if no such international organization existed.

This last statement is not difficult to document. The armistice which marked the cessation of hostilities in Palestine was certainly due to the conciliation machinery of the United Nations; so was the solution of the Indonesian crisis and the establishment of a new national entity, the United States of Indonesia. The quarrel between India and Pakistan over Kashmir has not yet been settled, but the fact that the United Nations is studying the question has certainly reduced, at least for the time being, the threat of overt conflict. It is true that aggression in Korea has not been prevented, but the policing action of the United Nations, though costly in human lives and resources, may be expected to have the salutary effect of demonstrating to the world that aggression no longer will go unpunished. Even the danger of war between the Soviet Union and the United States has been rendered less likely because of the existence of an international platform from which grievances may be aired. We are all justifiably impatient at the slow pace of action, but there is hope as long as the representatives of different nations continue to talk together, and take advantage of the international machinery which makes such talk possible.

It is important that the successes of the United Nations should be more widely realized and understood, because that would contribute to our hope and faith that a third World War may still be averted. Such hope and faith are badly needed, since the belief that war is inevitable is itself one of the causes of war. Professor Gordon W. Allport of Harvard University has stressed the role of "expectancy" in his contribution to the volume on *Tensions That Cause Wars*, published for UNESCO under the editorship of Professor Hadley Cantril of Princeton University. Allport speaks of the development of a state of cynicism "wherein men despair of ever achieving their desire for peace. They expect war—and this expectancy itself brings war." He goes on to suggest that "only by changing the expectation in both leaders and followers, in parents and children, shall we eliminate war." International organizations, including the United Nations and its specialized agencies, represent the possibility of a change in our attitudes so that we will expect not war but peace; such a possibility will be realized, however, only if we believe in these organizations, if we substitute faith and cooperation for skepticism. "The success of the United Nations," says Allport, "will be guaranteed as soon as the people and their leaders really *expect* it to succeed."

One may summarize the possible contributions of the United Nations to the solution of international tensions, therefore, by pointing to three specific functions; first, the direct handling of an international conflict through conciliation or mediation; second, the provision of a forum for discussion; third, the creation of an expectancy of peace instead of an expectancy of war.

There are obvious difficulties in the way of developing this expectancy of peace. People of one nation are suspicious of another, or they have false notions of what other nations are like, or they have aggressive attitudes which prepare the way for war. These aspects of international tensions are not fully understood, but the attempt is being made, notably by UNESCO, and specifically by the UNESCO Project on Tensions Affecting International Understanding, to investigate their nature in greater detail.

This Project was initiated by the General Conference of UNESCO in Mexico City in 1947, and modified slightly the following year in Beirut. The resolutions passed at Beirut in 1948 read as follows:

The Director-General is instructed to promote enquiries into:

the distinctive character of the various national cultures, ideals, and legal systems;

the ideas which the people of one nation hold concerning their own and other nations;

modern methods developed in education, political science, philosophy and psychology for changing mental attitudes, and into the social and political circumstances that favour the employment of particular techniques;

the influences which make for international understanding or for aggressive nationalism;

population problems affecting international understanding, including the cultural assimilation of immigrants;

the influence of modern technology upon the attitudes and mutual relationships of peoples.

The Project made a definite start in the early months of 1948, and since then a number of activities have been initiated, and in some cases carried to completion. A critical account of previous studies relevant to this whole area has been published by the Social Science Research Council under the title *Tensions Affecting International Understanding: A Survey of Research.* Early publication is planned for a bookshelf of monographs on the "Way of Life" of a number of different nations; a study of individual communities in four countries, with special reference to attitudes toward the "stranger" or "foreigner"; a series of booklets presenting the scientific facts concerning race and racial differences; a survey, of the public opinion type, referring to the "stereotypes" held by members of one nation concerning others; an analysis of the effect of technological change on mental and social adjustment; an account of what happens in connection with the cultural assimilation of immigrants; a study of intergroup tensions in India, of race relations in Brazil, etc. This list could be considerably expanded, but it gives at least a partial picture of the scope and variety of the activities which constitute the UNESCO Tensions Project. Through the cooperation of social scientists in many countries, there is gradually being accumulated a body of information which will help in the understanding—and, it is hoped, in the control—of international tensions. This is a long-term project, and one from which practical results are not to be expected in the immediate future. At the same time it represents an important application of scientific techniques to a complex area of human relations. As such, it, too, holds out some hope for a future "expectancy of peace."

The United Nations and UNESCO may perhaps best be considered as agreeing in their aims, but differing in their methods of approach to international tensions. The United Nations acts at the political level; UNESCO makes use of education, science and culture in order to bring people of different nations closer together. For this purpose it has engaged upon a series of undertakings which may seem to be unconnected, but which have the common aim of increasing international understanding. So, for example, UNESCO has aided in the founding of international organizations in the field of the natural and the social sciences, as well as in humanities and the arts. It has arranged for international fellowships so that students from one country may study in another. It has facilitated the purchase of books from other countries, and has encouraged the translation of important books into other languages. It has conducted seminars on educational problems in the field of international relations, and has given special attention to the development of an educational program relating to the United Nations. It has undertaken an active campaign of publicity and exposition, through the use of mass media, of the most important aspects of the Universal Declaration on Human Rights. It has aided in the educational reconstruction of countries devastated by the war. It has helped to set up international "villages" where children of many nations can live and work together. It has prepared, and made widely available, factual material concerning various national cultures so that international cooperation may be based on knowledge and understanding. Once again this is only a partial list, but it is by no means an unimpressive one. Though its approach is somewhat more indirect than that of the United Nations, UNESCO has a very real part to play in connection with international tensions. Whereas the United Nations deals with situations of tension as they arise, UNESCO is attempting to create, through education, science, and culture, an atmosphere of cooperation and friendliness which will reduce the likelihood that tensions will develop.

The approach of other specialized agencies to international tensions is still more indirect, but their possible contribution should not be minimized or lightly dismissed. The World Health Organization, for example, in addition to its program of prevention of epidemic diseases and its attempts to improve sanitation, maternal and child health, conditions of work, etc., also describes its task as including the fostering of "activities in the field of mental health, especially those affecting *the harmony of human relations*" (italics ours). It states further that: "Health is a state of complete physical, mental, and social well-being. The health of all peoples is fundamental to the attainment of peace and security." It is clear that for the World Health Organization health is not only of value in itself, but also as a means to the end of reducing international tension. Mentally healthy people are better prepared for cooperation with others, and less likely to welcome the opportunity to express aggression against an "enemy." This view has been stated most explicitly in the phrase: "No peace without mental health," in an early memorandum published by the World Federation for Mental Health, an international non-governmental body working in close cooperation with both the World Health Organization and UNESCO. W.H.O., in line with the general viewpoint expressed above, has worked closely with UNESCO on the Tensions Project, particularly on that aspect of the Project which raises the question as to "the influences which make for international understanding or for aggressive nationalism." Certainly it would be dangerous, in any attempt to understand these influences, to overlook the part played by the varying degrees of mental and social adjustment of the individuals concerned. It is not far-fetched to state that any contribution to mental health is a contribution to peace.

Similarly, any contribution to physical and economic well-being, other things being equal, is also a contribution to peace. Satisfied people are less likely to become aggressive (again it must be stressed, *other things being equal*) than those who are dissatisfied. In this sense many of the other specialized agencies of the United Nations also have a part to play in the reduction of international tensions. The Food and Agriculture Organization lists among its goals: "raising levels of nutrition and standards of living," and "bettering the condition of rural populations." The International Labor Organization states explicitly that "Poverty anywhere constitutes a danger to prosperity everywhere." The International Monetary Fund has as one of its purposes "to contribute to the development of the productive resources of all members." These organizations, if they succeed even in part, will be helping in the establishment of a more stable, international economic situation in which states of tension will be less likely to arise.

This account, brief though it is, of what the United Nations and its specialized agencies are doing to reduce friction among nations and to create conditions conducive to better understanding, should give us some basis for hope. It is a striking fact, revealed by a careful investigation of public opinion on world affairs (reported in *American Opinion on World Affairs in the Atomic Age,* by L. S. Cottrell, Jr., and Sylvia Eberhart) that those who are well-informed are on the whole more optimistic. This is an encouraging sign, and one which justifies a program of the widest possible dissemination of relevant information on the International situation. In such a program, increased knowledge regarding the United Nations, UNESCO, W.H.O., and other related agencies must occupy a position of fundamental importance.

For specialists in the psychological sciences there is another encouraging sign. Psychiatrists and/or psychologists are serving on the secretariats of the Economic and Social Council of the United Nations, of UNESCO, and of W.H.O.; they have been included in national delegations to the General Conferences of both of the latter two organizations; they have been called in frequently as advisers and consultants. There is hope in the fact that those who have specialized in the scientific study of human relations are beginning to have a voice in international affairs.

UNITED STATES

Gardner Murphy, Ph.D.

Professor of psychology and Chairman of the Department, City College of New York; Past President of the American Psychological Association and of the Society for the Psychological Study of Social Issues.

THERE are at least two senses in which it may be thought that the world is in a near-psychotic condition.

On the one hand, the scientific and educational skills of modern societies might easily and quickly achieve a higher standard of physical and social well-being for the human family. The economy of abundance is now technically possible, and so is worldwide education to a rather high level; and a good life which could easily be attained for all. Why do we not simply take it? It may be urged that it is only a psychosis affecting the *will* which prevents us from doing so.

On the other hand, it might be maintained that the trouble is with our inability to *see*. We see only as far as the ends of our noses and know nothing about the kinds of lives we might plan for the members of our society; our state of mind resembles those psychoses in which external reality is repudiated and a world of unreality cultivated instead.

These are interesting points of view, but they are based on certain assumptions as to the ways in which normal human beings behave. These assumptions require scrutiny. There are other assumptions which might be cultivated just as well; and all such assumptions need careful testing in the light of experience.

First of all, it might be worthwhile to develop a tentative idea as to how the world situation looks to those United States leaders charged with responsibility for economic, political, and above all, international affairs; then to formulate a hypothesis about the way in which these matters probably appear to the leaders of Soviet life; then to consider the intersection of the two viewpoints. We could then proceed to ask ourselves where the psychotic tendencies actually lie.

The viewpoint of the American leaders, then, appears to be this: the Russian Revolution did not stop in Russia, but extended and still extends far beyond the confines of the Soviet Union. It was the aim of the world revolution to seize a favorable occasion in Germany, Hungary, and elsewhere after World War I, where resort to revolutionary methods temporarily made headway. The occasion for class war arose or was created in many other places, even in Switzerland, where it would not have been easy to foresee it. It was the evident purpose of Communists to engineer revolts on the basis of very limited spearheads of effective power. It was not their practice to wait for majority votes. In fact, they had rejected the appeal to majority vote even in their own revolutionary movement in 1917. Partly as the result of struggle with the Trotskyites, but also partly on its own account, the world-wide Stalinist organization has remained eager to watch revolutionary possibilities. Spain and China were two obvious instances. Europe and Latin America bristle with revolutionary possibilities.

From the point of view of American leadership, it has continued to be reasonable to be very apprehensive as to how far the movement might spread. It was not irrational for the western powers to regard the Soviet Union as a very doubtful ally in relation to the growing power of the Nazis. Would Soviet leaders choose to fight Hitler first, or the structure of Western society? After Munich came the Soviet-Nazi non-aggression pact, and the U.S.S.R. did not fight the Nazis until invaded by them. There began to be evidence in 1944 and 1945 that the forced alliance against Hitler could not actually endure long. The Moscow demobilization of the Comintern did not actually change long-range policy at all. A hard bargain had, of course, been driven at Yalta; and after peace had been made on both fronts in 1945 it was clearly a question of seeing how much each side would be able to demand and secure in a power struggle in which both sides claimed and occupied spearheads of extraterritorial power. The Red Army's reluctance to withdraw from Iran and the Communist refusal to participate in the plebiscites in Greece and Korea were representative of the desire of the Kremlin leadership to battle things out in its own way.

There was nothing so surprising, then, about the fact that the United States was unable to build, through the United Nations, a world scheme on the basis of the utilization of majority power. The use of the veto by the Soviet Union, sometimes with and sometimes without the cooperation of its satellites, was foreseen. The history of atom-bomb espionage and the history of inflammatory diplomatic utterances and press dispatches, along with the record in Bulgaria, Rumania, Hungary, and Berlin, made it appear likely to the leaders of the Western Powers that Soviet pressure might actually soon lead to a military showdown; or at any rate might well do so as soon as the U.S.S.R. produced the atomic bomb.

It was therefore not surprising that those charged with the responsibility for defense of Western society, knowing exactly what might happen to the whole fabric of that society in all its phases—economic, political, ideational, educational, religious—began to grow acutely alarmed. No matter what their political complexion, those sharing such responsibility thought that the time had come to deny further possibilities of compromise or appeasement. When finally the pressure upon Czechoslovakia terminated in the extension of power over that country, along with diplomatic pressure upon Sweden, Turkey, and other states, and when the Soviets attempted to squeeze the Western Powers out of Berlin, the "cold war" openly took the form of a military power struggle.

If this sketch represents at all fairly the way in which the situation is viewed by American leaders, it is scarcely surprising that vigorous countermovements should have developed, especially since 1946. In fact, looking back over history at the ways in which nations manage their affairs, it is the old story of diplomacy, armaments, and the threat of force.

Now let us try to look at the same situation as it probably appears to Soviet leaders.

One may again go back to 1917 and recall the invasions by the Western Powers (and the invasion by Japan) which followed the October Revolution. One may recall the desperateness of the situation at the time of the invasion of the Soviet Union by Poland in 1920, remembering the open sympathy of the Western Powers for the invaders. We must remember also the vitriol which was poured on the Soviet Union by the press, and the lack of diplomatic or any other effective type of normal intercourse with the United States for over a decade.

Then, when the situation became somewhat stable and the United States finally joined the group of those which had recognized the Soviet Government, the reconciliation was jeopardized by the question of what was to be done with Germany. In fact, the rearming of Hitler, so alarming to the Soviets, was not taken seriously enough to lead to any strong American countermovement. When Chamberlain finally made his arrangements with Hitler at Munich, excluding the Soviet Union, the United States offered no opposition. It became very evident that no protection was to be afforded to the Soviet Union against Hitler's advance. In fact, Munich might well mean that if the East was to be invaded, a temporary respite would be afforded to the West. The Nazi-Soviet non-aggression pact did buy a little peace and a little time for rearming. But when finally the mass of the Hitler attack fell upon Russia, it was a long time before much was done about achieving an effective "second front"; and the assumption of the West seemed frankly to be that it would help with its billions of dollars, but that the main human cost could well be afforded by the Soviets.

In the general struggle for consolidation of power after V-J Day, it became evident to the Soviets that the United States was determined to obtain bases over all the world, including those at Okinawa and Iceland, for example, which were so close to the Soviet Union as to constitute very easy means of attack, whether by B-29's or by atomic-bomb-carrying planes. And of course the question of guided missiles was openly discussed by

American generals and many others; the contents of magazine articles about such possibilities are not lost upon the residents of the Kremlin.

In other words, there was nothing to cause any change in the mind or heart of the Soviet leaders as regards the kind of attitude and the kind of treatment which they thought might be expected in the postwar period. If there was reason for skepticism and hostility toward the Russian Revolution for political, economic, or social reasons, these reasons continued to exist after World War II; and the Soviet leaders, as Marxists, could hardly be so naive as to overlook the economic expansion of the United States which came with victory in World War II.

In this connection it would be worthwhile to ask ourselves how the various processes of American diplomacy and armament would inevitably appear to any Marxist leader charged with responsibility for the defense of the Soviet Union. Such a leader can hardly regard the rise of one American leader or another to a position of political responsibility as the fulfillment of purely personal or capricious political forces. He will look for reasons in Marxist terms. He will note that John Foster Dulles, Republican expert on foreign affairs and a prominent representative of the United States with the United Nations, is directly identified with one of the largest economic establishments having to do with the rebuilding of industrial Germany. This may, in fact, be accidental; but from the point of view of a Marxist leader, viewing the problem of the rebuilding of industrial Germany in terms of its possible threat to his own country, such a situation would not seem accidental.

Again, one might ask oneself what view a Marxist leader would take of the fact that Mr. Louis Johnson was named by President Truman as Secretary of Defense. Soviet leaders were interested in the question of the general stand which Mr. Johnson took with reference to armaments considered appropriate for the United States. They knew that Mr. Johnson had been closely identified with the American aircraft industry, and also with the pressure for a seventy group air force, which plays so large a part in budgetary considerations relative to American armament.

It may have been accidental that Mr. Johnson was chosen at that time for the powerful position of Secretary of Defense. We do not know whether it was accidental or not. But what we do know is that it would not appear to a Marxist leader to be accidental, any more than a Soviet political move will appear accidental to an American leader.

If, therefore, a Marxist leader regards the prominence and power of Mr. Dulles and Mr. Johnson, so directly related to the immediate problem of German industrial and war potential and of air force expansion, as symptomatic of a situation, it would be utterly naive to regard these responses of his as psychotic. Indeed, it would only be a psychotic leader who could be indifferent to considerations of this sort, just as it would be only a psychotic American leader who would be indifferent to the expansion represented by events in Korea, Iran, Poland, and Czechoslovakia. Actually there is no psychosis. There is good historical precedent for the tendency of persons in such a situation to become nervous, frightened, and desperately determined to make themselves as strong against attack as they can be made, and to be relatively unaware that their own desperate behavior is in some degree the basis for the desperate behavior of their antagonists.

From this point of view, then, there is about as much psychosis in the international situation as there is in the behavior of two men who know that they are likely to meet each other at midnight in a lonely spot and arm themselves in advance so that they will not be overpowered. For psychology and psychiatry to interpret phenomena of this sort as war hysteria is politically and historically naive.

But let us look at the other possibility of psychosis; the possibility that there is something psychotic or neurotic about our collective inability to perceive the desperateness of the situation. From this point of view one might ask, for the sake of perspective, about similar blindness in the past. What view did the British take during the 1750's, '60's, and '70's regarding the increasing hostility of the American Colonies, and what steps did they take to prevent the rupture which seemed likely to occur? The answer is that except for Burke and Pitt there were no British statesmen of authority who even took the trouble to protest effectively against the stupidity of the Crown. One might ask about the French blindness in 1869–70 with regard to the growing power of Bismarck's Germany. Again the answer is well-known; the French leaders simply waited naively and even said things which were easily fanned to the flame requisite to mount the attack upon the French. Again, one might remind oneself of the general naiveté of the British, and especially of the Americans regarding the impending war of 1914; and one might remind oneself of the long struggle during the 1930's in which Americans tried to persuade themselves that they were really safe, that no Second World War would come, and that if it did come it would not touch us.

Actually all this is nothing more than the tragic and human story of wishful thinking and self-deception. One might, if one wishes, argue that this kind of ostrich-like avoidance of danger is psychotic. But if one does so, then everyday wishful thinking would likewise have to be called psychotic. There is actually no reason to believe that modern man, in his unwillingness to think very much about the danger of war, is essentially different from men of other periods. He does in fact have more scientific information, and perhaps a few of his number have a little more perspective as to the world picture. In this sense he may be slightly less "psychotic" than his ancestors. Yet it may be maintained that a striking feature of the general blindness of the American public is its willingness to let matters drift on from bad to worse; the lack of public interest in the day-by-day course of world events, the general readiness to let political, economic, and military leaders take one move after another in a warlike direction. It may be maintained that it is only blindness which allowed the preparation and signing of the Atlantic Pact and the increasing readiness of Western Europe and the United States to gird themselves for war against any possible aggressor. It is not clear, however, that there is anything else that the general public can do. The public does not understand economics very deeply; but it does watch the map, and does know what has happened to defenseless states. If one has observed the recent history of Poland and of Czechoslovakia, and if one is concerned at all about the maintenance of his own traditional way of life—economic, political, religious, educational, etc.—if one feels that he does not wish to be forcibly overrun and ideologically swamped, and if he happens to feel that military defense is the only way which has yet been found to stop such expansion, it is hard to see what is psychotic in such behavior. From the point of view of the Russian public, with the facts at its disposal, the same is true; the Russian public likewise is normal, not psychotic, in its fears.

It might be concluded that the present outlook involves no comfort and no hope; it may seem that we have been pleading for the acceptance of the status quo regarding war preparations as a normal and natural part of everyday psychology, and assuming that they must go on to their natural and inevitable conclusion in World War III. But there are in fact two possibilities of escape. Neither one of them can be counted upon with any certainty; both are, as a matter of fact, small voices in the whirlwind that may be of no avail. But they must be considered. These two possibilities are social-science research and long-range compromise. It is likely that neither one will prove of any use without the other. It is likely that we shall be told, and correctly, too, that social science is too young to do very much, and that compromise belongs to a period before a cold war has actually begun. Actually, however, social-science research is a new idea in the world that is rapidly developing tremendous possibilities. On the other hand, compromise, the oldest of human techniques for avoiding strife, might prove to be a somewhat different technique in an era in which people have some glimmering of understanding of the social sciences.

Let us consider what the social sciences might offer. We have the enormous development within recent years of cultural anthropology, showing the cultural roots of attitude and value systems; psychiatry and psychology, concerned with half-conscious and unconscious factors which profoundly aggravate every possibility of discord, may in the same way point the way to reduction of hostility and to the grasp of more rational viewpoints.

Considerable headway has been made by the UNESCO International Tensions Project and by the World Federation for Mental Health. More specifically, it is possible that social-science research on Russian culture and institutions may help us to understand them more fully, finding more accurately what makes them tick and learning how to persuade them—as we in the meantime persuade ourselves—that there are ways which are better than the present ones. If time is granted, it is likewise possible that social-science research may give the Russians more understanding of what makes us tick, and may enable them to persuade us—while they persuade themselves—that there are ways which are better than the present ways. Today one notes the development of the Russian Institute at Columbia and the Russian Research Center at Harvard. Here long-range studies in the hands of highly competent investigators are concerning themselves with the problem of Soviet leadership—recruitment and training of personnel, the structure of economic and political power, the analysis of individual personality factors which play a part in the selection, grooming, promotion, transfer, discouragement or liquidation of various kinds of leaders; the circumstances which sift and select in such a way that particular kinds of leaders appear in particular types of posts. Such data help to make possible long-range predictions regarding the kinds of men representing the various kinds of compromise or intransigence which may be expected from new leadership as it emerges. It will therefore become much more feasible to predict where the areas of compromise are likely to be discovered—to predict, for example, where trade agreements or scientific or medical collaboration might at least get a tentative start. In the same way one may learn to predict where the major concentrations of explosives, in the psychological sense, may be found, and perhaps more effectively avoid them.

In the same way social-science research may make it possible to get along better with the British, the French, the Chinese, or anyone else. This sort of study, however, is especially necessary in relation to ourselves. Why should not we ourselves, as well as our friends in other lands, study American leadership in the same way? This has not yet been done to any serious extent. We do an enormous amount of public-opinion research all the time, but we do less at the top of our society than at the bottom. Here and there a little investigation of American business or political leadership, or even of journalistic and literary leadership, has been attempted. But we could do a great deal more. If it is worth our while to study, psychologically speaking, the halt, the lame and the blind, it is also worth our while to study the people who are making destiny for us; to study the middle and top leaders, making use of all the tools of psychology, psychiatry, and sociology at our disposal. Here again we can hope to discover where intransigence comes from, where areas of possible compromise may be defined, what kinds of leaders express the will of the American public more effectively. It is a slow haul, of course. But public-opinion research has already shown its community value; and if community research can be done on the higher leadership levels, it can also make clear to ourselves and to the world the spots in which American leadership is less aggressive, less intransigent.

It may, for example, be possible, through social-science research, to do a little here and there to show where there is relative—I do not say absolute—freedom from economic determination in the formulation of foreign policy. Studying, for example, the development of David Lilienthal's ideas regarding the national utilization of atomic energy, and noting ways in which the spirit of his inquiry leads into questions of world economics in terms of community service rather than private profit, it may be possible to find the material out of which a deeper and more enduring world compromise could be constructed.

Another large area for social-science research is the use of psychology in relation to conference procedures. Anyone familiar with international conferences will know how often each side may consciously or unconsciously adopt the tactic of putting the other in the wrong; emotionally interested in "making a case" with their own public, they may ultimately defeat every purpose, even the purpose of making a case. Here the study of conference procedure would at least have made clear to all concerned what the inevitable results of such tactics must be. So often when there was a little furtive hope of agreement, stupidity or lack of information regarding conference methods made real communication impossible. At lower conference levels, as has already been shown at the United Nations, much is already known regarding those kinds of conference procedure which get results. Later the same knowledge may be obtained for middle or even top levels.

Again let me emphasize that social research and compromise are two aspects of one process. Certainly compromise of a radical sort is not something which either side would say it wanted at present. Social-science research will have to show specific possibilities for kinds of compromise which do not as yet exist, but which could be made. These would arise partly from understanding of national character and the discovery of things which the Russians—and ourselves—would rather have than the continuation of the impasse.

Up to this point we have been primarily considering American and Soviet leaders, and how social-science research might be used in relation to both. Actually, the matter is a world affair; all social scientists, whether British, French, Chinese, Indian, Arab, or Brazilian, will have to be given their share and encouraged to do whatever they want by way of research. With regard to the study of intercultural misunderstandings and hostilities, UNESCO's tension project is already beginning to blaze a trail. The Economic and Social Council of the UN has likewise suggested a study of problems related to the reduction of international hostilities. If a toehold can be gotten on little things here and there, perhaps in time the demonstration that such research collaboration on an international basis is feasible might lead into bolder and bolder attempts.

One aspect of the immaturity of the social sciences is, however, especially troublesome at this point; the technique of formulating and testing hypotheses. When a natural scientist makes a prediction and things do not occur as he expects, he discards his hypothesis and goes to work with a new one. If a social scientist, however, makes a mistake, he is likely to grow hot under the collar, justify himself, or resort to other irrational behavior. Often he is not clearly aware that most of his "statements of fact" are in reality simply hypotheses waiting to be tested. Most of the hypotheses about Russian behavior and about American behavior lack verification by the only means which can bring conviction: namely, prediction of specific steps which Russians, or Americans, will take—prediction with a degree of success demonstrably greater than is possible *without* such hypotheses.

With regard to the prevention of war, an essential step is the cultivation of the habit of formulating predictions about international developments based on explicit hypotheses, and the prompt admission and specification of the nature of the errors made at the time that an error becomes evident. If the social scientist were to proceed in a systematic way to predict, a couple of months at a time, the course which would be taken by international discussions and economic, political, and military moves —if he were to say, "When *A* does this, *B* will have to do that," and if he were prepared to record his prediction—he might learn by his errors and make better hypotheses. If teams of experts would get the habit of being explicit regarding the system of forces which they believe to be operating at a given time, and the reasons why they think that one rather than another eventuality will occur, they could then check as they went along the areas of relative accuracy and relative inaccuracy of prediction. This point may seem very elementary; but I cannot see that those working with the problem of international relations are as yet actually doing this to any great extent. Here and there, however, one encounters a social scientist who is doing this, and who is consequently revising his hypotheses in a realistic direction; and with these men lies the hope of the future.

Finally, there is a little word of hope regarding the possibilities of extensive adult education of the public. It is essentially a new idea to do research on the *process of communicating to the public* what it desperately needs to know. Here is one of the major scenes of powerful social science contributions. Insofar as there really is a psychosis relating to international affairs, research on ways and means of educating the public regarding cultural diversities and regarding types of national leadership should be a device for helping to prevent its spread. With all the active groups now at work on conveying to the public an aware- ness of the present world predicament, what is chiefly needed is research to see which methods of public education are most effective. The Federation of Atomic Scientists is an example; to its concern with the acts of government it joins a concern with the question of studying how the public can be guided towards understanding.

CONCLUSIONS

George W. Kisker, Ph.D.

Director of the Clinical Training Program; Associate Professor of Psychology in the Graduate School of Arts and Sciences, University of Cincinnati; Psychological Consultant to the United States Veterans Administration.

THE melancholy truth about the course of world history is that we are well along the road to disintegration. Poised on the brink of chaos, we are morally and ethically bankrupt. Forces are loose which might easily result in total destruction. In the opinion of Dr. George Brock Chisholm, Director-General of the World Health Organization, "The human race is threatened as it has never been before."

While the destruction of humanity would appear to be the ultimate catastrophe, there is serious question in many minds as to whether civilization is really worth saving. It might be argued that it is of little consequence whether mankind continues as it is, whether it progresses, retrogresses, or completely disappears. Since the human race is a mere accident of nature, its disappearance would be of no greater importance than its appearance some millions of years ago. Those who hold this view are convinced that man is becoming obsolete and that the situation is truly hopeless. These people say that we might as well "eat, drink, be merry" and go down recklessly in one stupendous cataclysm.

We cannot, however, with self-respect take such a defeatist attitude toward what is happening in our world. The great mass of the world population is emotionally committed to the idea that civilization and the human race must continue to exist and to progress. For this reason, there is grave concern about the world-wide symptoms of psychological and social disintegration.

The forces driving us to destruction are not new. The history of our world has been a history of violent leadership—of an Attila, Genghis Khan, Alexander the Great, Caesar, Napoleon, or Hitler. The cult of force, excessive nationalism, and collective irrationality have had their prototypes in many previous eras. The unique thing about contemporary civilization is that these destructive forces are aggravated beyond anything previously known in history. There has been a universal deterioration of personal, political and social morals. We live in a climate of tension and hostility. Labor disputes, aggressive picketing, family discord and divorce, movies of crime and gangsterism, and magazine, radio, and television stories of murder and pathological behavior are reflections of the tensions sweeping our world. Wherever one looks, there are symptoms of this basic sickness of contemporary society. A falling birth rate, increasing unemployment, subordination of the individual to the industrial and administrative machine, the development of numerous modes of evading life, along with a compulsive urge toward war-making, betray the degenerative and regressive trends in our present civilization.

There is good reason to believe that we are going "mad" on a world-wide basis. Fear, uncertainty, and anxiety grip us as individuals and as groups. Dr. William C. Menninger, eminent past President of the American Psychiatric Association, recently said, "Nationally and internationally, our relationships are marked with tension, mistrust, suspicion and selfishness." And the distinguished Brazilian psychiatrist, Dr. Henrique de Brito Belford Roxo, professor of psychiatry at the University of Brazil, informs us that the entire world is in a state of nervous excitement. It was not without reason that the late President Franklin Delano Roosevelt, in his address to the Congress of the United States in January, 1941, declared that the Fourth Freedom was the freedom from fear. He knew the dangers of the ever-increasing mass insecurity, feelings of personal inadequacy and inferiority, loss of faith and hope, disgruntlement, panic, and social distress which pervaded the world at the time, and which have since increased to an almost intolerable degree.

The insecurity, anxiety and psychological instability of the masses is reflected, on the international level, by the shifting tension spots on the face of the globe. Trieste, Korea, Greece, Israel, Indonesia, Pakistan, India, and China are examples that are only too well known. Nor can we ignore the serious tensions being generated in present-day Germany. Lord William Beveridge, a man not given to exaggeration, speaks of Germany as "a center of misery generating hate." Mr. Richard Law, one of the most respected of the conservative statesmen in Great Britain, describes it as a "moral vacuum." And who remains untouched by the overpowering tension being built up as a preface to the rapidly approaching death-struggle between the United States of America and Soviet Russia?

Harold Ickes, in a speech to the National Council of America-Soviet Friendship in New York City, in November, 1943, said: "The fate of civilization, and the lives and well-being of future generations, depends upon the relations between the United States and the Soviet Union." A year later, on the day before the 1944 presidential election in the United States, Stalin categorically stated that the United States had nothing to fear from a Russian-based ideological war against constitutional systems of free enterprise. He stressed his government's desire for close cooperation and understanding with the United States. Yet today the drums of war are being beaten in the very antechambers of Premiers, Presidents, and Prime Ministers. The realization that a new World War is being deliberately engineered by frustrated or irresponsible statesmen is a bitter pill. But it is a pill that every realist must sooner or later swallow.

We are forced to conclude that our civilization is a reversion to savagery of the most degenerate type. Professor Pitirim Sorokin of Harvard University describes our century as the bloodiest and most inhuman of the twenty-five hundred years of human history. He believes that our existing cultural framework is so rotten and is becoming so increasingly destructive and painful that mankind cannot be expected to live within it for any length of time. Small wonder that destructive tensions develop in such a social, psychological, economic, and political climate.

While the great majority of specialists in human behavior are convinced that there are important parallels between the disorganized behavior of groups and the disorganized behavior of individuals, there are those who question the existence, or at least the significance, of such parallels. Professor Albert Einstein believes that a meaningful analogy cannot be made between individual and social psychopathology. And Professor Einstein's view is shared by others. The Belgian psychiatrist, Dr. Marcel Alexander, President of the Belgian League for Mental Hygiene, believes that the disorganized behavior of the group is so entirely different from individual psychopathology that the psychiatrist has little to offer toward an understanding and solution of problems at the international level.

It is, of course, a mistake to conclude that world tension is additive, that it is nothing more than the sum of a great number of tense individuals making up the nations of the world. A tense nation is considerably more than a group of tense individuals. In this respect, the warning of Professor Einstein as to the danger of formulating uncritical analogies is quite in order. But the extreme position of Dr. Alexander is unnecessarily pessimistic. There is a most urgent need to apply our knowledge of individual psychopathology to social problems. Dr. William C. Menninger has likened war and prewar tension to a psychosis. And Dr. Nicola Perrotti, psychiatrist and member of the Italian Parliament, has pointed out that the behavior of conflicting groups in the world today reminds him strikingly of the psychology of the neurotic. A similar point of view has been advanced by Dr. A. M. Meerloo, the Dutch psychiatrist, who believes that war tension is an outcropping of mass hysteria. He looks upon the symptoms one finds in the mental hospital as being exactly the same as those found, in exaggerated form, in the masses and in whole nations.

It should be kept firmly in mind, however, that tension is something that happens to *individuals*. Social, political, economic, and military disorganization can be nothing more than a symptom. The problem of war and peace can be solved only in the mind of the individual man, woman and child. UNESCO recognized this fact when it included Archibald MacLeish's much-quoted sentence in the preamble to its constitution: "Since wars begin in the minds of men, it is in the minds of men that the defences of peace must be constructed."

While pathological tensions are generated by mistrust, hatred, suspicion, guilt, and prejudice, it should not be forgotten that there are "normal" forms of human tension. Both Dr. Perrotti of Italy and Dr. Oscar Forel of Switzerland have very wisely emphasized this point. Normal tension may be observed in all forms of competition, in the anticipation of the lover, the feeling of expectancy as the curtain rises in the theater, the excitement of a school graduation, the moment before the kick-off in the stadium, and the glow of pride when the flag passes in parade. These are wholesome, desirable, and constructive tensions. Unfortunately, the major tensions gripping the world today are neither wholesome nor constructive. Rather, they are vicious and destructive.

If the world is to save itself from its own destruction, it is imperative that we seek the underlying causes of these negative tensions. We must arrive at a more mature understanding of what is happening to us. Almost every kind of economic, political, technological, ethical, and sociopsychological factor has been cited as being responsible for world tension and for the conflicts growing out of such tension. Nationalism, race prejudice, cultural differences, imperialism and economic penetration, war propaganda, militarism, totalitarianism, and innate aggression have all been emphasized. We sometimes forget that a factor is not necessarily a cause simply because it is present when war starts. Too often the variables belong to different types of phenomena or to different levels of abstraction. While a multiple-causation theory of tension can never be completely satisfactory, a great many factors will have to be examined before social and psychological scientists will be in a position to spell out clearly and concisely the conditions ultimately responsible for world tension.

From the social point of view, there are many contributing factors to the creation and maintenance of individual and group tension. Poverty, housing shortages, low living standards, the monotony of industrial life, hyper-urbanization, and the chaotic disintegration of social life brought on by rapid advances in communication and transportation have had a far-reaching influence on the human personality. The breakdown of family life, the lack of emotional bonds, the increased valences away from home, and similar trends are additional reflections of the disruption brought about by changes made possible by modern technology.

Cultural conflict is also an important source of tension. Both Dr. Tsuneo Muramatsu of Japan and Dr. Abdullah El-Koussy, Dean of the Institute of Education at Cairo, Egypt, have shown that serious tensions have been generated by the existing conflict between Oriental and Occidental cultures. Dr. El-Koussy is concerned primarily about "cultural imperialism." He is unquestionably correct in assuming that attempts to reform other nations from a religious, economic, and cultural point of view are dangerous. President Harry S. Truman's Point Four Program, described in his inaugural address on January 20, 1949, as a "bold new program" for making the benefits of the scientific advances and the industrial progress of the United States of America available for the improvement and growth of underdeveloped areas of the world, is indeed bold, if not entirely new. From the point of view of many so-called underdeveloped nations, the program appears simply as another source of tension. The hard lessons of reality have made it difficult for these areas to see in such a program any motive other than power politics or economic penetration.

There are many who believe that war tension is essentially a political phenomenon. According to Karl von Clausewitz, the Prussian military theorist, war is merely a continuation of "political intercourse." President Dwight D. Eisenhower of Columbia University takes substantially the same position when he says that war is "an extension of political policy to the field of force." However, not only the militarists think of war and tension as political phenomena. Dr. Georg Schwarzenberger, Director of Studies of the London Institute of World Affairs, and

Vice Dean of the Faculty of Law of University College, London, views peace as the consequence of successfully completed negotiations by which a state of peace is established between contracting parties. And Professor Gilbert Murray of Oxford University believes that war is a deliberate political act decided on by a government after prolonged consideration. The political point of view also receives a degree of support from social and psychological scientists. Professor E. Tchehrazi, an Iranian psychiatrist, has demonstrated how the selfish tendency of governments to extend their spheres of political influence often results in the suppression of the rights and interests of small nations, thus becoming an important factor in the development of world tension.

The economic interpretation of world tension is based on such concepts as capitalism, imperialism, international cartels, arms trade, international finance, and large-scale movements of capital. The distinguished French economist, Jacques Rueff, goes so far as to say that the basic cause of world tension is an unbalanced budget. According to this point of view, deficit financing is an evil so serious that it eventually leads to loss of liberty and war. The Greek psychiatrist, Dr. George Philippopolos, has expressed his fear that collective inferiority complexes are being created in nations forced by circumstances to accept economic assistance. We should not be unaware of the dangers lurking in world-wide economic schemes such as the Marshall Plan. Quite apart from the ultimate desirability of economic rehabilitation, the matter of the psychological consequences of such aid must be taken into consideration. The day is rapidly approaching when national and international politico-economic agencies will recognize the desirability, if not the necessity, of giving psychologists and social scientists high-level staff representation.

The most extreme economic view is that human tensions arise fundamentally from material causes, and that they can be dealt with adequately on that level. Marxism maintains that economic and social reform is the key not only to the alleviation of international tension but also to a lasting and enduring peace. At a symptomatic level, Marxist theories of war and tension are correct when they emphasize the aggravating effect of capitalistic monopoly and economic materialism. Such factors unquestionably reinforce the tension inherent in any system of power politics.

The difficulty with the Marxist approach, as well as with the political approach, is that the problem of tension is attacked at several levels of abstraction removed from the basic reality. There is a growing recognition among economists that statistical considerations and the problem of sequences are insufficient for a meaningful economics. Dr. Robert Mossé, Professor of Economics at the University of Grenoble, France, has said: "Decisive progress toward the understanding of relationships will only be achieved if a major current of research is deliberately directed to the study of life and the mind, drawing its inspiration from biology and psychology." The mind of man is the instrument through which economic and political realities function. Dr. Carl Evang of Norway, in his Presidential Address to the World Health Assembly in Rome in June, 1949, commented on the economic approach by saying, "Let not the economists make us forget the human being." He also said, "Unless the peoples of the world enjoy a certain degree of mental and physical health which they have by no means reached, all the plans of the economist will be in vain, all his programs will go to pieces."

Without attempting to deny the importance of non-psychological factors in the development and maintenance of tension, it is clear that politics and economics are nothing more than expressions of personality in action. Such factors exert their powerful influence on human thinking through indirect means. If we are to reduce tension in the world, we must seek to understand the minds and motives of men. It is only then that we will be getting at the most fundamental levels of the problem.

One of the major difficulties is that present-day man is not fitted psychologically or otherwise to use the limitless power that science has placed in his hands. Our world is marked by a high degree of scientific maturity on the one hand and by political, social, economic, and philosophical immaturity on the other hand. While we have made great strides in perfecting the means to destroy, we lag far behind in the knowledge of how to live together constructively and peacefully. We cannot deny the great advances made in public health, medical science, engineering, physics, chemistry, and indeed in all of the physical and mathematical sciences. Yet we too often persuade ourselves that psychological man has progressed accordingly. The fact is that the phenomenally rapid advance in the physical sciences has operated to depress and destroy the psychological man. We are foundering in our attempt to deal with the social and psychological implications of recent developments in physical science. Our utter helplessness with respect to the atom bomb, the hydrogen bomb, and the rapidly approaching era of nuclear power confirms the suspicion that we have not advanced socially and psychologically to a point where we can deal adequately with the philosophical problems created by the advance of physical science. We are operating with concepts and standards which were outmoded many centuries ago.

The complexities of the world have become too great. They are beyond our comprehension. The rapid extension of the individual environment through improved communications and transportation has so overwhelmed us that we can do nothing more than grasp frantically at isolated bits of reality in our feverish effort to hold our world together. According to Dr. Hugo Lea-Plaza, Professor of Psychiatry at the University of Santiago, Chile, the cause of the collective neurosis in the world today is the discrepancy between the paradise pointed out to us by science and the abyss in which we actually find ourselves. Dr. Franz Alexander, Director of the Chicago Psychoanalytic Institute, agrees that the discrepancy between the development of the natural sciences and that of psychology and the social sciences is largely responsible for the disasters we are witnessing.

Granting that the world is sick, we are faced with the problem of therapy. A great many experts in the fields of political science, history, economics, sociology, ethics, religion, and education have assumed the role of doctor to the world's ills. Immanuel Kant, in his *Essay on Eternal Peace,* not only outlined the specific conditions he considered necessary to insure peace among nations, but he also made an analysis of the philosophical principles which underlie these conditions of peace. More recently, such widely differing remedies as the universal state, outlawing war, restoring balance of power, mediation and arbitration, disarmament, absolute pacifism, and a world federation of states have been suggested. The foundations of peace are too often looked for in diplomatic compromises, international agreements and legislation, and cleverly devised institutions and machineries to attain justice and peace. Such remedies, unfortunately, are entirely symptomatic. While they get at the surface problems of world tension, they completely neglect more basic causes.

Before entering into the problem of how world tension might be reduced or eliminated, it should be remembered that there are those who maintain that it would not be wise to get rid of war and tension even if we could do so. The militarists insist that war makes nations strong, hard, vital, and dynamic. Others agree that war is desirable, necessary, and even beautiful. Some state flatly that it is a social obligation. The English philosopher Thomas Hobbes pointed out that war is the normal activity of mankind, with peace nothing more than a breathing space, a time when people are tired and disillusioned. Late in the nineteenth century, the Prussian Field Marshal Count Helmuth von Moltke wrote: "Eternal peace is a dream, and not even a beautiful dream; war is a part of God's world-order. The noblest virtues of mankind are developed in war: courage, fidelity, and the willingness to sacrifice oneself." And in 1915 Nikolai Lenin said, "The experience of war, like the experience of every great crisis in history, as every great disaster and every sudden turn in human life, stuns and shatters some but enlightens and hardens others." The two World Wars within our own generation have testified to the grim truth of Lenin's—if not Moltke's—words. Mankind has learned how to mobilize itself materially and psychologically for large-scale destruction, but it has been almost completely impotent in the matter of mobilizing for peaceful and constructive purposes.

How can such a paradox ever be resolved as long as there are those who believe that war is not only necessary, but that it is a beautiful and esthetic experience? Filippo Marinetti, a senator in Fascist Italy and poet laureate of the Fascist State, said, "War is beautiful because it creates new architectures—the flying geometries of an airplane, the spiral smoke of burning villages; because it completes the beauty of a flowering meadow with the passionate orchids of machine-gun fire. War is beautiful because it makes a symphony of fusilades and cannonades—pauses choked by silence and the perfume of putrefaction." And Vittorio Mussolini, the son of Benito Mussolini, wrote in his diary, "War is the quintessence of beauty. I recommend it to everybody. War has been a sport for us; the most beautiful and complete of sports." It is impossible to read such lines without being overwhelmed by the primitive, infantile, and regressive mentality that is revealed. One becomes shockingly conscious of the superficiality of cultural forces and civilizing influences. Yet in spite of the basic viciousness of mankind, the great mass of the world population recognizes that war and destructive tensions must somehow be abolished.

Where can we turn for help in dealing with world tension and war as expressions of social behavior? Professor Michael Fordham of England said, "It would be desirable to find somebody who is not affected by the crisis and who could dispassionately evaluate it for us; but on this occasion all of the civilized peoples of the world are involved, and in consequence we have, like the hero in the belly of the monster, to cut ourselves out from within with what weapons we can hastily improvise." Certainly one of the most effective of these weapons is our growing knowledge of human behavior. As Dr. Nicola Perrotti of Italy pointed out, millions of people today have lost all faith, all idealism, and all safety. They look to science, and particularly to psychology, with trust.

As long ago as 1935, the Committee for War Prophylaxis, sponsored by the Netherlands Mental Hygiene Association, prepared a manifesto which was circularized to the leading statesmen of all nations. This document was signed by 339 psychiatrists from 30 nations. It emphasized the unintelligence of war, the danger of war-planning mentality, the instinctive and unconscious factors impelling toward war, and the responsibility of statesmen to solve international difficulties by reason. The manifesto concluded with the statement that "We psychiatrists declare that our science is sufficiently advanced for us to distinguish between real, pretended, and unconscious motives—even in statesmen."

Quite obviously, psychologists and psychiatrists are not destined to save the world from calamity. Yet it does seem reasonable that scientists who have specialized in the field of human relations are better equipped to analyze the problems of group conflict than are specialists in political science, economics, military strategy, or even professional diplomacy. Psychologists and psychiatrists have made extraordinary strides in understanding individual tension. Similarly, we must look to these specialists for insight into group tension at the community, national, and international level. This point of view has been stressed by the Committee on International Relationships of the American Psychiatric Association in the following statement: "Psychiatrists endeavor to understand the psychological causes of difficult and faulty interpersonal relationships, and should be able to offer some advice on their improvement. Such knowledge and advice should be acceptable whether the adjustment difficulties are between individuals or groups of individuals." Further support has been given by Dr. Thomas Parran, Surgeon General of the United States Public Health Service, who said, "The science of mental hygiene is one of our newer disciplines, concerned with the human mind and emotions. Even in its present early stage of development it helps man adjust to his environment, to live in greater harmony with his family, his community, his world. This science of mental hygiene needs urgently to be developed and applied as a basic element in preventing war and destroying seeds of war."

The role of the psychologist and the psychiatrist is all the more important because some of the most important tension-producing influences, whether in the masses or in the leaders, lie deep in the basic tendencies of human nature. Every child brings into the world an extraordinary capacity for hostility and violence. In times of war, this capacity shows itself as a veritable blood-lust. Professor Sigmund Freud pointed out that the primitive history of mankind is filled with murder. In fact, the history of the world which our children learn in school is little more than a series of race murders. Professor Freud said, "The very emphasis on the commandment *Thou shalt not kill* makes it certain that we spring from an endless ancestry of murderers with whom the lust for killing was in the blood, as possibly it is to this day with ourselves." This same thought was expressed in an exchange of letters between Albert Einstein and Freud. The Committee on International Cooperation of the League of Nations asked Einstein to select an outstanding thinker and invite him to answer the question "Why War?" The question as put to Freud was "Why is it so easy to work up a war fever? Is it because man has within him a lust for hatred and destruction?" Freud agreed that this was the case. He also indicated that the desire for war is quite unconscious in most people. War is a form of man's effort to resolve many of his unresolved, unconscious conflicts on a wholesale scale.

In another place, in his essay on *Thoughts on War and Death,* Freud wrote, "In our unconscious, we are like primitive man— simply a gang of murderers." Freud believed that destruction for its own sake is one of the strongest human motives. War represents man's unconscious desire to destroy himself. Professor Ernest Jones of England agrees that there is in mankind a permanent capacity for hostility, aggression, and cruelty towards his fellow creatures. According to this view, human beings can live together peacefully only when this innate destructiveness is turned outward. Internal national peace, therefore, depends upon international warfare.

While other psychologists and psychopathologists have not gone to the extreme position of Freud and Ernest Jones, there is considerable support for the fact that aggression is a basic, if not innate, part of human nature. Professor William McDougall, the Anglo-American psychologist and psychiatrist, pointed out that there is an instinct of pugnacity which impels us to attack that which injures us or interferes in any way with the attainment of our desires. Dr. Siegen Chou, Professor of Psychology at the National Central University in China wrote, just before the ultimate success of Communist revolutionists in his country, that he fully supported the views of McDougall, and felt that these views could be used to throw light on the psychodynamics of the international tension we are now experiencing. World tension is regarded as a result of the tightening of powerful springs which represent repressed primitive instincts. These instincts are destined eventually to break loose from the forces that have controlled them. Inherent in this thinking is the belief that nations that have too long or too assiduously cultivated peace must sooner or later relax to the barbarisms of war in order to relieve the pressure of the accumulated tensions.

The powerful and pervading influence of aggressiveness in the development of world tension can be accepted without subscribing to the theory that such aggression is inborn. The English anthropologist, Professor Bronislaw Malinowski, believed that war and tension are undoubtedly cultural phenomena and that their main determinants are not rooted in human nature. Similarly, Dr. Oscar Forel of Switzerland emphasizes that there is no instinct of aggression. A few years ago, two thousand American psychologists subscribed to a manifesto which included ten principles on human nature and peace. The first of these principles proclaimed "War can be avoided; it is not born in man—it is built into man."

Learned or unlearned, aggressive impulses spring from the deepest layers of man's nature. There may even be, as Professor Clyde Kluckhohn of Harvard University suggests, a certain amount of "free-floating aggression" in every human society. Or, to follow the British psychiatrist, Dr. Edward Glover, man's attitude both to war and peace may have its basis in fear and anxiety resulting from repressions and distortions. Unconsciously motivated sadism and masochism may indeed be the essential causes of world tension, with economic and similar factors merely being a "screen" for underlying psychological causes. Such a point of view is supported by Dr. Franz Alexander, who considers basic human behavior as the constant factor and sociological factors as the variables in the development of world tension and international warfare.

The regressive elements in the development of world tension are closely related to the aggressive elements. The development of a primitive mentality and emotional immaturity is one of the basic conditions for war and prewar tension. Dr. Hjalmar Helweg, Professor of Psychiatry at the University of Copenhagen, Denmark, describes such behavior as a form of psycho-infantilism. It is no accident that Dr. Klaus Conrad of Germany speaks of group relationships as being "childlike," that both Dr. John Bostock of Australia and Professor Bernard Notcutt of South Africa see an analogy between international tension and tension in the nursery, and that Dr. Ernest Jones finds that the prototype of the struggle of all mankind is the infant's struggle between helplessness and omnipotence.

Both aggression and regression have a powerful impact on world affairs through the medium of leadership. It is a grim truth that the foundations of international relations are being undermined to a considerable degree by psychologically incompetent men in key positions. There is an astonishing amount of self-interest, pettiness, shortsightedness, narrowness, bigotry and greed exhibited by highly placed persons in many of the world's great powers. World diplomacy today is largely a matter of words and conduct that are manifestly chaste but latently indecent. Governments use distressingly little judgment in the selection of those who represent them in international affairs. Unfortunately, there are few signs that the quality of world leadership is improving or is likely to improve in the near future. Madame Charlotte Muret, the French commentator, has likened our world politicians to a pack of cards: the longer the cards are played the greasier they become; but invariably the same old faces come out of the shuffle!

The appalling incompetence of many of the so-called "leaders" of the world has been emphasized by Dr. George H. Stevenson of Canada, Dr. Oscar Forel of Switzerland, and Dr. Klaus Conrad of Germany. Dr. Conrad, observing events in his country during the past fifteen years, has good reason to believe that a group embarking on a neurotic development will select a leader who is a self-asserted neurotic. Dr. Conrad is convinced that a sick nation chooses psychopathic and neurotic leaders. The American psychiatrist Dr. C. S. Bluemel has also emphasized that one of the major causes of world tension is that national leadership frequently falls to men of abnormal mental make up. There is ample evidence that the psychological instability of the heads of states, and those who engage in war propaganda, is responsible, to a large degree, for the maintenance of tension in the world population.

The major political bungling at the international level can be laid directly at the door of our leaders. Prior to World War II, the world was treated to the unpalatable demonstration of international political shortsightedness in the handling of the Spanish Civil War, the Italian invasion of Ethiopia, the Japanese invasion of China, and the Munich Pact. The mishandling of these events led directly to World War II. And now, with that war still fresh in our minds, we have been forced to watch colossal diplomatic stupidities connected with the situations in Germany, Greece, China, Palestine, Pakistan, and other tension spots. The greatest folly of all, the incredibly ambivalent handling of United States—Russian relationships, cannot conceivably lead to anything but World War III.

Dr. Jaime Torres Bodet, Director-General of UNESCO, has emphasized the need to understand our leaders and their motives if we are to learn how tensions and wars develop. Moreover, there is an increasing recognition of the fact that the world's leaders must be selected on a basis other than emotional appeal, political manipulation, or historical accident. Dr. George H. Stevenson of Canada suggests that such leaders hold certificates of competency; Dr. Klaus Conrad of Germany recommends that an international council evaluate and appraise the qualifications of leading statesmen; Dr. Demetrios Kouretas, Professor of Psychiatry at the University of Athens, Greece, believes that any citizen aspiring to the direction of his nation's destiny should be made to undergo an examination by psychologists and psychiatrists; and Dr. F. W. Zeylmans van Emmichoven, Director of the Institute of Psychology of Peoples at the Hague, Netherlands, suggests that political leaders be advised by a board of psychological experts.

These are daring recommendations. The professional politicians, career military men, economic royalists, and other government-makers are not likely to take kindly to such ideas. Nor are they apt to relinquish their grip on the people of the world. Nevertheless, if mankind is to progress, there must be an increasing realization that the true leaders of the world are the thinkers, the scholars, the scientists and the creative artists.

A hundred and fifty years ago, Johann Pestalozzi, the Swiss educational reformer, pointed out that social reform could be brought about through the education of the individual child more readily than by political revolution. This point of view receives substantial support from present-day educators. Most problems of world tension have their counterparts or prototypes in such social microcosms as the family, the classroom, and the community. Human beings, in the course of their social education, acquire many habits, attitudes, beliefs, and motives which can be used either for large-scale social construction or for widespread social destruction.

Whatever the ultimate merit of education, it is a sad commentary on our civilization that education as a means of social reform has, for the most part, failed. The educational systems of even the most advanced countries of the world are largely obsolete; they are not geared psychologically to electronics, nuclear energy, atomic and hydrogen bombs, round-the-world airplane flights, and supersonic speeds. They were designed for the restricted community life of a past era. But such education cannot furnish the kind of minds and men needed to grasp the complexities of world affairs. We must agree with Arthur Koestler, who insists that our textbooks and our methods of teaching are mere relics of an earlier conception of the world. And Dr. Nic Waal, a Norwegian psychiatrist, is convinced that modern educational practices foster latent anxiety, guilt feelings and hate. In her opinion, a complete reorientation of our educational system is needed in order to allow children to be natural, to permit the satisfaction of aggressive needs, and to prevent potentially destructive drives from becoming dangerously hidden and suppressed.

A major indictment of present-day education is the fact that the majority of adults now living in the world are unable to think about any problem larger than themselves. Some manage to deal with problems at the community level. A few capable people have risen to the national level; distressingly few are capable on the international level. As Dr. Gardner Murphy of the United States has suggested, there is urgent need for a comprehensive program of world-wide adult education. Recognizing this need, UNESCO has sponsored an International Conference on Adult Education.

Men, women and children must be taught to stand up against the racial, religious, and political persecution, hatred, and bigotry which exist in flagrant form in every part of the world. A substantial segment of the world population is philosophically and practically dedicated to the perverted notion that a colored man is something less than a white man. The representatives of this considerable segment of the population are in the vanguard of those clamoring for world peace. They make eloquet speeches opposing bigotry, narrow-mindedness and prejudice existing in other countries. Yet the prototype of all world tension, world disorder, and even war itself flourishes within their own homes and within their own minds. As Dr. George H. Stevenson has pointed out, putting our own homes and minds in order is the stuff out of which world peace is made.

Another significant failure of education has been its inability to utilize constructively the channels of world communication. Newspapers, magazines, motion pictures, international radio broadcasts, and other media have too often been used to tear down the emotional bonds between the various peoples of the world rather than to strengthen them. This has been particularly true in the motion picture industry, where poor taste, psychological illiteracy, and questionable judgment have been consistently displayed. Millions of feet of film are fed to a worldwide audience. Yet these films, which potentially are a most powerful weapon for peace, deal with trite, hackneyed, sub-standard fare. Many of the warped and distorted attitudes held by millions of people in the world towards the United States are the direct result of the infantile, narcissistic, and totally unrealistic productions of Hollywood. As Dr. John Bostock of Australia has pointed out, American films sow seeds of tension by misrepresenting the American scene. No other medium of communication has so recklessly flaunted its disregard for its social obligation. We can only hope that the future of international television will not be as dismal and as impotent as has been the relatively brief history of motion pictures.

The most hopeful sign in the slow trend to destroy the provincialism that has blocked progress in the field of mass communication has been the creation by UNESCO of a Commission on Technical Needs of the Press, Film, and Radio. The work of this commission could do much to stimulate cross-cultural research in this vitally important area.

International education and cooperation must be encouraged through the strengthening of such international organizations as the United Nations, World Health Organization, International Labor Office, International Union for Child Welfare, World Federation for Mental Health, International Federation of Children's Villages, and all similar agencies having a true international orientation. Most important with respect to an understanding of world tension is the UNESCO study of tensions affecting international understanding.

Professor Hadley Cantril of Princeton University, the first director of the UNESCO Tensions Project, and a committee of eight internationally known social and psychological scientists came to the conclusion that there is no evidence to indicate that wars are necessary and inevitable consequences of human nature. Moreover, they agreed that the problem of peace is the problem of keeping group and national tensions and aggressions within manageable proportions, and of directing them towards ends that are at the same time personally and socially constructive. Another important finding of this group was that tensions between nations and groups of nations are fostered by many of the myths, traditions, and symbols of national pride handed down from one generation to another. Emphasis was put on the fact that parents and teachers find it difficult to recognize the extent to which their own attitudes and loyalties (often acquired when they were young and conditions were different) are no longer adequate to serve as effective drives to action in a changing world. Positive suggestions were made for the cooperation of social scientists on broad regional and international levels, the creation of an international university, and a series of world institutes of social science under international auspices.

It is not possible to leave the subject of international education without reference to religion as an educative force. In an address to the Second World Health Assembly in Rome during the summer of 1949, His Holiness, Pope Pius XII, said, "The spiritual well-being of mankind is a condition of world-wide peace and general security." Similar views have been expressed by religious leaders in every part of the world. It is important that it be recognized clearly that the reduction of world tension—like all other human virtues—is non-sectarian. While Christianity has had a most powerful impact on so-called Western civilization, the doctrines of Buddhism, Hinduism, Mohammedism, Confucianism, and many other religious ideologies are equally valid as a basis for world peace.

Admittedly, religion is a potentially powerful weapon against world tension. Yet the experience of history has been that as war tension grows, religion frequently becomes distorted and finds itself an ally of the very forces it started out to oppose. The frequency with which war takes a religious turn is readily observed. Dr. Nicola Perrotti of Italy has pointed out that the most atrocious cruelties during war are often performed in the name of Christian love. And Professor E. Tchehrazi of Iran, who has had a first-hand opportunity to watch religion being used to create discord and strife in the Near East, recognizes religion as a potent force in the promotion of imperialistic aims. Religious differences and fanaticism have been used in many areas of the world to create enmity among men. Dr. Abdullah El-Koussy of Egypt is convinced that the invasion of Egypt and other countries by European religious doctrine has served to bring insecurity, conflict, frustration and misery to the people. Such infiltration of religious doctrine shakes the roots of the people's faith in their own traditions and culture without being able to supply a really stable substitute. Dr. El-Koussy deplores the sending of missionaries to effect religious conversion. He sees in the missionary an attempt to smuggle imported religious and foreign creeds under the guise of medical treatment, social hygiene, education, and other welfare projects.

A most telling blow against the concept of the morality and religious ethics of Western civilization as an instrument of peace was made by Dr. George Brock Chisholm when he pointed out that the great burden which keeps humanity from the vital step to maturity and a peaceful society is the combination of inferiority, guilt, and fear created by a morality which overemphasizes the concept of right and wrong. We must free ourselves from outmoded types of morality and from the magic fears of our ancestors. Dr. Chisholm insists that religion has failed us because it has managed to entrench the concept of "sin" throughout much of the world.

While it is conceivable that the fountainhead of peace may eventually be found in a controlling philosophy of life and in the spiritual convictions of man, it is folly to hope that tension will be reduced by this means so long as these convictions are at such sharp variance with one another and religious sects are unable to apply their own teachings in their relationships towards one another.

Observation of the contemporary international scene can lead only to pessimism with reference to the possibility of enduring world peace. It has been pointed out that since intelligence and good sense have never held sway for more than brief periods in human affairs, there is little reason to believe that such intelligence and good sense are likely to predominate in the near future. Considering the psychological and social immaturity of mankind, it is naive to hope that men in our time can learn to live at peace with themselves or with others.

World War I and World War II have been mere phases in a

psychological ferment involving the entire world. The undercurrents of world revolution are in motion, and conflict is unavoidable. The trend of Russian policy, the distintegration of Germany, the anarchy in China, industrial unrest in the United States and Europe, revolutionary upsets in South America, and the upsurge of the socially, politically, and economically depressed masses of Asia point to an era of psychological, economic, and political collectivism.

While World War III is well on its way, the long-range possibility of reducing world tension and discouraging international warfare is not inconceivable. There is little hope that our present civilization will see the condition of universal peace. Yet universal peace is not beyond the potentialities of mankind.

INDEX

Italic figures following the name of an author indicate the location of his article in this book.